DISCARDED

Between Theater
and Philosophy

Between Theater and Philosophy

Skepticism
in the Major City Comedies
of Ben Jonson and Thomas Middleton

Mathew R. Martin

Newark: University of Delaware Press
London: Associated University Presses

© 2001 by Rosemont Printing & Publishing Corp.

All rights reserved. Authorization to photocopy items for internal or personal use, or the internal or personal use of specific clients, is granted by the copyright owner, provided that a base fee of $10.00, plus eight cents per page, per copy is paid directly to the Copyright Clearance Center, 222 Rosewood Dr., Danvers, Massachusetts 01923. [0-87413-739-X/01 $10.00 + 8¢ pp, pc.] Other than as indicated in the foregoing, this book may not be reproduced, in whole or in part, in any form (except as permitted by Sections 107 and 108 of the U.S. Copyright Law,and except for brief quotes appearing in reviews in the public press).

Associated University Presses
440 Forsgate Drive
Cranbury, NJ 08512

Associated University Presses
16 Barter Street
London WC1A 2AH, England

Associated University Presses
P.O. Box 338, Port Credit
Mississauga, Ontario
Canada L5G 4L8

The paper used in this publication meets the requirements of the American National Standard for Permanence of Paper for Printed Library Materials Z39.48-1984.

Library of Congress Cataloging-in-Publication Data

Martin, Mathew R., 1970–
  Between theater and philosophy : skepticism in the major city comedies of Ben Jonson and Thomas Middleton / Mathew R. Martin.
    p.   cm.
  Includes bibliographical references and index.
  ISBN 0-87413-739-X (alk. paper)
    1. Jonson, Ben, 1573?–1637--Philosophy. 2. Skepticism in literature. 3. Middleton, Thomas, d. 1627--Knowledge--London (England). 4. Jonson, Ben, 1573?–1637--Knowledge--London (England). 5. English drama--17th century--History and criticism. 6. English drama (Comedy)--History and criticism. 7. Middleton, Thomas, d. 1627--Philosophy. 8. Middleton, Thomas, d. 1627--Comedies. 9. Jonson, Ben, 1573?–1637--Comedies. 10. London (England)--In literature. 11. City and town life in literature. I. Title.

PR2642.S55 M37 2001
822'.309353--dc21   00-053241

PRINTED IN THE UNITED STATES OF AMERICA

To Tamara,
who bore this work with me

Contents

Acknowledgments	9
Introduction: Theater's Janus Face	13
1. *Volpone* and the Dystopian Turn of Utopian Discourse	23
2. "[B]egot between tirewomen and tailors": Commodified Self-Fashioning in *Michaelmas Term*	39
3. *Epicoene* and Knowing by Tradition	58
4. The Rise of *Homo economicus* in *A Trick to Catch the Old One*	78
5. Play and Plague in *The Alchemist*	95
6. Paradox, Wonder, and the Reproduction of Patriarchy in *A Chaste Maid in Cheapside*	115
7. Skeptical Laughter in the Brave New World of *Bartholomew Fair*	133
Conclusion	154
Notes	157
Bibliography	176
Index	186

Acknowledgments

I would like to thank the University of Alberta and the Social Sciences and Humanities Research Council of Canada for the scholarships and fellowships that made this work financially possible. Early versions of chapters 2 and 5 appeared in *Early Modern Literary Studies* 5, no. 1 (May 1999) and *English Studies in Canada* 26 (December 2000), respectively, and I would like to thank the editors of both these journals for their permission to reprint them here. To Rick Bowers, Patricia Demers, and David Gay go my thanks for their constant support and guidance. To Tamara I owe more than can be expressed on an acknowledgments page.

Between Theater
and Philosophy

Introduction:
Theater's Janus Face

If I have been fascinated by skepticism, perhaps like a deer frozen by the headlights of an oncoming vehicle, then in my defense I can plead only that I am in very good company. Skepticism critically illuminated Hellenistic philosophy. The spectral foe of modern philosophy from Francis Bacon and René Descartes to Wittgenstein and beyond, skepticism is a perennial possibility, the seductive song of mental boundaries of all sorts, not a dogma but a mood. Accordingly, I have chosen a quotation from Sir Thomas Browne's *Religio Medici* to be this study's weathervane. Looking back on the intellectual fashions of the first half of the seventeenth century, Browne comments that "though our first studies and *junior* endeavors may stile us Peripateticks, Stoicks, or Academics, yet I perceive the wisest heads prove at last, almost all Sceptics, and stand like Janus in the field of knowledge."[1] Browne's retrospective summary locates the inherent instability of the movements that constituted his cultural and intellectual inheritance. The spirit animating the Renaissance revival of antiquity and its philosophical dogmas ultimately carried those caught up in it away into uncharted seas of epistemological exhaustion and perplexity. For Browne, though, skepticism is no North Star by which to navigate, no synthesis superseding what preceded it. Rather, skepticism is a wisdom that emerges out of discursive contradiction to operate upon the ever-shifting boundaries of culturally specific discursive knowledge. In the following pages I follow two early-seventeenth-century playwrights, Ben Jonson and Thomas Middleton, in the distinctly skeptical moods of their dramatic careers. These moods are deeply affected by their time yet emerge through non sequitur, contradiction, and paradox to a self-reflexive awareness of the temporality and constructedness of knowledge, an awareness that is perhaps timeless knowledge's poor but only substitute. More specifically, I explore the skeptical energies of the two playwrights' city comedies, which constitute the bulk of their dramatic output for public theater in the opening decade of James I's reign. In their city comedies, both Jonson and Middleton mobilize theater to interrogate the production of early modern English culture's key discourses as knowledge, the construction of the knowing (and doubting) self, and the impossible epistemological fantasies of power.

The history of skepticism's development provides a useful context for Jonson's and Middleton's skeptical theater. As A. A. Long discusses in *Hellenistic Philosophy: Stoics, Epicureans, Sceptics*,[2] skepticism was an influential strand of thought in Hellenistic and post-Hellenistic philosophy, developing alongside and in opposition to the two major dogmatic philosophies of the period, Epicureanism and Stoicism. Long distinguishes two traditions of skeptical thought: an extreme skepticism first articulated by Pyrrho of Elis in the fourth century B.C. and a more moderate skepticism developed in the Platonic Academy in the third and second centuries B.C. The Jacobean intellectual had three main primary sources to which to turn for the presentation of ancient skepticism: Diogenes Laertius's thumbnail sketch in his *Lives of Eminent Philosophers*, Cicero's presentation of academic skeptical arguments in *Academica* and other works, and Sextus Empiricus's summary of Pyrrhonian skepticism in *Outlines of Pyrrhonism*. Cicero and Sextus differ most significantly in the conclusions they reach through skeptical argument: Cicero argues for a probabilistic form of knowledge based on appearances, while Sextus suspends judgment on all assertions of knowledge in order to attain tranquillity, an ethical goal that the Pyrrhonists shared with the Stoics and Epicureans. Sextus defines skepticism as "an ability, or mental attitude, which opposes appearances to judgements in any way whatsoever, with the result that, owing to the equipollence of the objects and reasons thus opposed, we are brought firstly to a state of mental suspense and next to a state of 'unperturbedness' or quietude."[3] Despite their differences, though, both Cicero and Sextus articulate skeptical arguments emphasizing the situatedness of the knower, the mediatedness of sensory knowledge, and the ungrounded rhetoricity of argument. In short, both expose the epistemological difficulties faced by material minds in a material world with no transcendental anchor for sense perception or reason. As I will argue throughout this study, Jonson and Middleton do likewise.

The two dramatists, however, lived and wrote in early modern England, not the Roman Empire, and their skepticism shares the inflections characteristic of the Renaissance reception of skepticism. According to Richard Popkin in *The History of Scepticism from Erasmus to Spinoza*, little interest was shown in ancient skeptical philosophy until Henri Estienne published a Latin translation of Sextus's complete works in 1569. After that, however, extreme skeptical arguments were appropriated as powerful and double-edged weapons in debates that had developed their own skeptical momentum.[4] The Reformation inevitably raised the issue of the bases of religious knowledge. Reformers invoked skeptical arguments to question the bases on which the Catholic Church asserted the certainty of its doctrines, thereby justifying their own interpretive procedures, and the counter-reformers replied in kind. Humanists used skeptical strategies derived from Cicero to debunk the pretensions of scholastic reason and to formulate the notion of a limited, prudential, and rhetorical reason that justified a humanist emphasis on language and literature. Other thinkers, however, turned skepticism, rhetoric, and the classics against the humanists, questioning reason's ability to arrive at even a limited kind of knowledge and using the multiplicity of classical texts recovered by the humanists to undermine their belief that the classics provided a fount of unified wisdom. Renaissance science experienced a similarly Pyrrhonian dialectic between those who used skeptical arguments to clear a space for their own non-Aristotelian theories and those who used skeptical arguments to assert the futility of all science. Renaissance thinkers, then, appropriated skeptical arguments primarily as limited tools for critical and even polemical ends. Few, notably Montaigne in *Apology for Raymond Sebond*, were willing to adopt the extreme Pyrrhonist position in all major fields of knowledge—theology, humanism, and science—and even in the *Apology* one can observe that Montaigne's skeptical project is rendered significantly different from Sextus's by the social, political, and economic contexts of its articulation. Montaigne's attack on dogmatism is a reaction not only to acrimonious philosophical dispute but also to bloody religious warfare, which closed or considerably constricted the Pyrrhonian passage from suspension of judgment to tranquillity by shattering the unity of Christian custom, by eliminating most if not all of the uncontested ground on which the skeptic could rest unperturbed after exhausting the resources of epistemology. The situatedness of the skeptic as well as the knower is a source of perplexity. To Montaigne, skepticism "is a desperate stroke, in which you must abandon your weapons to make your adversary lose his, and a secret trick that must be used rarely and reservedly."[5]

In this study I will frequently follow Montaigne's lead by analyzing Jonson and Middleton's contestatory and critical uses of skepticism. Yet although I here place the plays in the context of a significant development in Renaissance thought and in the chapters that follow will have occasion to place them in more specific intellectual contexts, this is not a study of the influence of the revival of Pyrrhonism on the two playwrights' works. Jonson and Middleton were doubtless aware of skeptical philosophy, if not through the classical sources then at least through Florio's translation of Montaigne, but this study's primary goal is to explore the connections between theater and skepticism at a more fundamental level. Skepticism is theater. Descartes begins his *Meditations* by describing the scene of his skeptical musings: "I am here, sitting by the fire, wearing a dressing-gown, with this paper in my hand."[6] He then transforms his den into a space of intense illusion, of dream then divine deception, in order to demonstrate the groundlessness of knowledge. Descartes himself faces—and struggles against—transformation: his doubts bring him into close proximity to "those insane persons whose minds are so troubled . . . that they constantly assert that they are kings, when they are very poor; that they are wearing gold and purple, when they are quite naked; or who imagine that they are pitchers or that they have a body of glass. But these are madmen . . ."[7] But he is not insane, he claims. He knows he is pretending, and he has deliberately donned his dressing-gown, grasped his paper, and seated himself by the fire in order to meditate on his nonidentity with his costume and his actions. Descartes, then, is not a madman but an actor. Three centuries later, Wittgenstein stages skepticism in a similar fashion, confining the problematics of radical doubt to special and withdrawn settings and associating the skeptical inquirer with madness: "I am sitting with a philosopher in the garden; he says again and again 'I know that that's a tree,' pointing to a tree that is near us. Someone else arrives and hears this, and I tell him: 'This fellow isn't insane. We are only doing philosophy.'"[8] For Wittgenstein, skeptical inquiry (indeed, all modern epistemology) is a game played in limited circumstances by misappropriating words and discursive strategies from the ordinary language games in which they normally (and intelligibly) function. Consequently, skeptical inquiry has the peculiar hollowness or dreamlike quality of lines spoken on stage or in a garden under a tree. Skepticism, like the theatrical speech act as J. L. Austin describes it, is "parasitic" upon the normal uses of space, time and language.[9]

Skepticism, then, is fundamentally theatrical; conversely, theater is fundamentally skeptical. If Plato in the *Republic* constitutes philosophical discourse in opposition to theater, which Plato declares ontologically derivative, disturbingly Protean and dangerously skeptical, then Aristophanes in *The Clouds* and later Lucian in *Philosophers For Sale* return the compliment by skeptically returning philosophy to the theater and the philosopher to the marketplace, in which he is revealed to be a greasy huckster selling his wares or a puppet performing inanities. Here philosophy and theater agonistically engage each other over the truth, each constructing the other as a fraud to be expelled—both from the stage and from society. In his postskeptical verdict upon philosophy, Bacon would later make the connection between philosophy and theater explicit: philosophical systems are "Idols of the Theater, because in my judgment all the received systems are but so many stage plays, representing worlds of their own creation after an unreal and scenic fashion."[10] But philosophy and theater seek different truths: philosophy finds truth in presence and being, theater in absence and ontological groundlessness. Indeed the qualities for which philosophy castigates theater as false are the avenues along which theater pursues its truths. Constructed by philosophy as a nonreal, parasitic ontological space, theater exposes the parasitism and ontological insecurity of the various presences and sites of being on which philosophy and other discourses build their epistemological edifices. Theater brackets the truth claims of "normal" discourses to disclose their performativity, situatedness, and functions in economies of power and exchange.

Obviously, not all stages at all times and places develop the parasitic conditions of their existence into theaters of skeptical disclosure. Costumes and curtains conceal as well as uncover, perhaps conceal as much as and at the same time as they uncover. Yet the Elizabethan and Jacobean professional stage developed in circumstances that favored the exploitation of the stage's skeptical potential. Steven Mullaney in *The Place of the Stage* details the liminality of the Elizabethan and Jacobean stage, its Janus-like position on the thresholds of a variety of physical and discursive spaces.[11] Occupying buildings in the Liberties, inside and outside London and the grasp of civic authority, the professional theater converted play into work, appearances into the reality of hard coin, and provided rogues of all sorts with a home and royal livery. The new professional theater was visibly parasitic; to many, it was outrageously parasitic. As Jonas Barish outlines in *The Antitheatrical Prejudice*,[12] parasitism was not a neutral philosophical term to the opponents of the new professional stages but rather a term of abuse whose social, political, and economic elaboration reveals those stages' ability to create considerable unease: players were parasites whose social mobility threatened the stability of a hierarchical social order based on the conception of a fixed social self; their acting, or hypocrisy, or lying, struck at the roots of that order not only by divorcing its legitimating ideologies from a grounding in truth but also by demonstrating the manipulability of all social signs and so suggesting a fundamental disjunction between being and appearance at the heart of social reality. Yet if the theater for which Jonson and Middleton wrote was constructed by its society as parasitic, sheer performance, then the strength of its metadramatic impulse indicates the extent to which its playwrights acknowledged, drew energy from, even flaunted this construction. The Elizabethan and Jacobean stage thrived on the edginess surrounding it.

A number of studies have been written on the skeptical complexities of English Renaissance drama. Not surprisingly, most of them have concentrated on Shakespeare, primarily the tragedies. Stanley Cavell's *Disowning Knowledge in Six Plays of Shakespeare* is the outstanding instance.

However, while Cavell's studies are masterful and illuminating, my shift away from Shakespeare and tragedy is also a shift away from Cavell's humanist approach to Shakespeare's plays as meditations on timeless epistemological problems. City comedy as a genre demands such a shift: if its New Comedy inheritance, with its emphases on wit, disguise, and deceit, draws attention to questions of perception and knowledge, then its use of humors psychology gives those questions a distinctly materialist slant, and its focus on contemporary urban realities embeds those questions in the changing material environment of Jacobean England.

My concentration on city comedy also entails a shift away from one of the main themes of New Historicist and cultural materialist studies: the making and interrogation of the self and society at the center and on the peripheries of royal power. Castiglione's *The Book of the Courtier* and Machiavelli's *The Prince* are key texts in this theme's elaboration. As a subtext, however, both register the effects of a commercial reality whose expansion in early modern England was altering the modalities of power as it had done in Castiglione and Machiavelli's Italy. In *The Civilizing Process*, Norbert Elias argues that the development and refinement of aristocratic manners were the result of European society's transition from feudal to more centralized and commercial organization, a transition that changed the aristocracy from a warrior class to the class of courtiers whose ideal behavior is the subject of Castiglione's work.[13] Similarly, though Machiavelli in *The Discourses* maintains that "the sinews of war are not gold, but good soldiers,"[14] in *The Prince* he discusses at length the increasingly contractual nature of the relationship between soldiers and their employers, attributing the Italian city-states' recent military setbacks to their preference for mercenaries, their habit of conceiving war in commercial terms. This study's focus on city comedy brings the commercial subtext of Castiglione and Machiavelli's works into the foreground. Jonson and Middleton's comedies are concerned with the making and interrogation of self and society, but in the context of a social reality undergoing subtle and not-so-subtle reconfiguration by an expanding capitalist economy.

Two aspects of these changes require comment here: their visibility and the ways in which they altered social relationships. The capitalization of agriculture created major changes in the relations between landlords and their tenants: in their drive to increase their income through increased productivity and higher rent, landlords favored large tenant farmers and limited, contractual rather than customary land-holding agreements; many smaller tenants became wage laborers, whose migrations in search of work became socially visible as the "masterless men" problem.[15] London became a major European trading center, the hub of an expanding network of import and export trade. The city also became the center of a diverse but increasingly integrated national economy.¹⁶ These two developments had important consequences, as Joyce Appleby outlines in *Economic Thought and Ideology in Seventeenth-Century England*.¹⁷ In this increasingly complex economy with its multiple layers of mediation between buyer and seller money took on a life of its own. Investment, usury (legalized in a limited form in 1571), and foreign exchange rate differentials created money that could not be reduced to tokens of barter transactions and ways of life that could not be slotted into traditional, hierarchical representations of society. Furthermore, as England became integrated into larger, European, and even global economies, the national economy became sensitive to forces, such as foreign exchange rates and economic downturns in major export markets, not subject to national control. The government's ability to subordinate the economic to the social, one of the central roles of the government in Tudor thought on the commonwealth, was gradually undermined, creating considerable ideological as well as economic distress. Indeed, James's attempt to intervene in the economy through monopolies became one of the most divisive issues of his reign, an issue that brought merchants and gentry together in opposition to the royal prerogative and James' absolutist ideology.

On a smaller scale, the expanding domestic economy and its integration through multiple layers of middlemen created a market for the products of artisans not subject to the regulations of urban guilds. Guild regulations placed economic activity firmly within larger social considerations, but competition from unregulated artisans such as those living in the liberties of London threatened to render the guild structure anachronistic and prohibitively uncompetitive. Such institutions as Gresham's Royal Exchange, built in 1568, were visible—and ambiguous—symbols of capitalism's developing power. Visited and named by Elizabeth in 1570, Gresham's Exchange was an impressive manifestation of the new power and position of capital in England's social order; yet, it and the later New Exchange created disorder by supplying anyone possessing the necessary money with commodities for the conspicuous consumption that defeated repeated government attempts to enforce sumptuary legislation, to regulate the appropriation and display of traditional signs of social hierarchy. The playhouses built in Elizabeth's reign possessed a similar visibility and ambiguity: a commercial venture patronized by the nobility and the queen, the theater drew the ire of London magistrates for the commotions it caused among the city's citizens and the condemnation of moralists for the social disruptiveness of its actors' mobility and the semiotic disruptiveness of their metamorphoses.

City comedy's relation to these economic changes and their consequences has been the subject of a considerable amount of critical commentary.

The main tendency has been to see city comedy or, more specifically, certain city comedies as moral critiques of capitalism mounted from the perspective of traditional social thought. L. C. Knights presents this position in *Drama and Society in the Age of Jonson*, contrasting "Jonson's general anti-acquisitive attitude" to the plot-driven amorality of Middleton's comedies.[18] Alexander Leggatt's *Citizen Comedy in the Age of Shakespeare* and Theodore Leinwand's *The City Staged: Jacobean Comedy, 1603–1613* present more complex variants of the moral thesis. Leggatt argues that "the assertion of morality and the subversion of morality are the poles between which citizen comedy moves,"[19] and Leinwand considers the satiric edge of city comedy as moral condemnation not of real London figures but of the demeaning and conflict-oriented stereotypes by which Londoners perceived each other. Brian Gibbons's *Jacobean City Comedy*, the first published study devoted exclusively to city comedy, still offers one of the most complex and insightful readings of the genre: according to Gibbons, Jonson and Middleton are moral critics who, as they explore and develop the genre, come to confront the inadequacy of inherited social and moral frameworks to describe let alone critique the new urban, capitalist reality.[20]

Recent studies, however, have pointed out that the moral thesis oversimplifies the relationship between city comedy and expanding capitalism because it fails to take into account the theater's and the playwrights' situatedness within England's changing economy. Douglas Bruster comments that "London's playhouses can best be understood in terms of commerce, as centers for the production and consumption of an aesthetic product."[21] Consequently, as Don Wayne observes, "While they may be satirizing the acquisitiveness associated with an incipient mercantile capitalism, the dramatists are themselves caught in something of a double bind concerning the place of their own work in this new economic, political, and social context."[22] Jonson and Middleton's city comedies seem obsessively aware of their own situatedness, and with this awareness comes an intimacy with the new commercial reality that extends beyond critique from a distant moral vantage. In *Worlds Apart: The Market and the Theater in Anglo-American Thought, 1550–1750*, Jean-Christophe Agnew argues that

> The professional theater of the English Renaissance became in effect a "physiognomic metaphor" for the mobile and polymorphous features of the market. But it did not merely represent those features; at its most venturesome, it dramatized representation and misrepresentation as the pivotal problems of its drama. For the first time, perhaps, theater made what Anne Righter has called the "idea of the play" its cardinal concern and, by thus confronting the conditions of its own performance, it invoked the same problematic of exchange—the same questions of authenticity, accountability, and intentionality—at issue in the "idea of the market."[23]

This study particularizes the insights of these recent arguments: each play I discuss explores in some way the epistemological difficulties created by the reconfiguration of social reality by the forces of exchange.

A word on the structure of the book is necessary. Each of the seven chapters focuses on a single play by Jonson or Middleton. When I began the research for this work I envisaged for it a very different organizational method, but as the work progressed I chose to organize my material around close readings of a small corpus of plays for a number of reasons. First, a focus on a larger cultural formation or episteme would lose touch with the radical particularity of skeptical inquiry. Furthermore, the emphasis on the particular reflects my critical methodology, which could be described as deconstructive and materialist. Deconstructive because, in a reversal of deconstruction's "normal" movement, it treats as "serious" philosophical meditations texts that have been consigned to the literary and often, because of their comic nature, the light literary. Close readings are therefore essential. Materialist because it situates these serious and comic, philosophical and literary pieces of theater within their material and cultural intertexts in order to tease out the social, political, and economic directedness of their skepticism. The close readings are therefore also points of departure and return for a hermeneutics that, by recognizing the particularity and contingency of its own skeptical strategies as well as those of the texts it engages, is free to and must follow various eccentric orbits.

The body of plays to which the following pages are devoted comprises four plays by Jonson and three by Middleton: *Volpone*, *Epicoene*, *The Alchemist*, and *Bartholomew Fair*; *Michaelmas Term*, *A Trick to Catch the Old One*, and *A Chaste Maid in Cheapside*. Other playwrights wrote city comedies, but none possesses the powerful skeptical dynamics of these seven plays. I have excluded John Martson from this study not because I do not find him challenging but because I find him most challenging in the absurd extremes of his tragedies, particularly the *Antonio and Mellida* plays and *The Malcontent*. Moreover, despite the centrifugal impulses of their skepticism, the seven plays I have chosen reveal as a group a certain thematic and theatrical unity. The city in these city comedies is certainly, in Gail Kern Paster's phrase, "a predatory trap" rather than "a visionary embodiment of ideal community."[24] Their urban fictional worlds are labyrinthine places of uncertainty, the opposite of Laurence Manley's "fictions of settlement."[25] If Manley's fictions of settlement domesticate and render knowable the bewilderingly new urban environment of early modern London, then the city comedies I explore are fictions of unsettlement that derive comic and critical energy from the city's resistance to knowledge. Within specifically urban worlds of appearance, the plays explore the roles of desire, commerce, and power in the production of knowledge. Middleton's fictional worlds are zones of conflict shaped by commodity forms and commercial mentalities. Jonson's worlds are more tightly circumscribed and intense but always situated within an exchange economy that threatens the possibility of a world overrun by appearances, utterly ungrounded in being. Middleton's plays derive their dramatic energy from time and contingency, parameters of performativity that Middleton manipulates to skeptical effect. Time and contingency are central elements in Jonson's dramaturgy, but so too is space, including the space of the theater, which serves as a paradigm for Jonson's explorations of the various malleable epistemological spaces at the heart of his plays: Volpone's bedchambers, the fashionable world of London's West End, Subtle's alchemical laboratory, and Bartholomew Fair.

The book begins by revisiting the quarrel between philosophy and theater. The first chapter explores *Volpone*'s Venice as an appropriation of and critical commentary on the ideal, just polis of Plato's *Republic*. Theater returns to Plato's polis not as alien but as the utopian city's enabling precondition. The second chapter examines the way *Michaelmas Term* reworks the inescapable theatricality of social order into a critique of Jacobean ideologies of social hierarchy. Both plays dramatize the self and society as improvisations in networks of power and exchange. The third, fourth, and fifth chapters shift emphasis slightly to focus on the knowing, the calculating, and the doubting selves. In the airless world of *Epicoene*, the knowing self is implausible, ridiculous, and most damningly, unfashionable. All are fools, and only those wits who grasp knowledge's potent theatricality can exploit folly successfully. *A Trick to Catch the Old One* probes the cynical, calculating self's disquieting irrationality as it navigates a world characterized by the disjunction between form and feeling. In *The Alchemist*, Descartes's madmen take the stage in plague-time London to reveal their kinship with the skeptic despite his denials. The last two chapters turn to the impossible epistemological fantasies of power. *A Chaste Maid in Cheapside* dramatizes patriarchal order's paradoxical reproduction, and *Bartholomew Fair* draws its comic energy from the perversely contradictory nature of the nationalist project to know and so to control others defined as aliens.

1
Volpone and the Dystopian Turn of Utopian Discourse

If not always nowhere, Utopia is always elsewhere: for Plato, in a realm of ideas; for More and Bacon, in the uncharted waters of the New World, longitude and latitude unknown or forgotten. Utopian worlds are not merely escapist, though. The voyage to Utopia is followed by the return to the here and now and completed by the voyage's retelling, bringing Utopia home as a more or less explicit critical commentary on contemporary society.[1] *Volpone* stands in a complex and ambivalent relationship to such utopian fictions. More specifically, the play critically uses but skeptically interrogates the notion of the unalienated or just self, which is both a microcosmic analogy and a necessary precondition of such utopian social orders as Plato's *Republic*, a work whose influence on More's *Utopia* ensured its paradigmatic status in the utopian imagination of the Renaissance.[2] Jonson's poetics are at their most problematically Platonic in *Volpone*. Like Plato's Socrates, who to pursue the issue of justice in the self and in society adopts the role of the "philosophic artist" and "[looks] frequently in both directions, that is, at justice and beauty and self discipline and the like in their true nature, and again at the copy of them he is trying to make in human beings,"[3] Jonson adopts the role of "comic Poet" whose office is "to imitate justice, and instruct to life."[4] The play is set in the Venetian Republic, whose symbolic ambivalence as the city of wealth and decadence, justice and oppression, and wisdom and deceit Jonson exploits to imitate the *Republic*'s double vision: until the final scene the play dramatizes a very unideal, unjust human world and examines the dystopian effects of the logic of an economy of accumulation and consumption; the final scene seems both to transform and to pronounce judgment on this dystopian world by imposing upon it a Renaissance version of Plato's just social order. Nonetheless, *Volpone*'s comic aesthetic is not straightforwardly utopian. The play not merely reproduces but also deconstructs Platonic double vision.

In Plato's republic, the just self and the just society are anchored in and produced by the prior knowledge of a realm of being and truth. In Jonson's Venice, the mind is thoroughly material and lacks any access to such a realm of being and truth; consequently, the just self and the just society are appearances of truth anchored in and produced by power. Jonson does not simply contradict Plato, however, but like Aristophanes and Lucian returns him to the marketplace and the theater. The play's bleak comic conclusion dramatically unfolds utopia's paradoxical theatricality, a dystopic dependence on representation that Plato the philosopher must acknowledge yet suppress. *Volpone* shows the realization of Utopia to be itself a dystopian moment within the larger economy of expenditure and death.

Volpone's Venice, like Shakespeare's Ephesus in *The Comedy of Errors*, is a labyrinth, a space of epistemological uncertainty. Ephesus is a

> town . . . full of cozenage
> As nimble jugglers that deceive the eye,
> Dark-working sorcerers that change the mind,
> Soul-killing witches that deform the body,
> Disguised cheaters, prating mountebanks.[5]

Even so, Shakespeare's skepticism does not run deep in this play. The inability to distinguish appearance from reality is "one day's error,"[6] a temporary aberration not a permanent affliction, and confusion ultimately gives way to the establishment of true identities and the renewal of society based on these identities. In Venice, another town full of cozenage and prating mountebanks, the rift between appearance and reality is fundamental, and epistemological uncertainty is a permanent condition which (as I will argue later) even the ending's unmasking of Volpone and Mosca does not redeem. Subsequent chapters will show that this construction of the city—as space in which knowledge has no anchorage—unites the seven plays I discuss even as it distinguishes them from such plays as *The Comedy of Errors*, which either domesticate or conquer the city by representing its space as transparent and unproblematic or by reducing it to the ultimately knowable. In Venice, as in the various London spaces dramatized by the other plays, the link between appearance and being remains elusive.

One of the play's enabling preconditions is the unreliability of sense perception. Volpone makes a career out of deliberately exploiting this unreliability through his various disguises as ailing magnifico, Scoto, and the commandadore. Most of the play's characters, though, are blissfully unaware of their senses' tenuous hold on reality. The legacy hunters are more than willing to trust their senses: when Mosca, shouting insults at a supposedly deaf and nearly dead Volpone, tells Corvino to "credit your own sense" (1.5.51), Corvino does so unhesitatingly. Bonario also gives his senses more credit than is due, believing the "personated passion" (3.2.35) that accompanies Mosca's highly ironic relation of the difficulties of being a sycophant: "What? Does he weep? The sign is soft and good! / I do repent me that I was so harsh" (3.2.18–19), Bonario exclaims. The epistemological uncertainty generated in these scenes and in other similar scenes throughout the play is to some degree artificial. Corvino, Bonario, and the others are victims of deliberate plotting. But the play represents the senses as unreliable at a more fundamental level. Sense perception, it seems, can be fashioned to fit any suggestion, no matter how absurd, and the play makes a potent comic principle out of Montaigne's maxim that "A strong imagination creates the event."[7] Having been told that her husband is "Rowing upon the water in a gondola, / With the most cunning courtesan of Venice" (3.5.20–21), Lady Would-Be shapes her perceptions to fit this story and so transforms Peregrine, Sir Pol's companion when Lady Would-Be locates him, into "a lewd harlot, a base fricatrice, / A female devil, in a male outside" (4.2.55–56). Once informed of her error, she refuses to abandon the story and provides eye witness testimony to support Voltore's claim that Celia (not Peregrine) had "baited / A stranger, a grave knight, with her loose eyes, / And more lascivious kisses" (4.5.146–48): "Aye, this same is she" (4.5.1), she states while pointing at Celia. The most spectacular example of the openness of the senses to suggestion is the "blue toad, with a bat's wings" (5.12.31) that flies from a supposedly demon-possessed Voltore in the play's final scene. The blue toad is quite obviously part of Volpone's desperate theatrics—he is attempting to discredit Voltore's written confession of Celia and Bonario's innocence—and yet two people other than Volpone (Corvino and Corbaccio) claim to see this demon, and even the avocatori are "full of wonder" (5.12.36) at the event.

To complicate matters, reason is as weak as the senses and is incapable of compensating for the senses' unreliability by providing a criterion by which to distinguish appearance from reality, falsehood from truth. The legacy hunters swallow any story Mosca feeds them; they persuade themselves that they and not Mosca have invented the plots by which they are gulled; and, ultimately, they come to believe the lies they tell to prevent their conspiracy from being discovered. Perhaps the most telling example of the utter confusion of truth and fiction in the legacy hunters' minds is the written confession Voltore submits to the avocatori after his hopes of being Volpone's heir have been dashed. The written confession is a curious blend of fact and fiction: Voltore claims that "the gentleman [Bonario] was wronged; /And that the gentlewoman was brought thither, / Forced by her husband: and there left" (5.12.2–4), but "that / Volpone would have ravished her, he holds / Utterly false; knowing his impotence" (5.12.5–7).

Even when Voltore attempts to tell the truth, he cannot arrive at it but remains lost in the "labyrinth" (5.10.42) of knowledge without any criterion of truth as guide. Indeed, that the senses are unreliable and appearances seem not to be anchored in being makes Volpone and Mosca's schemes possible; that the mind is weak makes them so easy. As Mosca comments, each of the legacy hunters

> Is so possessed, and stuffed with his own hopes,
> That anything to the contrary,
> Never so true, or never so apparent,
> Never so palpable, they will resist it -
>
> (5.2.24-27)

This problem is not confined to the legacy hunters but extends beyond the play's world to the world at large. Separating the factual from the fantastic was as much a problem for the Jacobean reader of Hakluyt as it is for Sir Politic Would-Be, whose wildly fertile mind constantly gives birth to stories that Peregrine fears will be "put i' the book of voyages" (5.4.5) and "registered, for truth" (5.4.6). It is significant in this regard that Bonario, one of the play's two unambiguously virtuous characters, has no special insight into the truth. In the play the mind possesses no inner light of truth and has access to no transcendent realm of ideas from which standards of truth might be obtained. Rather, the mind is material, an organ on the same level and with the same unreliability as other sense organs. Ironically, Lady Would-Be, who like the Collegiates in *Epicoene* is all surface, provides the lecture on the inner workings and epistemological problems of the material mind:

> There's nothing more doth overwhelm the judgement,
> And clouds the understanding, than too much
> Settling and fixing, and (as 'twere) subsiding
> Upon one object. For the incorporating
> Of these same outward things, into that part,
> Which we call mental, leaves some certain faeces,
> That stop the organs, and, as Plato says,
> Assassinates our knowledge.
>
> (3.4.105–12)

This view of the mind raises insoluble epistemological difficulties. If the mind is an organ, who is to decide "who have half-stopped the organs of their minds with earthly oppilations" (2.2.60–61) and who have not? The mind cannot reach beyond its material conditions to measure the truthfulness of its reasoning. In *Volpone* there can be no turn from the cave to the sunlit world, from shadows to things in themselves; all are confined to living in a "waking dream" (1.1.18).

The disjunction between appearance and being in *Volpone*'s Venice is not merely an epistemological problem, however. The material mind and its waking dreams are fashioned by and integrated into the material world of Venice's commercial exchange economy, a dystopian, anti-Platonic economy that values an object not by the extent to which it has being by participation in an Idea but by the extent to which it *appears* valuable. In the exchange economy an object's being is consumed by its appearance. Gold is the "dumb god" (1.1.22) of this economy: the motor, token, and end of exchange, gold is the measure of all things, including "the price of souls" (1.1.24). The circular structure of gold's value—valued for its (scarce) appearance, paradoxically it becomes the standard of value—corrodes value's ontological ground, transforming "all style of joy, in children, parents, friends" (1.1.17) into a "waking dream" (1.1.18).

At the center of gold's fashioning of dreams are Volpone's bedchambers. The wealth and the seemingly decaying body that these rooms contain are the objects on which the legacy hunters fix their minds and around which they shape both their hopes and their perceptions of their world. But, although an object of fixation, these chambers are not the site of knowledge (even though they contain the two characters who do seem to know.) As Lyle observes, Volpone's chambers are a "world of art" in which Volpone is artist, even demiurge.[8] The demiurge's creation, however, is governed by its god and remains in the realm of appearance. Strangely both parasitical on and the center of Venice's exchange economy, Volpone's bedchambers are dedicated to gold, the god of appearance, containing a "shrine" (1.1.2) to this dubious "saint" (1.1.2) which is both an echo and (according to Volpone) an intensification of a similar shrine, Saint Mark's treasury, located at the center of Venice.[9] In this space dedicated to appearance, Volpone works to inhabit a dream of the golden age. "Well did wise poets, by thy glorious name / Title that age, which they would have the best" (1.1.14–15), Volpone exclaims to his heap of gold in the opening scene, and for the rest of the play he works to recreate, through the economy of which gold is god, his version of the golden age. Like Hesiod's "golden race of mortal men" who are "untouched by work or sorrow,"[10] Volpone "wound[s] no earth with ploughshares" (1.1.34). Volpone's sexual fantasies, in which he and Celia metamorphose into the shapes of various gods and their lovers, locate Volpone's world of art in a golden mythic past. Volpone goes so far as to dream of drinking gold: "our drink shall be prepared of gold and amber" (3.7.216), he tells Celia. Volpone too lives a gilded, waking dream.

Volpone's bedchambers are not, then, a utopian enclave of being in a dystopian world of appearance. Rather, Volpone's dream of a golden world is a dream of a world in which gold and other objects are fetishized for their appearance, for the exchange value that has sedimented around them but that has little if any relation to their intrinsic properties. In the play's opening scene Volpone with Mosca's help attempts to distinguish himself and his activities from the commercial world around him—Volpone "gain[s] no common way" (1.1.33)—and many critics have taken him at his word, arguing that the sterility of Volpone's "secondary world" sets it completely apart from the larger productive world of Venice.[11] As the play develops, however, we see quite the opposite to be the case. Volpone's secondary world concentrates and thus makes visible the sterile economy of expenditure (the economic equivalent of what Freud called the death instinct) underlying Venice's apparently productive exchange economy.[12] The source of the wealth accumulating in Volpone's vault is the surplus wealth generated by the community of Venice. Throughout the play the money given to Volpone by the legacy hunters is figured as investment capital. In these terms Corvino attempts to persuade Celia to prostitute herself to Volpone: "respect my venture" (3.7.37) he tells her. In the play's first scene Volpone makes explicit the commercial nature of his game with the legacy hunters: his project

> draws new clients, daily, to my house,
> Women, and men, of every sex and age,
> That bring me presents, send me plate, coin, jewels
> With hope, that when I die (which they expect
> Each greedy minute) it shall then return,
> Tenfold, upon them; whilst some, covetous
> Above the rest, seek to engross me, whole.
>
> (1.1.76–82)

Tellingly, the legacy hunters can hope for a return on their investments only at Volpone's death. The occlusion of production in Volpone's secondary world clarifies this relationship between capital and death. Volpone does nothing productive with the wealth in his vault; production, the economic link between capital and consumption, has dropped out of the economy of this secondary world only to reveal consumption, expenditure, and death to be the ultimate end of the economy of exchange. Nowhere is this more apparent than the imaginary banquet Volpone sets before Celia in his attempt to seduce her. Here Volpone's rhetoric supplies the function of production, translating the wealth in his vault into commodities to be either literally or figuratively consumed. What is to be consumed in this magnificent if grotesque feast, however, is the appearance of the object—the exchange value of "A gem, but worth a private patrimony" (3.7.199), or the exotic appeal of "The heads of parrots, tongues of nightingales, / The brains of peacocks, and of ostriches" (3.7.201–2)—rather than the object in itself, whose substantiality or being is negated by its appearance (how peacock brains actually taste is irrelevant for Volpone.) Celia herself attracts Volpone's desire to possess her primarily because she is a scarce commodity with "so rare a face" (1.5.107) and "kept as warily as is your [Volpone's] gold" (1.5.118). Even sex for Volpone is consumption—not of Celia herself but of Celia in a multiplicity of costumes.

The economy of consumption finds its double in Volpone's protean, alienated subjectivity. Like the economy of consumption, Volpone's subjectivity is anti-Platonic. For Plato, the ideal, just individual presents a unified continuum of bodily appearance which manifests the inner harmony of a soul governed by reason.[13] Greene argues that this ideal, centered self exhibits "an inner moral equilibrium" and is incarnational: reason or the word is continually made flesh, and the full presence of the individual's being is manifested in her or his appearances.[14] Volpone's theatrically produced self, on the other hand, is the antitype of the Platonic self and revels in the multiplicity of appearances. The anti-incarnational, protean self of which Volpone is the paradigmatic example is, according to Greene, "without core and principle and substance."[15] Greene's definition of the protean self is, however, somewhat inaccurate, especially as it applies to Volpone: the anti-incarnational self is not entirely without principle but exploits the gap between word and flesh rather than seeking to close it. The alienation of Volpone's subjectivity does not consist in a simple disjunction between appearance and being or the abdication of reason in the control of behavior. Volpone glories in his "cunning" (1.1.31) and strives to bring every aspect of his bodily appearance under its control. Volpone's alienation is similar to the alienation that splits Descartes' knowing subject. In *Discourses on Method*, Descartes divides the individual into two entirely separate realms: the subject or *cogito*, of whose existence alone can we be certain; and the body, the uncertainty of whose existence places it as alienated and supplementary Other to the subject.[16] Francis Barker comments that this alienated and supplementary body thus becomes inarticulate and incomprehensible in itself, an otherness that will remain troublingly mysterious until captured in the self's network of signification: the Cartesian body "cannot itself signify, but becomes an object for discursive practice, present to discourse only across the distance of representation."[17] For the subject conceived exclusively as reason, the body is either a textualized object or a disturbing otherness; this subject is anti-incarnational, always plagued by the gap between the word and the flesh.[18]

Volpone's subjectivity is considerably more ludic than Barker's angst-ridden Cartesian subject (Volpone has more fun with his anti-incarnational self), but Volpone is nonetheless alienated, his relation to his body both bifurcated and caught up in a capitalist economy of accumulation and consumption. Volpone's body is an object of his own discursive practice, a text that is also a carefully crafted commodity exchanged for the legacy hunters' gold. In the play's first scene we watch the first of a number of scenes scattered throughout the play in which Volpone fashions that text/commodity as he takes upon himself the signs—the "furs" (1.1.97), the "caps" (1.1.113), the "ointment for your eyes" (1.1.114), "my feigned cough, my physic, and my gout, / My apoplexy, palsy, and catarrhs" (1.1.124–25), and "this my posture" (1.1.126)—of extreme decay by which "this three year, I have milked their hopes" (1.1.127). Significantly, when in act 2 Volpone chooses to transform his body into something other than the ailing magnifico, he plays Scoto the mountebank, a role designed not only to sell *"oglio del Scoto"* (2.2.126) but also to allow him to acquire a scarce commodity, a look at Celia. And Volpone's final role, his appearance as himself in front of the avocatori, precipitates another transaction: "all are sold" (The Argument 7). Volpone's attitude toward his body as semiotic object to be consumed does not change even when he throws off his disguise to seduce Celia. Rather, his body becomes another text composed of costumes and Ovidian tales whose end is death—"we may, so, transfuse our wandering souls, / Out at our lips, and score up sums of pleasures" (3.7.233–34)—and translation into another text, a fragment of a poem by Catullus:

> That the curious shall not know,
> How to tell them, as they flow;
> And the envious, when they find
> What their number is, be pined.
>
> (3.7.235–38)

The play is full of images of Volpone as both consumer and object to be consumed: gulling the legacy hunters, declares Volpone, is "better than rob churches yet: / Or fat, by eating, once a month, a man" (1.5.91–92) and affords Volpone many a "rare meal of laughter" (5.2.87); and for the legacy hunters Volpone is both "carcass" (1.2.90) and "carrion" (5.2.66). Skulsky argues in "Cannibals vs. Demons in *Volpone*" that through these images the play explores consumption and being consumed as modes of selfhood: to fill the void in one's self one can either consume others (cannibalism) or be consumed by others (demon possession, occupying others by having them ingest you).[19] I would qualify this argument by pointing out that what is being consumed is appearance, not substantiality or being: the legacy hunters consume the appearance of a "carcass," and Volpone's "rare meal of laughter" is the spectacle of the legacy hunters' disappointment and large financial loss. Volpone and the legacy hunters are locked in an economy of accumulation and consumption in which feasting and being feasted upon are modes of the endless articulation of selfhood in a world of commodified appearances.

Controlling the semiosis of Volpone's body, its articulation in the world of appearances, is not the precocious interiority of a Hamlet but a largely instrumental reason whose goal is the maximization of accumulation and consumption and whose pleasure is the shiver of the one passing into the other. It is no surprise, then, that Volpone takes as much pleasure in the thought of Celia's destruction as he would have in enjoying or consuming her: for him there is no difference. The alienated self's control over its textualized body, however, is precarious. During Volpone's first encounter with the avocatori the physicality that Volpone has attempted to textualize returns as something other, from without, ironically afflicting him with the pains whose signs he was attempting merely to represent:

> 'Fore God, my left leg 'gan to have the cramp;
> And I apprehended, straight, some power had struck me
> With a dead palsy.
>
> (5.1.5–7)

Greenblatt observes that Volpone, who has attempted to be "nothing, a bodiless fiction," has suddenly experienced "a sign that the body resists the will and thus that the fiction is collapsing. For Volpone, to sense the body's resistance is to sense death," the inescapable return of the bodily Other he has tried to suppress.[20] This incident leads Volpone to assert control over his body by further alienating himself from it. At several points in the play Volpone withdraws to the position of spectator when not himself performing. This position is one of passivity but also, at least momentarily, one of spectral power. In act 5, scene 3 Volpone withdraws too far, however: the "dead" Volpone "peeps from behind a traverse" (5.3.8) to observe the implementation of the plan he devised primarily to shake off the effects of his encounter with his body and only secondarily to torture the legacy hunters. In this case, Volpone's spectral alienation from the textual production of his (dead) body comes back to haunt him as Mosca attempts to "bury him, or gain by him" (5.5.14). The author finds his textual body circulating in contexts beyond his control.

Having explored the dystopian extremes of the exchange economy, *Volpone* in the final scene executes a sharp utopian turn in the direction of a restored Platonic justice antithetical to the exchange economy. In the *Republic* justice is both social and individual: social justice consists in a hierarchical social organization in which each individual minds her or his own business; individual justice is minding one's own business on a smaller scale, the identity of an individual's being and appearance. For Plato, just individuals are necessary for a just state; consequently, anything that threatens individual justice—acting, sophistry, most forms of poetry—must be eradicated from the state.²¹ In *Volpone*'s final scene Jonson dons the mantle of the "philosophic artist" in order to perform "the office of a comic Poet, to imitate justice" (Dedication 112), and the order imposed upon Volpone's Venice replicates the ideal, just order of Plato's *Republic*. Significantly, the avocatori's sentences do not punish for violations of the law but for deviations from ideal justice; their punishments are designed not to conform to the legality of the commercial world—the characters are not, strictly speaking, "mulcted" (Dedication 111) or fined in accordance with established law—but to restore individual and social justice in Platonic terms. Thus, Volpone is punished not for attempting to rape Celia but for appearing other than he is (which is not in itself illegal). His punishment forcibly restores the identity of his being and appearance: "Thou art to lie in prison, cramped with irons, / Till thou be'st sick and lame indeed" (5.12.123–24). Mosca is punished for the Renaissance equivalent of not minding one's own business, for violating Venice's social hierarchy: Mosca has "abused the court, / And habit of a gentleman of Venice, / Being a fellow of no birth or blood" (5.12.110–12) and his punishment is to be put back into his proper place, to "be whipped; / Then live perpetual prisoner in our galleys" (5.12.113–14). Similarly, Corvino and Corbaccio are punished not for their perjury but for their stupidity; their punishments are designed to make their true inner conditions visible to themselves and to others. Lastly, Voltore, that consummate actor and sophist, is banished from the republic.

Yet Utopia's transition from the nowhere of a critical ideal to the somewhere of an actual social order is difficult. *Volpone* performs Jonson's intention to "put the snaffle in their mouths, that cry out, we never punish vice in our interludes" (Dedication 106–8), but in so doing it raises questions about the results. The utopian nature of the justice imposed in the play's concluding scene is discordantly suspended between its unideal, dystopian causes and effects: the avocatori who impose the justice are conspicuously fallible, thoroughly immersed in a material world of appearances unanchored in ideal being, and the effects of the justice—Volpone and Mosca will suffer cruel physical punishment and confinement or enslavement—seem unduly harsh. As Barish has commented, the concluding scene noticeably lacks the "judicial integrity" that would legitimate the avocatori's social engineering as justice.²² This ironic inadequateness between the form of justice and its material causes and effects situates *Volpone* as a complex, self-reflexive exploration of the genre of utopian fiction, on par with More's *Utopia*. Krishan Kumar observes that "anti-utopia has stalked utopia from the beginning," the product both of skepticism about the possibility that Utopia can ever be realized and of the fear that "utopia *can* be attained, and that it will be a nightmare."²³ More's *Utopia*, for instance, is not an exercise in social engineering so much as a highly ironic examination of utopian modes of thought. Hythloday emerges as a paradoxically isolated figure, a social philosopher who is unable and unwilling to promote his social vision in a world equally unable and unwilling to listen to him. His utopia cannot exist anywhere but elsewhere—which is nowhere.[24] And indeed even its realization elsewhere is problematic: this utopia that is supposedly eutopia has patriarchy, slavery, and preemptive Machiavellian warfare as fundamental elements. Novels such as Huxley's *Brave New World* and Orwell's *Nineteen Eighty-Four* extend this kind of analysis of the darker, dystopian aspect of Utopia.

The *Republic* is less obviously ironic and pessimistic, but here nonetheless the transition from nowhere to somewhere is aporetic. The problem surfaces in book 7 of the *Republic*, as Socrates struggles to assert that his vision of an ideal, just society is not "merely an idle dream" (354). Socrates' struggle points to a curious duality that structures Plato's dialogue, a duality in the status of imitation or representation that shifts the convergence of being and appearance in an ideal social order into an impossible, paradoxical future. Plato's construction of a just society in which being governs appearance involves a theory of representation that places representation at the furthest remove from being and truth: material reality imitates ideal form, but representations imitate material reality and are (at best) imitations of the appearances of imitations. Representation's tenuous hold on being pushes it into the creative nonbeing of fiction—or, in the terms of Plato's utopian epistemology, of lies, dangerous perversions of reality that constantly threaten to insinuate themselves between being and the appearances it should structure and so to break the link that renders the individual and society just. Yet, marginal or banished though representation may be in Plato's utopia, Socrates' struggle draws our attention to the fact that the utopia from which fiction is banished is itself a fiction, that a philosophical artist is still an artist, unnecessary and undesirable in Plato's ideal society. The margins of the *Republic*, the fictional frame of its dialogue, implies a radical inversion of the theory of representation articulated *within* its utopian fiction. In the space of the frame, representation's fictionality indicates not representation's but reality's distance from being, suggesting a dystopic lack of being at the heart of reality that renders utopian fiction possible and even necessary as a mode of participation in the ideal and yet that preempts the possibility of utopian fiction's realization. In book 7 Socrates contends that the ideal, just society is realizable, albeit with difficulty, if "political power should be in the hands of one or more true philosophers" (354). Yet at the end of book 9, Socrates shifts his ideal society's location irretrievably inward: "it is laid up as a pattern in heaven, where he who wishes can see it and found it in his own heart. But it doesn't matter whether it exists or will ever exist; in it alone, and in no other society, could he [the truly just individual] take part in public affairs" (420). Utopia is realizable only if utopian conditions already obtain, and, as Socrates' discussion of imperfect societies in book 8 demonstrates, they never do except in a mythic past or fictional future. Only by the nonbeing of representation can the imperfections of existing societies be measured. Paradoxically, then, Socrates' utopian urges are both enabled and frustrated by a dystopian ontology whose repudiation within his utopian fiction is at the same time a rejection of the fictionality by which it is repudiated. Utopia cannot escape the ambivalent nonbeing of representation, and the philosophical artist is an exile from both the dystopia he rejects and the utopia that rejects him.

The aporetic nature of imitation's duality structures the multiple ironies of *Volpone*'s conclusion. *Volpone*, however, is a bleaker work than the *Republic*, foregrounding not the utopian space that can be carved out in representation but utopian imitation's double deformation in an inescapably dystopic world. *Volpone* is dystopic, even in its concluding utopian turn. The conclusion replicates Platonic justice but in entirely anti-Platonic circumstances. Like the rest of the play's fictional world, the Scrutineo is part of a world of appearances unanchored in being. Although the avocatori are not flagrantly corrupt—they neither are offered bribes nor expect them—they are characterized as much by their sensitivity to appearances, to their own and others' perceived social status, as by their desire for justice. They quickly alter their treatment of Mosca, for instance, once they are told that he is dead Volpone's heir. The play makes quite clear the Scrutineo's disjunction from any ideal exemplar: the "consciences" (4.6.16) and "heaven, that never fails the innocent" (4.6.17) to which Celia and Bonario appeal "are no testimonies" (4.6.18) in the avocatori's court. This disjunction is most tellingly revealed in the avocatori's epistemological weakness. The avocatori are more gullible than corrupt, and because of their epistemological limitations their imitation of justice turns out to be a parody that inverts the crucial relationship between truth and power that must ground a just, Platonic society. The avocatori are in as weak an epistemological position as the play's other gulls, material minds lost in a world of appearances. Before Volpone reveals himself in the concluding scene, they listen to four different versions of the events surrounding Volpone's attempted rape of Celia. In the first trial they listen to two accounts: Celia and Bonario's, followed by Voltore's. Voltore's rhetoric defeats Celia's pleas to heaven and Bonario's plain speaking, and the avocatori adjourn having accepted Voltore's account as truth. When they reconvene, they are presented with a third version of the play's events, Voltore's confession, and then a fourth, Voltore's retraction of his confession as the product of demon possession.

Mystification rather than clarification is the result, each version eliciting from the avocatori phrases such as "The like of this the Senate never heard of" (4.5.1), "These things, / They strike with wonder" (4.6.153–54), "This same's a labyrinth!" (5.10.42), and "What maze is this!" (5.12.43). The avocatori are inclined to believe the most recently presented version because they have no way of distinguishing truth from falsehood other than calling more witnesses, whose appearances and testimonies are as uncertain as the claims and accounts which they support or contradict.

Then the heckling commandadore decides to "uncase" (5.12.85) in front of the court, announcing

> I am Volpone, and this my knave;
> This, his own knave; this, avarice's fool;
> This, a chimera of wittol, fool, and knave.
>
> (5.12.89–91)

The avocatori proclaim this to be the "miracle" (5.12.95) or sign that unequivocally points out the truth. But Volpone's uncasing cannot function as this kind of miraculous, unambiguous sign, cannot bear the epistemological weight the avocatori attribute to it. Its function is belied by the epistemological uncertainty of the world in which it appears. The courtroom scenes preceding Volpone's uncasing emphasize the avocatori's inability to distinguish truth from falsehood, their fascination with the spellbinding surfaces of words, clothes, and power, and Volpone's uncasing does not carry within itself the significance that would warrant the attribution of demystifying power. Volpone does not provide another account that somehow explains the preceding ones: his revelation consists of mere assertions of identity, and, as we have seen, assertions of identity are extremely problematic in the play. Volpone uncases, strips off the commandadore's costume—to reveal what? He offers no unmistakable tokens of his identity, such as the birthmark, the family heirloom, or the piece of knowledge only he could know, that characterize the recognition scenes of other Renaissance comedies, including several of Jonson's own. He has been known to all the play's characters, except Mosca, only through the elaborately crafted appearances of his various costumes; throughout the play he *is* the sum of his costumes. The avocatori know Volpone only in his heavily made-up appearance as an ailing old man. By stripping away his costume Volpone strips away the substance of his identity, the appearances by which he might be recognized as someone or another, to reveal nothing at all. Certainly, he reveals nothing possessing a greater degree of certainty or self-evidentiality than the preceding revelations and counterrevelations. Consequently, the avocatori's decision to accept the uncasing commandadore's assertions of identity as truth is epistemologically unmotivated: they have no more and no less grounds for accepting them than the grounds they had for accepting any of the other accounts they have heard.

For the avocatori, then, perception of the truth does not ground their exercise of power; rather, their exercise of power creates the appearance of truth, just as it would have if Volpone had played it safe after the first court session and Celia and Bonario had consequently been punished as guilty of the fabricated charges brought against them. In both cases justice is thoroughly dystopic: working without a criterion of truth, the machinery of justice produces the effects of truth through its public authority and its power to act *as if* it knew the truth. Not being in a position to know, the avocatori arbitrarily decide to recognize the commandadore as Volpone and to produce this as the truth by using their power to inscribe on the commandadore/Volpone's body the marks of his identity. As Foucault puts it, "'Truth' is linked in a circular relation with systems of power which produce and sustain it."[25] The play has not turned from a world of appearance to a world of being, or from the self as text to the self as fullness of being. Rather, it has shifted from one dystopia to another, to a Hobbesian universe in which power vested absolutely in the sovereign body—here the avocatori—fixes appearance and constrains the text to one absolute and univocal interpretation.

The audience, of course, knows that the avocatori's arbitrary decision is, in fact, the right one, but this privileged epistemological perspective is entirely the product of Jonson's art. Jonson provides the audience with a behind-the-scenes vantage impossible in the play's fictional world, and only from this artistically constructed vantage point is the true imitation of ideal justice, the imposition of order based on a prior cognition of the truth, possible. To place the audience in this privileged position constitutes an artistic choice on Jonson's part: dramas as diverse as Jonson's own *Epicoene*, Middleton's *A Chaste Maid in Cheapside,* and Agatha Christie's *The Mousetrap,* intent on immersing the audience in the epistemological difficulties of their characters, deny the audience this type of perspective. Jonson, however, removes the audience and with it the possibility of true imitation of justice from the play's dystopian fictional world. At the same time, this removal renders highly visible the dystopic, parodic nature of the avocatori's imitation of what appears to be utopian justice: only from its privileged position is the audience fully able to perceive the extent of the avocatori's epistemological weakness.

The audience's removal into the realm of art is part of a larger disjunction between the play's fictional world and Jonson's artistic design. The comic poet's artistic design lacks an adequate objective correlative, an adequate agent, in the play's dystopic reality. As we have seen, the avocatori are far too limited to serve as agents of ideal justice. Although virtuous, Celia and Bonario are ineffective: neither Celia's prayers nor Bonario's honest speeches make any impact on the course of the avocatori's proceedings. They are, as Watson puts it, "exiles from the world of sentimental melodrama, which is the only place their sort of virtue has any real relevance or force."[26] Even a hypothetical divine providence does not serve. Although the play's conclusion might appear to be a providential answer to Celia's prayers[27] or, as Broude contends, a divinely ordained working out of the truth fully in line with the conventions of a dramatic tradition that Broude isolates under the rubric of the Triumph of Truth play,[28] in *Volpone* there is a critical difference, a disjunction between such conventions and the world in which they appear to operate. In the Triumph of Truth plays discussed by Broude, the final perception of truth is organically connected to the world in which that truth is perceived: though the revelation of truth is accidental, its signs are unmistakable, irrefutable within the terms of the play's fictional world.[29] In *Volpone*, however, the gap between the equivocally signifying "miracle" of Volpone's uncasing and what the avocatori decide to make of it foregrounds the absence of any compelling spiritual force at work within the play's dystopic fictional world. Along with the audience's privileged epistemological position, Jonson removes divine providence, the rough equivalent of Plato's Good from which all other Ideas, including justice, receive their being and force, into the realm of artistic convention.

Yet even artistic representation cannot remain the uncontaminated medium of ideal imitation. The material conditions of its production ensure that it too becomes only a moment in the dystopian economy of the production and consumption of appearances. More decisively than the *Republic*, *Volpone* as theater is alien to Plato's ideal society. Volpone's appearance on stage to deliver the epilogue and invite the audience to "fare jovially" (Epilogue 6) is a reminder that the comic poet who can "feign a commonwealth" must do so to make a living.[30] Significantly, it is Volpone who delivers the epilogue, Volpone after whom the play is titled, and Volpone's magnificent and completely unjust performances, not the harsh justice of the play's conclusion, that gain the audience's applause. Jonson, like Plato, knows that "unstable and refractory" (*Republic* 434) characters, not reasonable and just ones, are the stuff of which entertaining theater, theater that brings applause and full box office coffers, is made. And it is this imitative dysfunctionality that integrates *Volpone* into the dystopian economy of appearances: Jonson has sold his play and the actors their appearances to provide the audience with the jovial fare they have bought and consumed. Like Plato's Socrates, Jonson the comic poet's utopian urges cannot escape dystopian deformation. Utopia inhabits the in-between space of an aporia, a vision consigned to art but whose artistic articulation is a sign both of its impossibility and its participation in what it would reject.

2

"[B]egot between tirewomen and tailors": Commodified Self-Fashioning in *Michaelmas Term*

Volpone and *Michaelmas Term* were both written, performed, and published between 1604 and 1607, and the two plays share enough features, such as intriguing master-servant relationships and backfiring death tricks, to lead critics to speculate about who copied whom. Rather than take up the question of influence, however, in this chapter I engage the ways in which Middleton in *Michaelmas Term* "rewrites" *Volpone*'s analysis of utopian discourse in specifically social terms. Both plays draw their comic energy from the disturbing disjunction between being and appearance at the heart of social reality, but Middleton's play addresses this issue in the context of Jacobean London and Jacobean ideologies of social order. The play particularizes the just self and the just social order as gentle birth and the ideology of divinely ordained social order based on birth. *Michaelmas Term* is as interrogative as *Volpone*, however, and Middleton as much as Jonson uses theater as his tool of skeptical inquiry. The play shows the queasy lightness of being at the heart of Jacobean London's fashionable world of courtiers and courtesans, dramatizing the social self and social order as the outcomes and instruments of conflict, the conventions of social dramas performed by the self-interested actors who populate the theatrical London that constitutes the plays' fictional worlds. Here, sartorial spectacle is the paradigm of a mode of self-fashioning that is also a mode of self-commodification. Assembled out of commodities and as a commodity, the self is integrated in early modern England's emerging but wayward and disruptive capitalist economy, an economy of accumulation and consumption that materializes ideologies of social order as unstable and manipulable scripts in social conflict.

Broadly, the play is concerned with the social dramas that blur or reinforce distinctions of social status, distinctions underpinning the society in which Middleton lived. Yachnin remarks that this early city comedy marks a turning point in the mode of Middleton's dramatic representation of social order, a "crucial transition from a sacramental to a scientific view of class differentiation. The sacramental view seeks to wed the social order to a divinely established universal order so that power and privilege can be presented as the natural and ordained concomitants of rank. The scientific view undertakes to divorce society from the ordained order of the universe."[1] Theatrical rather than scientific, though, best characterizes Middleton's altered perspective. The sacramental view joined social order to divine order through the notion of birth. A person's social position at birth was divinely ordained and endowed that person with an innate social essence that defined his or her social trajectory. By birth one was a commoner, a member of the gentry, or a peer, and consequently birth determined one's position in the scheme of distribution of goods, power, and privilege. Departure from one's native place and prescribed vocation sinfully disrupts the commonwealth's divinely sanctioned order. The sacramental view, then, was fundamentally anti-theatrical, ideally eliminating slippage between birth and the social roles an individual might play and consequently legitimating the existing social order as natural and just. Social mobility has the potential to disrupt this sacramental view of society, and *Michaelmas Term* breaks the link between social order and its legitimating ontological ground by taking the performativity implicit in social mobility as the norm for all social status. For Middleton, even gentle birth, the crucial dividing line between those fit to govern and those not, is a matter of appearances.

Early modern England witnessed unprecedented social mobility.[2] England's emerging capitalist economy pried people from their "natural" places in a number of ways, allowing people to create for themselves new social roles and identities. London's rise as a hub of international and domestic trade and a center of manufacture was accompanied by the expansion of the number of men of business whose "trade" the traditional guild structure could define only inadequately if at all, men whose wealth had little to do with the craft of the guild to which they nominally belonged but was rather capital garnered from and pumped back into the importing and exporting of commodities, developing new industries outside guild regulations, and moneylending.[3] A few of these men amassed spectacular fortunes, and merchant wealth in general was on the rise.[4] Through the crown's dependence on these wealthy Londoners for revenue in the form of loans, taxes, and customs duties, this wealth was translated into power and influence beyond the civic sphere not easily accounted for in conceptions of the commonwealth in which the lines of power were hierarchical and unidirectional. Some merchants took advantage of a real estate market quickened by the dissolution of the monasteries to buy their way into the aristocracy.[5] The Tudor monarchs' reliance on "new men," educated but less-well-born public officials, to administrate the increasingly complex machinery of centralizing government provided other opportunities for social mobility. James took this process several steps further by selling knighthoods and peerages.[6] Birth, then, could be seen not as a natural essence completely defining one's social trajectory but as an acquired social position, a commodity to be gained or lost. In this period the aristocracy in general was caught up in these ideologically disruptive socioeconomic changes, not only as victims through their heavy borrowing but also as active participants through investments and their development of capitalist agriculture.[7] And if as borrowers they increased the market for and hence numbers of money-lenders, as capitalist farmers, through contractual rent agreements and enclosure, they also increased the number of vagrants, another group whose transgressive social mobility was highly visible and disconcerting.[8]

Parvenu, middleman, money-lender, "new man," vagrant: these socially mobile and socially dislocated individuals traversed hierarchical boundaries of social order or existed in their interstices. Such figures created ideologically threatening disjunctions between birth and social role, disjunctions all the more threatening for their visibility. Rogue literature expressed an anxiety about the vagrant that focused on the vagrant's rootlessness and the performative existence it enabled (and necessitated). *A Caveat for Common Cursitors Vulgarly Called Vagabonds* (1566), for example, written by Justice of the Peace Thomas Harman, responds to the vagrant's disturbing social mobility by locating points of origin for the vagrants with whom Harman comes into contact and exposing their disguises as the sick, the poverty-stricken, or even as respectable members of the commonwealth.[9] As Paul Slack documents, Tudor and early Stuart policies were directed against the vagrant's protean existence, attempting to fix the vagrant's identity by judicial spectacle and by returning the vagrant to a determined point of origin: "Vagabonds were now to be whipped . . . and then returned to the place where they were born or where they last lived for at least three years. The qualification for settlement was reduced to one year in 1598, but otherwise this remained the usual medicine for vagrancy throughout the period."[10] Equally perplexing was the visible power and wealth of the upper echelons of London's merchants, commercial capitalists, and moneylenders rather than artisans and mere retailers. Rivaling the aristocracy in wealth, having little in common with the rank and file of the companies to which they belonged, but often of humble origins, these figures had no clear position in the commonwealth. Their ambiguous position called forth a body of Elizabethan imaginative literature—prose fiction and drama—that attempted to find a place for them but could not pass beyond the invention of such paradoxical figures as the merchant knight errant, figures that Jacobean dramatists found absurd and burlesqued in plays like *The Knight of the Burning Pestle*.[11] Similarly, the writers of tracts on gentility and the ideal gentleman perceived the "new men" to be a potentially destabilizing force but in reply could only assert the basis of gentility to be birth while paradoxically arguing that birth must be cultivated and supplemented by such cultural attainments as education and manners. Ironically these tracts, which could be treated as how-to manuals, only heightened the sense that gentility was performative, a role that could be played by anyone and must be played even by those whose natural birth might seem to exempt them from the consideration of social appearances.[12]

The developing capitalist forces reshaping England's economy, then, broadened the possibilities for theatrical modes of existence, played out most visibly on the nation's largest stage, London. As the nation's political and economic capital London was the ideal home or terminus for the socially mobile, and as a developing center of conspicuous consumption London did not merely accommodate but positively encouraged theatrical existence.[13] Conspicuous consumption privileges social appearance over innate social essence: being seen to consume is what is important, and London provided the largest audience available. Furthermore, the social mobility concentrated in London transformed consumption, formerly the exclusive mark of those born into the upper reaches of society, into a signifier subject to appropriation and manipulation by anyone with enough money or enough wits to obtain the credit to finance his or her social performances. London was the site in which a crisis in the category of birth was most visible, the theater of a crisis in social perception.[14]

Most perceptions of the problematic nature of birth did not result in the kind of skepticism found in *Michaelmas Term*. As we have seen, more often than not such perceptions resulted in calls for measures to restabilize the category, to produce and enforce its central, socially determining position. Nonetheless, the anxiety and urgency of these calls are matched by the difficulties they encounter in restoring the category's essentiality and naturalness. Philip Stubbes's discussion of clothing in *Anatomie of Abuses* (1583) nicely illustrates this. In Stubbes's moral framework the abuses of dress occupy a prominent position as the most egregious of those abuses that threaten to plunge England into divinely sanctioned chaos: "The greatest abuse which both offendeth god most, [and] is there not a little aduaunced, is the execrable sinne of Pride, and excesse in apparell, which is there so ripe, as the filthie fruits thereof have long since, presented themselves before the throne of the maiestie of God, calling and crying for vengeance day and nighte incessantly."[15] This is not merely a function of Stubbes's moral severity. For Stubbes, dress as a mode of conspicuous consumption is the most visible register of the disruptions and displacements afflicting birth and the modes of social perception founded on it. Stubbes writes that

> now there is such a confuse mingle mangle of apparell in Ailgna, and such preposterous excesse therof . . . so that it is verie hard to knowe who is noble, who is worshipfull, who is a gentleman, who is not; for you shall have those, which are neither of the nobylitie gentilitie, nor yeomanry, no nor yet anie Magistrat or Officer in the commonwealth, go daylie in silkes, velvets, satens, damasks, taffeties and suchlike, notwithstanding that they be both base by birth, meane by estate & servyle by calling. This is a great confusion & general disorder, God be mercifull unto us.[16]

Behind Stubbes's complaint lies the vision of a society in which each individual's social appearance is an unequivocal expression or sign of her or his social position determined by birth. The "great confusion & general disorder" that Stubbes describes is caused by the failure of this ideal social language. The link between signifier and signified has been rendered uncertain and open to manipulation. Stubbes indicates the seriousness of this ontological and semiotic rupture by connecting birth and power: the inability to know who is noble and who is base is also the inability to know who is master and who is servant, who rules and who is ruled. Who, then, knows whom to obey and whom to command? Power itself is at stake in the play of social signs. Stubbes, though, does not doubt the adequacy of birth as a key social category but rather insists that the current semiotic confusion be remedied. In this at least Stubbes and the government concurred: according to Stone, "Elizabeth issued no less than ten Proclamations during her reign enjoining the enforcement of the 1533 Sumptuary Act."[17] Yet Stubbes's own discourse reveals birth's inadequacy. On the one hand, if birth is to remain an essential category in spite of the "confuse mingle mangle of apparell," then social signifiers must be inessential, accidental to birth, ornamental. On the other hand, appearances and signs are all social actors have to go on. Were birth itself immediately visible, apparel would be trivial, generating neither anxiety nor regulative legislation. Birth, then, vanishes behind or is overwhelmed by the appearances that become its irreplaceable substitutes.

If *Anatomie* is a conservative moral critique of a disorderly society, then *Michaelmas Term* turns that disorder back into a skeptical critique of the social epistemology underlying Stubbes's conservatism. The point at which Stubbes's discourse unravels, the supplementarity of appearances, is Middleton's play's point of departure. More precisely, it is the play's enabling comic presupposition and the focus of the play's skeptical analysis of birth's ideological inadequacy and illegitimacy. In *Michaelmas Term*,

Middleton deploys city comedy's doubleness (things are rarely what they seem to be), its dramatic speed, and its emphasis on conflict and the contemporary—especially merchant-gentry conflict—to produce a play that insistently queries birth's status as an innate social essence. The play's skepticism does not take sides: as Theodore Leinwand argues, "Middleton's city comedies . . . are not directed against status groups so much as they examine the effects of a status society itself under pressure."[18] Broadly, Middleton transforms the static oppositional conflict between merchants and gentry into a frenetic circular motion that exposes the positionality of all birth. The play draws two stereotypes of this conflict—citizen as cozener versus gentry as gull, citizen as impotent hoarder versus gentry as fertile profligate—into cycles of transience and illegitimacy, two cycles of accumulation and consumption that transform birth, the boundary between citizen and gentry, those who rule and those who do not, into an empty sign incapable of signifying as a natural category within the ideology of aristocratic social formation.

One of the play's fundamental comic principles is that birth and inheritance are no match for the instability of social position across generations. Even in Elizabeth's reign, the pace of social mobility, especially gentrification, was enough to render it disturbingly visible. Thomas Smith in *De Republica Anglorum* (1583) notes that "as for gentlemen, they be made good cheape in England."[19] In James's reign they had become much cheaper. Stone argues that during this period "families were moving up and down in social and economic scale at a faster rate than at any time before the nineteenth and twentieth centuries,"[20] pinpointing the decade between 1610 and 1620 as the decade in which the rate of social mobility peaked. Social mobility in itself need not pose a threat to hierarchical societies. As Bacon comments in "Of Nobility," time in this context can be a great conservative force: "For new nobility is but the act of power, but ancient nobility is the act of time. Those that are first raised to nobility are commonly more virtuous but less innocent than their descendants, for there is rarely any rising but by a commixture of good and evil arts. But it is reason the memory of their virtues remain to their posterity, and their faults die with themselves."[21] For Bacon as much as for Andrew Lethe, forgetfulness, Time's less famous daughter, is essential to complete gentrification. But time is precisely what Middleton does not allow his socially ambitious characters, removing gentrification's cloak of naturalness with the speed at which his characters acquire gentrification's material trappings. The Induction presents to us

> A fellow
> Shrugging for life's kind benefits, shift and heat,

> Crept up in three Terms, wrapt in silk and silver,
> So well appointed too with page and pander.[22]

This "fellow" becomes one of the play's main characters, Andrew Lethe, who has transformed himself from the son of a tooth-drawer into "Master Andrew Lethe, / A gentleman of most received parts" (1.1.157–58). The Country Wench is allowed even less time, a mere three acts to Lethe's three terms. Her rapid transformation from a "Northamptonshire lass" (1.2.12) into a "Lady" (4.1.40) is more unsettling than Lethe's metamorphosis because it occurs entirely within the play's fast-paced dramatic time. The Country Wench makes the leap from commoner to gentlewoman in the first half of what is at most two hours' traffic upon the stage, and the play thus foregrounds the performativity of her gentrification.

The play's critical use of accelerated time is not limited to the acquisition of gentry status. The play dramatizes the equally rapid consumption of the accouterments of gentrification, locking accumulation and consumption into a vicious (not virtuous, as Bacon would have it) circle of social rise and fall motivated by citizen-gentry conflict. Throughout his oeuvre Middleton delights in the circular futility of his comic worlds.[23] In *Michaelmas Term*, however, the circularity is particularly devastating: what one generation accumulates in wealth, land, and status, the next consumes, forcing the third to begin the cycle once again. In the play there is no time to naturalize gentry status, which is thus exposed as raw and transient positionality. Thus, the Country Wench must enter a trade, "wholesale" (4.2.15), to regain the "name and state" (2.2.23) that her father has rioted away. Middleton develops the cycle in more complex directions in the play's main conflict, the struggle between Quomodo the citizen cozener and Easy the gentry gull for Easy's Essex lands. Here the play not only works to demystify gentry status but also provides a strongly ironic reading of Bacon's already ambiguous contention that "virtue" as opposed to "innocence" is the means of status acquisition. The only virtue by which Quomodo gains, albeit momentarily, Easy's land is a debased Machiavellian *virtù*, the con artist's ability to cheat successfully. But despite his virtue Quomodo cannot break the cycle, even though he is the character in the play most aware of it. He cheats Easy of his lands not only for sport and his own gain but also eventually to elevate his son Sim to gentry status. What we learn of Sim's education indicates that Quomodo has been fashioning his son for his new social position: Quomodo declares Easy's Essex lands are "an excellent place for a student, fit for my son that lately commenced at Cambridge, whom now I have placed at Inns of Court" (2.3.84–86). Yet, as Quomodo prophetically muses and perversely takes steps to confirm, the "cozenage in the father" by which the citizen obtains land from the gentry "wheels about to folly in the son, our posterity commonly foiled at the same weapon at which we played rarely" (4.1.82–84). In order to "break destiny of her custom" (4.1.87), Quomodo feigns death, intending to nip in the bud his son's riotous, profligate tendencies. With typical Middletonian irony, the death trick precipitates the event it was designed to forestall, and almost immediately after the bells announcing Quomodo's death have rung Sim is cheated out of the Essex lands by Quomodo's servant Shortyard. By regaining his lands Easy may seem to break the cycle—but only for now. Rowe points out that "We watch the prodigals being engulfed in a hellish London, but we never see any of them make a symbolic journey 'home' to the countryside."[24] Easy may not have been hooked this time, and he may have taken Quomodo's lectures about bonds to heart, but the play offers no assurance that he will leave the gallant's life of consumption and waste. In *Michaelmas Term*, then, gentle birth is transitory, and gentle inheritance is more likely to be consumed than passed down through the generations. "Oh, worse than consumption of the liver! / Consumption of the patrimony!" (2.1.116–17), Rearage exclaims between tosses of the dice.

The other fundamental comic principle of *Michaelmas Term*'s fictional world is what Chakravorty calls the "sex-money calculus. What a merchant gains in money, he loses in virility; what the prodigal heir loses in estates, he gains in sex."[25] In the play's induction, Michaelmas Term presents one version of this calculus: "Where bags are fruitful'st there the womb's most barren; / The poor has all our children, we their wealth" (24–25). Quomodo revises Michaelmas Term's equation by aligning money and sex, "Revenue" and "Pleasure,"[26] not with the wealthy and the poor but with the (wealthy) citizen and the (poor) gentry and by expressing the equation as part of the class conflict between these two groups:

> There are means and ways enow to hook in gentry,
> Besides our deadly emnity, which thus stands:
> They're busy 'bout our wives, we 'bout their lands.
>
> (1.1.107–9)

It would be misleading, however, to maintain that Middleton's alignment of revenue with citizens and pleasure with the gentry is an absolute disjunction of sexual and economic forces. The matches between Thomasine and Easy and Susan and Rearage can perhaps be seen as unions of revenue and pleasure: Easy and Rearage are certainly after wealth, and Thomasine and Susan are quite obviously not (although it is not clear whether they are motivated by pleasure or by the desire to acquire status). For the most part, however, sexuality and economics are merely different modes of the cycle of accumulation and consumption. Quomodo does not lack sexual desire but channels it into his economic operations. Land, the goal of his economic activity, becomes the fetishized object of his sexual fantasies: "Oh, that sweet, neat, comely, proper, delicate parcel of land, like a fine gentlewoman in the i'th'waist" (2.3.81–82). Quomodo's fraudulent acquisition of Easy's lands is, then, a lucrative form of cuckolding, a reversal of the ostensibly unidirectional sexual dynamics of citizen-gentry conflict. On the other side of the cycle, Rearage and the other gallants are engaged in the "consumption of the patrimony" (2.1.117) in both economic and sexual senses. They waste their economic patrimony on "feasts" and their sexual patrimony on "drabs" and begetting the citizens' illegitimate children.

Of course, in Middleton sexuality is almost always an economic affair, with large economic and social implications. In *A Chaste Maid in Cheapside*, for example, Middleton manipulates the sexual economics that both maintain and undermine the socioeconomic status quo. Parodying New Comedy romance's sublimation of socially threatening sexual desires into socially acceptable forms, the play charts the progress of Touchwood Senior, a gentleman whose amazingly potent "fatal finger"[27] has beggared him, separated him from his wife because of his poverty, and has disrupted the rural economy by impregnating and so disabling a significant portion of the work force during harvest. His fortunes are restored when he is offered four hundred pounds (3.3.137–39) by Lord and Lady Kix to dispense a "fertility drug" to Lady Kix to remedy the couple's childlessness and so to prevent Sir Walter Whorehound from inheriting their estates. This arrangement renews the community, providing the Kixes with heirs and Touchwood Senior with a permanent and productive outlet for his sexuality and an opportunity to reestablish his marriage:

> Sir Oliver: Master Touchwood, hear'st thou this news?
> I am so endear'd to thee for my wife's fruitfulness
> That I charge you both, your wife and thee,
> To live no more asunder for the world's frowns:
> I have purse, and bed, and board for you;
> Be not afraid to go to your business roundly;
> Get children, and I'll keep them.
>
> (5.4.76–82)

The wink and nudge of innuendo and the shared gentry status of the Kixes and the Touchwoods work to tame the subversiveness of the play's sexual economics, but the play nonetheless shows how much, both economically and socially, depends on birth, while simultaneously exposing as a convenient fiction the purity which it is necessary to attribute to birth in order to render it so important. If the formula of Shakespeare's festive, romantic comedy is, as Barber puts it, "through release to clarification,"[28] then *A Chaste*

Maid In Cheapside moves through ejaculation to skeptical clarification, demystification.

The sexual economics of *Michaelmas Term* have equally disturbing and, because expressed in generalized terms, more widespread implications. Disguised as a wealthy citizen, Shortyard declares to Quomodo that "I am of those citizen's minds that say, let our wives make shift for children, an they will, they get none of us; and I cannot think but he that has both much wealth and many children has had more helps coming in than himself" (4.1.34–38). If this is the case then the consequence is that the bastard children of the gentry will inherit the land and gentry status that the citizens have fraudulently gained from the children's profligate fathers. This cycle of illegitimacy as much as the "destiny" (4.1.87) Quomodo fears undermines Quomodo's utopian fantasy of the reconciliation of revenue and pleasure, capital and land. After gaining Easy's lands, Quomodo dreams of

> A fine journey in the Whitsun holidays, i'faith, to ride down with a number of citizens and their wives, some upon pillions, some upon sidesaddles, I and little Thomasine i'th'middle, our son and heir, Sim Quomodo, in a peach-color taffeta jacket, some horse-length or long yard before us; there will be a fine show on's, I can tell you; where we citizens will laugh, and lie down, get all our wives with child against a bank and get up again.
> (4.1.70–76)

Quomodo dreams of gentrification underwritten by merchant capital and of legitimate heirs to inherit this reconfigured social order. "Destiny"—the comic law of biter bit projected across generations and modulated by class conflict—ensures that this utopian vision remains a dream, but questions of legitimacy create the suspicion that this dream, even were Quomodo to keep Easy's lands, is a delusion. Like Jonson's Volpone, Quomodo thinks that everyone is self-deluded and ripe for gulling—except himself. Having himself articulated the sexual dynamic of citizen-gentry competition, he does not suspect that this dynamic may apply to him personally. "What a wife hast thou, Ephestian Quomodo! So loving, so mindful of her duty" (5.1.58–59), Quomodo exclaims after having caught glimpses of Thomasine's behavior after his faked death. The dramatic irony of Quomodo's exclamation is almost painful. Unlike Quomodo, the audience has witnessed Thomasine rush to marry Easy even as the coffin supposedly containing Quomodo's corpse is being carried to the grave. Earlier on the play hints that the citizen-gentry sexual dynamic may in fact apply to Quomodo. Thomasine is disgusted by Lethe's sexual advances not because they are immoral but because "'tis for his betters to have opportunity of me" (2.3.7–8). We have only Quomodo's word for it that Sim, on whom Quomodo pins his utopian hopes, is his legitimate "son and heir" (4.1.72–73).

For citizen and gentry alike, then, birth proves to be a problematic category, lacking the real, "natural" referent it needs in order to function as the anchoring link between a hierarchical social configuration and the sacramental ideology invoked to justify the distribution of power and privilege in that configuration. Approaching the play from a slightly different perspective, Paster reaches a similar conclusion. She writes that "the traditional social hierarchy so much a part of the characters' thinking has little real value or substantiality except as a specious justification for appetitive behavior and mutually self-destructive rivalry."[29] Yet in some ways Paster's conclusion misses the point. The circular futility of citizen-gentry conflict delegitimates birth and the social hierarchy of which it is the central category, but birth is not therefore rendered valueless. In the play, the social distinctions based on birth are not just "mental furniture"[30] or the coordinates of an antiquated, purely subjective world view. As we shall see, "birth" continues to have value—not a natural, inherent value but the value of an exchangeable commodity, a value based on appearances but with material efficacy. This commodity is not so much the justification of appetitive behavior as its cause. At the least, the commodification of status incites the desire to acquire it, a desire structured by the cycles of accumulation and consumption governing London's exchange economy. As Slights puts it, Middleton "casts the concept of the fashioned self into a commercial context,"[31] specifically London. But the issue concerning self-fashioning in the play is not, as Slights argues, Middleton's moral evaluation of the process but rather his examination of the ideological consequences of the increasing underwriting of status by capital which enables his characters to fashion themselves. As the theater of conspicuous consumption, Middleton's London is both the site of birth's delegitimation and the mechanism of its revaluation, both a "man-devouring city" (2.2.21) and the womb or mint of strange, new births.

On its stage London practices a black magic of commercial transformation or, more precisely, performs the illusionist's art of reducing substance to appearance. The practice of law reduces the fruits of the earth to a "silver harvest" (Induction 10), a crop of coins whose value is a function of appearance—as rare and attractive metal, as authorized token—signifying in the context of commercial exchange. London's other acts and venues work a similar alchemy on the social self. London not only supplies the gentry with the means to express their birth through performance, with modes of and spectators for extravagant expenditure, but also creates an environment in which such performance becomes a necessity. In *De Republica Anglorum*, Thomas Smith's discussion of the gentleman charts this slide into the necessary supplementarity of appearances: Smith begins by defining gentlemen as "those whom their blood and race doth make known"[32] but concludes by stating that "a gentleman (if he will be so accompted) must go like a gentleman."[33] Smith's conclusion summarizes the lesson Easy learns from his London adventures. Arriving in London a "pure, fresh gull" (2.1.171), Easy must learn to go like a gentleman, must learn the manners of a London gallant, the defining characteristic of which is conspicuous consumption. Shortyard (alias Blastfield) is his willing tutor. During his first stint of gambling, Easy threatens to "forswear dicing" (2.1.105) after he loses. Shortyard corrects him: "What? Peace, I am ashamed to hear you. Will you cease in the first loss? Show me one gentleman that e'er did it! Fie upon't, I must use you to company, I perceive; you'd be spoil'd else. Forswear dice?" (2.1.106–9).

As expensive as Easy's education proves to be, however, its expense does not represent the limit of consumption. The supplementarity of appearances is never satisfied. Even two cynical gallants such as Rearage and Salewood need to be instructed about their inadequate standards of consumption. "Are you not knights yet, gentlemen?" (1.1.188), Lethe asks them. To Salewood's "Not yet" Lethe replies "No? That must be looked into, 'tis your own fault" (1.1.190). Lethe's question has a pointed topicality. Writing in Elizabeth's reign, Thomas Smith could still remark that knighthoods, which were nonhereditary titles, were bestowed as royal recognition of deserving public virtue: "Knightes therefore be not borne but made, either before the battle to encourage them the more to adventure their lives, or after the conflict, as advauncement for their hardinesse and manhood alreadie shewed: or out of the warre for some great service done, or some good hope through the vertues which do appeare in them."[34] For Smith, knighthoods function much as Stubbes thought clothing should function, as true signs of the qualities of their bearers, signs that significantly are not mere markers of wealth: "No more are all made knightes in Englande that may dispende a knightes land or fee, but they onely whom the king will so honour."[35] In James's reign, however, Smith's description must have seemed antiquated at best. James created more knights in 1604 alone than Elizabeth had created during her entire reign. More unsettling was the manner of their creation: James bestowed knighthoods whimsically and destabilized the unambiguous significance Smith attributed to them by treating them as commodities. Hard up for cash, James used knighthoods as an indirect means of raising crown revenue by granting to courtiers as rewards the privilege of recommending candidates for knighthoods; the courtiers could then charge what they wanted for their nominations, and they often sold their privileges to others, who would then attempt to make a profit by selling the knighthoods at an even higher rate. In 1606, for example, Lionel Cranfield purchased the making of six knights for three hundred and seventy-three pounds, one shilling, and eightpence.[36] Honor was there for the buying, and Lethe's question to Salewood and Rearage, whose only means of gaining knighthoods is surely by purchasing them, has all the anxiety-raising casualness of the luxury goods salesperson for whom the latest high-priced fashionable commodity is a necessity. Even the gentle-born are subject to the inflationary pressures of the traffic in titles.

As in Stubbes's discourse, necessary supplementarity soon becomes irreplaceable substitute. "Birth" is emptied out into appearances and becomes wholly a product of commodified self-fashioning or, in Bruster's terms, "the commercial inscription of identity."[37] The Country Wench and Andrew Lethe are the play's most obvious examples of this, and the transformations they undergo concretely dramatize the relations between the body and commercial transactions that were, according to Jean-Christophe Agnew, beginning to be theorized in the writings of Bacon, Thomas Wright, William Scott, and others: "As a locus of representation and misrepresentation, the body had become, in effect, a commodity—a double-stitched garment the social value of which fluctuated according the mysterious movements of a placeless market. In its own, albeit figurative way, the human body had become the newest of England's new draperies."[38] Hellgill the pander brings the Country Wench to the city from "a poor thrummed house i'th'country" (1.2.5–6) with the promise to make her "pass for a gentlewoman i'th'city" (1.2.6–7) in exchange for her virginity. London's market supplies the material of her rebirth: "Why, Northamptonshire lass, dost dream of virginity now? Remember a loose-bodied gown, wench, and let it go; wires and tires, bents and bums, felts and falls, thou shalt deceive the world that gentlewomen indeed shall not be known from others" (1.2.12–15). At this point in the play, Hellgill still distinguishes between those who are gentlewomen and those who merely pass as such. However, once he sees the end result of the Country Wench's retailoring, he declares this distinction untenable: "You talk of an alteration; here's the thing itself. What base birth does not raiment make glorious? And what glorious births do not rags make infamous? Why should not a woman confess what she is now, since the finest are but deluding shadows begot between tirewomen and tailors?" (3.1.1–5). The Country Wench's natural birth is superseded and rendered irrelevant by her sartorial self-fashioning. "Now," the self that the Country Wench has purchased, is all that counts. The Country Wench's self-fashioning is verbal as well as sartorial, and her use of "the true phrase and style of a strumpet" (3.1.27) also works to erase signs of her origins: "Out, you saucy, pestiferious pander! I scorn that i'faith" (3.1.25–26), she exclaims in reply to Hellgill's assertion that "this fine sophisticated squall came out of the bosom of a barn and the loins of a hay-tosser" (3.1.23–24). The Country Wench's and her father's failure to recognize each other indicates the thoroughness of this rebirth. London replaces kinship ties with commercial relations, natural parents with "tirewomen and tailors." Furthermore, the Country Wench fashions herself not only through commodities but also as a commodity, Lethe's "underput" (3.1.72). She is not merely Lethe's mistress but also his prostitute, from whom he expects to reap profit by selling her services to other gallants. Her gentle appearance is essential to her trade. Lethe uses the Country Wench's bought status as gentlewoman to increase both her marketability and his own social capital: she is, Lethe tells Salewood and Rearage, "a gentlewoman of a great house, noble parentage, unmatchable education, my plain pung" (3.1.73–74). The Country Wench herself embraces this peculiar combination of ennoblement and degradation: "Though it may be a hard fortune to have my keeper there a coward," she tells Shortyard, "the thing that's kept is a gentlewoman born" (3.1.169–70).

Like the Country Wench, Lethe has also been begotten "between tirewomen and tailors." Son of Walter Gruel, "an honest upright toothdrawer" (1.1.255–56), London has rechristened him "Master Andrew Lethe" (1.1.157). Lethe, whose transformation the induction prefigured, has

> crept to a little warmth,
> And now so proud that he forgets all storms;
> One that ne'er wore apparel but, like ditches,
> 'Twas cast before he had it, now shines bright
> In rich embroideries.
>
> (1.1.61–65)

Lethe's rags-to-riches story is just that, a story not of hard work or divine blessing, valor or loyalty, but rather of a change of clothes. As Thomasine informs us, Lethe's rise began in Quomodo's drapery shop where he "brought two of his countrymen to give their words to my husband for a suit of green kersy" (2.3.9–10). London's market supplies Lethe not only with his rich embroideries, the clothes necessary to establish him as a gallant, but also with the opportunity to acquire and display the manners necessary to establish him as a "gentleman of most received parts" (1.1.158). Lethe acquires his status as gallant through his conspicuous consumption, through his dicing, whoring, and feasting. And Rearage, whose dislike of Lethe is generated as much by the fact that Lethe is his rival for the rich draper's daughter's seven hundred pounds as by social snobbery, fully participates in Lethe's acquisition. When they "taste," "waste," and "cast" (1.1.197) venison at the Horn with Lethe, are gambling away their money to him, or are courting Lethe's "plain pung," Rearage and Salewood, even though they may despise Lethe behind his back, publicly accept Lethe in their fraternity so long as his mode of consumption matches or even outgoes theirs. Lethe's retailoring, like the Country Wench's, works to efface the signs of his origins. "Know you not me, good woman?" (1.1.267–68), Lethe asks Mother Gruel in the play's first scene; "Alas, an't please your worship, I never saw such a glorious suit since the hour I was kersened" (1.1.269–70) she replies. For the rest of the play, employed as Lethe's drudge, she fails to see through his "glorious suit," and even at the play's end she acknowledges him as her son only because she is forced to do so. Albeit less explicitly than the Country Wench's, Lethe's remaking of himself is also verbal. Some critics have assumed that Lethe is Scottish, a plausible inference from Lethe's connection with debased knighthood. Actually, the play only vaguely indicates Lethe's point of origin: according to Rearage, his father "brought him up below" (1.1.154), outside of London, but the play is not more specific than this. But if Lethe is Scottish, his speech does not betray him. Middleton does not use differences in dialect or level of speech to distinguish between (base) Lethe and the (naturally gentle) gallants, although speech differences quite clearly do separate the humble Mother Gruel from her son. Lethe has acquired the language as well as the clothes of a London gallant. Furthermore, like the Country Wench, Lethe has remade himself as a marketable commodity. He has parleyed his bought status as gallant into a lucrative position as courtier, gaining "Acquaintance, dear society, suits and things" (1.1.176), influence, wealth, and an opportunity to marry Susan Quomodo for her money.

The Country Wench and Lethe are relatively simple examples of commodified refashioning. In a dramatic context in which innate qualities of birth find ways to assert themselves, these two characters' refashionings might be considered merely disguise or play-acting. Leinwand argues that "The comic spirit informing city comedy does not despair over a world of endlessly shifting roles that are nothing but roles; it locates a secure self in the gentleman, the sponsor of prevailing ideologies."[39] But this is not the case, at least not for *Michaelmas Term*. The play's world is pure theater, in which to be is to be seen, even for the finest. Easy provides the play's most complex and powerful example of this irreplaceability of appearance. Having learned that naturally gentle birth is not enough in London, he soon discovers it threatening to become nothing at all. Under Shortyard's tutelage, Easy establishes himself as a gallant through consumption; shortly, however, "the continuing of this gentleman's credit in town" (2.3.155–56) brings Easy into debt and leads him to alienate that which established his natural gentle birth, his land. This, of course, has been Quomodo and Shortyard's plot all along. Significantly, Easy's father is dead (1.1.43) and his mother completely absent from the play. Shortyard states that he and Easy are "man and wife" (2.3.152), but Shortyard is more Easy's parent or creator than his spouse. "Methinks I have no being without his ["Blastfield"'s] company" (3.2.6), Easy comments, and Shortyard has ensured that

Easy's new "being," his "credit" as a gentleman, is a product for which he will pay dearly and from which Quomodo will profit. Shortyard creates Easy as a London gentleman, and Easy's rebirth, entirely a function of London's economy of accumulation and consumption, threatens to supplant and even eradicate his natural parentage. After Quomodo has pulled together the last strands of the plot to cheat Easy of his land, Shortyard taunts Easy with his rootlessness: "I should seek my fortunes far enough, if I were you, and neither return to Essex to be a shame to my predecessors, nor remain about London to be a mock to my successors" (4.1.14–17).

Like Witgood in *A Trick to Catch the Old One* Easy regains his land, but not because he has any natural right to it and not through the exercise of qualities inherent in his natural birth. Easy finally succeeds because he behaves as the typical amoral gallant into which he has been fashioned, seizing and exploiting the opportunities that present themselves. In short, he beats Quomodo at his own game and merely reinforces the power of that game as arbiter of destiny and identity. When Witgood declaims "Thou soul of my estate, I kiss thee, / I miss life's comfort when I miss thee,"[40] he kisses the mortgage not his lands; likewise, Easy's redemption is mediated by contracts:

> Here's good deeds and bad deeds, the writings that keep my
> Lands to me, and the bonds that gave it away from me.
> These, my good deeds, shall to more safety turn,
> And these, my bad, have their deserts and burn.
>
> (5.1.52–55)

Witgood and Easy regain their birthright in commodified form, as extensions of London's exchange economy and through the manipulation of that economy's dynamics.

Michaelmas Term's London, then, is a microcosm of Stubbes's Ailgna. Its ontological preposterousness, like Ailgna's, reconfigures modes of knowing and their intersections with power. Knowing becomes a form of accounting, an apprehension not of the being of a person or thing (in the play persons and things are interchangeable) but of how they are "accompted," to borrow Thomas Smith's term. This is most obviously the case in an exterior sense, in the sense of knowing or not knowing others by their exteriors. But interior knowledge, self-knowledge, is also reconfigured. The commonplace Renaissance injunction, "*nosce teipsum*," implies a distinction between the social self and a private, personal remainder, Hamlet's "that within which passeth show,"[41] but in *Michaelmas Term* nothing passes show. Knowing as accounting dissolves the division between interior and exterior, and self-knowledge becomes merely a reflexive form of the social account others take of the self. Thus, the Country Wench's refashioning has the same effect on her knowledge of herself as it does on others', specifically her father's, knowledge of her: "How can he [her father] know me when I scarce know myself?" (3.1.31–32).

Even such apparently interior dimensions of the self as memory are flattened into the surface of commodified appearances. As Lethe's name implies, a fashioned memory is as essential an accessory of his social self as a fashionable physical appearance. He comments that

> I have received of many, gifts o'er night
> Whom I have forgot ere morning; meeting the men,
> I wished 'em to remember me again;
> They do so, then if I forget again
> I know what helped before, that will help then.
> This is my course, for memory I have been told
> Twenty preserves, the best I find is gold.
> Ay, truly! Are you not knights yet, gentlemen?
> (1.1.181–88)

Memory, like cloth, can be bought and sold. Its integration into Jacobean London's exchange economy creates a new commodity compounded of knowledge and power: recognition, the knowledge or taking into account of oneself by a powerful social other. Moreover, as the last line of the above quotation suggests, the commodification of memory extends beyond the individual social self. Thomas Smith acidly remarks that those who purchased knighthoods and other honors also purchased fabricated but authorized genealogies from the College of Heralds: to one who "will bear the port, charge and countenance of a gentleman" (27), "a king of Heraulds shal also give him for mony, armes newly made and invented, the title thereof shall pretende to have been found by the said Herauld in perusing and viewing of olde registers" (28).[42] The play provides one example of this in Quomodo, who desires not only to reconfigure the future but also to rewrite the past: at his funeral is a "herald richly hired to lend him arms / Feigned from his ancestors" (5.3.6–7). Time, like the social self, collapses into the now of commodified appearances; "history," like "birth," becomes a simulacrum, a fashionable and refashionable, sellable and resellable product of the present.[43] "Had I not the better memory, / 'Twould be a wonder I should know myself" (1.1.178–79), Lethe states, but in fact only the possibility of the dispersal of Lethe's memory, his ability to sell pieces of it, allows him to buy the "better memory" by which he knows himself as Master Andrew Lethe. In London's market, one knows oneself by the birth and memories one buys and sells.

Much of the play's humor is generated by Lethe's only partially successful attempts to forget his natural birth—or, more precisely, to have others forget his natural birth—and to know himself by his better memory. The public humiliation that Lethe suffers at the play's end, as his base birth is announced in court, hovers pigeonlike over all of Lethe's strenuous efforts of self-fashioning, threatening to "drop my staining birth upon my raiment" (1.1.277) at any moment. It may seem that this strain of humor, taken with the play's end, ultimately affirms birth as a natural category, at least in Lethe's case. Yet *Michaelmas Term*, like *Volpone,* is and is not a socially corrective comedy; gentle birth, like the just self, is exposed as a product of power and appearances through the excesses of its very imposition. Just as Easy does not regain his lands because he is naturally gentle, so too Lethe's parentage is exposed not through any workings of his birth itself. Lethe's actions throughout the play are no more (and no less) base and churlish than Rearage and Salewood's. Lethe is exposed because Rearage finds it profitable to do so. Rearage writes a letter in which "Andrew Lethe is well whipped" (3.5.3) and entertains the Country Wench's father's "device" (4.3.43) to have Lethe and the Country Wench arrested on the morning of Lethe's planned wedding to Susan not out of any sense of honor or moral duty (Rearage is hardly in a position to serve as a mouthpiece for moral sentiments) but out of purely economic motivation: with Lethe out of the way, he is free to marry Susan for her money. Watching as Lethe is "taken with his Harlot" (stage directions to 5.2), Susan exclaims to Rearage that "now the difference appears too plain / Betwixt a base slave and a true gentleman" (5.3.9–10). The emphasis here should be on "appears," for Rearage, the play's witty playwright figure, has scripted the whole event, casting Susan as the audience, himself as satiric presenter and moral scourge, and Lethe as the vicious humors character in need of purging. The script provides Susan with only a partial perspective, one that allows Rearage to construct a difference between himself and Lethe far more decisive than the play itself has constructed for its audience, which knows that there is little to differentiate the two companions in dicing, feasting, and whoring. (Rearage himself aggressively courts the Country Wench earlier in the play.) Taking no chances, Rearage uses force—the officers—to stage, for Susan's benefit but primarily his own, the first scene of the concluding judicial spectacle that puts a halt to Lethe's performance of the gentleman and compels him to play another, equally contrived role: the "villain" (5.3.153). The play's end reveals not that natural birth is inescapable but that self-fashioning is not entirely within the individual's control.

The concluding court scene's public proclamation of Lethe's parentage continues the judicial drama begun by Rearage. The scene dramatizes not the Stubbesian fantasy of authority effectively intervening in the world of appearances and restoring it to an order guaranteed by birth's self-evident social essentiality but rather authority's failure to transcend appearances even as it gives them a kind of fixity through the exercise of power. Throughout the play Mother Gruel has failed to recognize her son, and even when Lethe to avoid corporal punishment appeals to her as his mother, she replies "Call'st me mother? Out, / I defy thee, slave" (5.3.144–45). Only through the intervention of the judge are Lethe and Mother Gruel restored to their natural mother-son relationship: "Wilt thou believe me, woman?" (5.3.152), the judge asks; after Mother Gruel's assent, the judge commands her to "know him for a villain; 'tis thy son" (5.3.153). The judge offers no reasons why Mother Gruel should believe him, and the audience similarly does not know how, within the fictional world of the play, this judge came about his knowledge of both Andrew Lethe's humble origins and the relationship between Lethe and the old woman standing somewhere on the peripheries of the stage. Such knowledge in itself is irrelevant in *Michaelmas Term*'s world of theater; only the possibilities and limits of performance matter. The judge's intervention, like the avocatori's, is effected entirely through the authority of his voice, the speaking of power, through which he has fashioned for Lethe a birth and identity that Lethe is now powerless to deny. The play's ending shows birth to be not a stable category with a real, 'natural' referent but a molding of appearances and a site of social and economic contestation.

3
Epicoene and Knowing by Tradition

In *Epicoene* Jonson continues to explore material minds in a material world. The focus, however, shifts from a skeptical interrogation of utopian discourse to a skeptical scrutiny of the assumptions on which the humanist project was based (a project that, in modified form, Jonson in his nondramatic writings endorses). It may seem willfully perverse to place such hermeneutic pressure on a play that some critics have considered lightweight in comparison to *Volpone* and other of Jonson's comedies.[1] Indeed, the god of *Epicoene*'s world is not gold but something that seems much more ephemeral, status, and the scope of this world is much smaller than *Volpone*'s, the small worlds of the collegiate ladies and Morose rather than the world that extends from Volpone's bedchambers to Venice's courtroom. But shrunkenness and triviality are very much to the point in a play that explores the particularity of epistemological space and the triviality of learning. In *Epicoene* Jonson not only presents learning (and lots of it—even the play's fools spew Latin) at its most trivial and ineffective, but also examines the ways in which the changing material conditions of the London in which he wrote worked to generate and limit discrete epistemological spaces and so at the very least severely to qualify the humanist notion of a transhistorical truth-bearing discourse. The play dramatizes the sociohistorical embeddedness of knowledge (the impossibility of a transhistorical discourse of universal truth) by examining the relationship between an epistemological space that problematizes humanist learning's status as knowledge and the material conditions that enable this epistemological space. In the play's world of fashionable urban gentry (Emrys Jones calls *Epicoene* "the first West End comedy"),[2] a world whose possibility depends on the wealth, leisure, anonymity, and increasing social stratification of the urban space of seventeenth-century capitalist London, the relationship between discourse and reality or being is less than straightforward, and knowledge is replaced by a performative being-in-the-know, a cruel *sprezzatura* whose characteristics are provisionality and success rather than universality and truth.

The humanist project depended for its legitimation on the value of the classical sources whose recovery and transmission formed the core of the project. Paul Kristeller states that the humanist project was "animated by the idea that the study of classical languages and literature provided valuable information and intellectual discipline as well as moral standards and a civilized taste for the future rulers, leaders, and professionals of its society."[3] For the humanists, ancient literature was valued as the fountain of truths that could be translated from the context of their articulation in antiquity to the vastly different sociohistorical contexts of Renaissance Europe. By the end of the sixteenth century, however, the humanist project confronted a number of problems, both external and internal. In *The History of Scepticism from Erasmus to Spinoza,* Richard Popkin treats at length what he sees to be the two major external problems: the Reformation and the rediscovery of Pyrrhonism. In their call for a return to gospel simplicity Luther, Calvin, and other reformers questioned classical—or pagan, as the Reformers would have it—literature's status as a source of truth, regarding it at best as a pale shadow of the truth revealed in the gospels and at worst an insidious source of error.[4] Furthermore, the Reformation raised the issue of reason's ability to decide between conflicting arguments, largely in terms of who had the correct interpretation of the scriptures. The sixteenth-century rediscovery of Sextus Empiricus's summaries of Pyrrhonist skepticism extended this issue into a problem besetting all knowledge generally, raising for all areas of knowledge the problem of knowledge's foundations. The academic skepticism of Cicero, which the humanists had used so well to establish the notion of prudential or practical reasoning as a substitute for certain knowledge, faced a stiff philosophical challenge from its more virulent Pyrrhonist sibling, and the grounds for resolving contradictions among competing arguments seemed to have vanished.[5]

And contradictions there were in the humanist project. In his account of Renaissance skepticism, Popkin emphasizes its externality to the humanist project, but other intellectual historians have seen it more in terms of the internal development of humanism, arguing that the humanist project itself contributed to the questioning of its legitimating assumptions. Copenhaver and Schmitt point out that as the humanists recovered more classical texts, it became increasingly apparent that consensus on the truth had been as unavailable to the ancients as to the scholastics whom the humanists despised for their contentiousness and that the contradictions among ancient authorities were many and resolvable only with difficulty if at all.[6] As W. Scott Blanchard argues in *Scholar's Bedlam*, the Menippean vein of such works as Agrippa's *De incertitudine et vanitate scientarum*, Montaigne's *Essays*, Rabelais's *Gargantua and Pantagruel*, and Burton's *Anatomy of Melancholy* is a manifestation of humanism's internal crisis.[7] Each of these works, in various ways, pours forth endless erudition only to present the conflicts among authorities ancient and modern and to leave these conflicts unresolved and, more or less explicitly, unresolvable. In these works humanist truth is shown to be fragmented at its origin, more a source of bafflement than truth, and only doubtfully applicable to the sociohistorical context into which it is translated.

Barbara Shapiro demonstrates in *Probability and Certainty in Seventeenth-Century England* that seventeenth-century English thinkers across a wide range of disciplines were sensitive to humanism's difficulties and sought to respond to them by revising in light of skeptical concerns both their estimation of reason and their relationship to classical authorities.[8] Reason shows itself to be not exalted but faulty (here one thinks of Bacon's four idols), capable of discovering only limited areas of knowledge with more or less limited certainty, and in need of methodological and/or mechanical aids to keep it from error. Methodology not antiquity becomes the ground of truth, and the discourse of knowledge is reconstituted as a discourse of the present, its transhistoricity or ahistoricity not negated but reversed as classical authorities are subsumed through a process of methodological sifting. "*Antiquitas saeculi iuventus mundi.* These times are the ancient times, when the world is ancient,"[9] Bacon states. Bacon's reorganization of knowledge in *The Advancement of Learning* and *The New Organon* is an instance of this sort of revision. To the skeptic Bacon concedes that "not much can be known in nature by the way which is now in use," but he does not abandon reason altogether: the skeptics "go on to destroy the authority of the senses and understanding; whereas I proceed to devise and supply helps for the same."[10] The help with which Bacon supplies reason is the method of true induction "which shall analyze experience and take it to pieces, and by a due process of exclusion and rejection lead to an inevitable conclusion,"[11] a method of induction in which experience and knowledge are dialectically related. Bacon's goal is to bring reality and its representations, things and words or concepts (Bacon at times does not clearly distinguish between the two, given his sensitivity to the ways in which language determines understanding), into true alignment: "I am building in the human understanding a true model of the world, such as it is in fact, not such as a man's own reason would have it be."[12] In this manner Bacon reconstitutes the discourse of universal truth as a discourse of the present or, more precisely, of the future, since Bacon's methodological guidelines lay the foundations for a discourse whose production would, Bacon saw, require a vast body of researchers with state funding working over a good deal of time to reach completion.

With his emphasis on methodology and experience, Bacon is not surprisingly critical of those whose faith in the authority of antiquity is such that their knowledge of the world is based not on judgment and experience but on what is found in the texts of antiquity handed down to them, on tradition. For Bacon, knowing by tradition has its roots in "credulity,"[13] one of several epistemological flaws to which the mind is prone and which the recovery and transmission of competing classical metaphysical systems has only exacerbated. These competing metaphysical systems Bacon calls "Idols of the Theater, because in my judgment all the received systems are but so many stage plays, representing worlds of their own creation after an unreal and scenic fashion."[14] Built with disregard or even contempt for experience, these systems are, for Bacon, poetic fictions that create their own more or less golden worlds rather than representing the world as it is. Bacon seems to consider idolatry of the theater to be a form of subjectivism and even solipsism (as we shall see, Morose is an example of this), the result of the mind's tendency to project its own desires and sense of order onto the world. Jonson, who admired Bacon's works, is equally critical of the credulity of the learned: "Nothing is more ridiculous, than to make an author a dictator, as the Schools have done Aristotle. The damage is infinite knowledge receives by it. For to many things a man should owe but a temporary belief, and a suspension of his own judgement, not an absolute resignation of himself, or a perpetual captivity."[15] In the passage from which the above quotation is taken, a condensed paraphrase of portions of Bacon's *The Advancement of Learning*, Jonson opposes judgment to knowing by tradition: we must "calmly study the separation of opinions; find the errors have intervened, awake antiquity, call former times into question."[16] In *Epicoene* Jonson moves his critique of knowing by tradition from the study to the Strand; his stage play recreates the unreal and scenic world of fashionable urban society in order to probe the epistemological emptiness that accompanies its material clutter. The play, though, problematizes rather than achieves the Baconian goal of leaving the theater for reality; constrained by the material conditions of its (re)production, knowledge cannot escape performativity.

Sir John Daw and Sir Amorous La Foole are the play's simplest embodiments of the lack of judgment and credibility created and maintained by the material environment the play's characters inhabit. Daw and La Foole are close kin to the humors characters of Jonson's comical satires, but the pathology of their credulity is more epistemological than psychological. John Enck observes that, unlike the humors plays, *Epicoene* "accepts human aberrations as a condition essentially comic but not wholly correctable."[17] As we shall see, the incorrigible nature of Daw and La Foole's folly has much to do with the material conditions of the world they inhabit. We are first introduced to Daw and La Foole through the Theophrastian character sketches drawn of them by Dauphine and Clerimont. What emerges from these character sketches is that the two are fools for the same reason: each is attempting to play a role, to be somebody, in London's town society but so lacks judgment that not only does he play his role ineptly but he does not realize this. Daw is "the only talking sir' i'th' town,"[18] a man who attempts to play the roles of scholar, wit, and statesman. His scholarship is limited to knowing "titles, and nothing else of books" (1.2.72); as we find out later on in the play, he is utterly incapable of distinguishing between major and minor writers, between classical and modern writers, and even between the titles of books and their authors. His attempts as a wit to court Epicoene reveal that he lacks the judgment to tailor his actions to the situation and to his intentions: "He would lie with her and praises her modesty; desires that she would talk free, and commends her silence in verses, which he swears are the best that ever man made" (1.3.14–17). He disqualifies himself as statesman material in the very act of expressing his desire to play that role: he "rails at his fortunes, stamps, and mutines why he is not made a counselor and call'd to affairs of state" (1.3.17–19)—in short, he throws a tantrum. La Foole is a simpler soul. His desire is to know and to be known, to be "one of the Braveries though he be none o' the Wits" (1.3.28). To that end he demonstrates a complete lack of the decorum, the ability to be sensitive to the moment and to govern "him selfe with that good judgement that will not suffer him to enter into any folly,"[19] that Castiglione found so essential to the courtier: "He will salute a judge upon the bench and a bishop in the pulpit, a lawyer when he is pleading at the bar, and a lady when she is dancing in a masque, and put her out" (1.3.29–31).

The rest of the play confirms the character sketches, and it is evident that Daw and La Foole's lack of judgment is the obverse side of their utter credulity, their readiness to believe whatever they are told about themselves and others. This credulity the three wits manipulate to effect their own designs: "Tut, flatter 'em both (as Truewit says) and you may take their understandings in a purse-net. They'll believe themselves to be just such men as we make 'em, neither more nor less. They have nothing, not the use of their senses, but by tradition" (3.3.87–91), Dauphine states. And throughout the play Daw and La Foole pass through a series of transformations into just such men as the wits require, metamorphosing into melancholy lovers, men whose honors have been offended, antagonists in a revenge tragedy, and ultimately lecherous gallants who have enjoyed Epicoene's favors. Because they know "by tradition," the two are puppets—

Clerimont calls La Foole "that precious manikin" (1.3.24) and Truewit states that Daw is "so utterly nothing, as he knows not what he would be" (2.4.138–39)—or characters in playlets scripted by the three wits. In *Discoveries* Jonson muses that "our whole life is like a play: wherein every man, forgetful of himself, is in travail with expression of another. Nay, we so insist in imitating others, as we cannot return to ourselves."[20] Daw and La Foole seem to be one step beyond this description of the human condition: they do not seem to have selves to forget. Their world is theater, of a less sophisticated sort than the theater of Bacon's metaphysicians but characterized by the same epistemological distance from the world "as it is." This epistemological distance is most evident in Truewit's "tragicomedy between the Guelphs and the Ghibellines" (4.5.26–27) in which Daw and La Foole are the unwitting antagonists. In this scene, the two take Truewit's word for reality, and nowhere is the distance between word and reality greater. Daw cowers in a closet to avoid an outraged La Foole "hung with pikes, halberds, petronels, calivers, and muskets" (4.5.100–101) while La Foole, in a closet on the other side of the stage, tempts his breeches to avoid a furious Jack Daw bent on strangling him with a towel. The tragicomedy reaches its happy conclusion when Dauphine, dressed in a carpet and a cushion, plays both angry revengers and delivers the negotiated number of kicks and nose tweaks. Significantly, even after the tragicomedy is over Daw and La Foole do not leave the theater, do not return to authentic selves or an authentic world. The two are provided with no way of detecting their epistemological error: they will learn of the theatrical nature of their (terrifying, to them) experience neither from each other—they have both been enjoined to silence—nor from the wits or collegiate ladies. This is another point at which *Epicoene* differs from Jonson's early humors plays: Macilente, whose task is accomplished when the "folly" of *Every Man Out of His Humour*'s humors characters has been "raked up in their repentant ashes,"[21] has been replaced by the three wits, whose goal is not to cure but exploit Daw and La Foole's foolishness; Daw and La Foole are never confronted with their epistemological error and are dismissed at the play's end not for their own credulity but, ironically, for supposedly taking advantage of the credulity of others with their tall sexual tales.

The absence of a feedback mechanism by which Daw and La Foole might have been cured cannot be attributed solely to the nastiness of the three wits, however. The world in which Daw and La Foole live is nearly epistemologically frictionless. It is what Tom Wolfe calls a "statusphere,"[22] a relatively self-enclosed social world generated by wealth, at the center of which is an arbiter of status whose judgments have no necessary connection to the judgments of other statuspheres or of a larger normative social world. As many recent critics have observed, the statusphere that Daw and

La Foole inhabit, at whose center are the collegiate ladies, is nearly as self-enclosed as, though more populated than, Morose's little world and is confined within the fashionable area of the Strand. Its inhabitants are wealthy but leisured, having no need to work and no opportunity to engage in "affairs of state" (1.3.19). Ayers states that the gallant, the typical male member of the play's sophisticated urban world, "is by birth and education a member of the gentry, but in certain respects a displaced one; he is a member of the traditional ruling class who has for practical purposes abandoned both his traditional power base and his traditional residence, his place in the country, together with its demands and responsibilities, in favour of the more exciting world of town life."[23] Freed from responsibilities, the members of Daw and La Foole's statusphere spend all their time in pursuit of status within the statusphere. As Haynes observes, the triviality of the goal in no way diminishes the intensity of the pursuit: "at issue is the definition and consolidation of polite social space, and, most of all, a competition for sway within it."[24]

The material conditions that enable this statusphere also generate epistemological limits for its inhabitants. Consequently, Daw and La Foole's world is a distorted version of the life of otium or contemplation; its lack of relation to any sort of action other than "nothing, or that which when 'tis done is as idle" (1.1.32) restricts opportunities for experience and the exercise of judgment and so diminishes the possibility that knowing by tradition will be transformed into some less credulous form of knowledge. For example, the only experience that calls for Daw to apply the learning for which he has acquired such a reputation occurs as he is being beaten by Dauphine, the moment during which Daw is most deceived about what he is experiencing: "What's six kicks to a man that reads Seneca" (4.5.265), Truewit cruelly remarks. Daw and La Foole's world is rendered even more frictionless by the nature of its inhabitants, who are either wits or fools. Significantly, to a certain extent the collegiate ladies must be placed in the latter category, their folly consisting in their inability to judge Daw and La Foole as fools and serving, then, to reconfirm the two in their folly by granting them the status they seek. The wits also reinforce Daw and La Foole's folly, not only for "sport" (5.2.79) but also for the status gained through such sport. If Daw and La Foole are "two yards of knighthood measur'd out by time to be sold to laughter" (2.4.135–36), then it is the wits who turn a profit on the sale. The two knights' tragicomic humiliation functions not only as entertainment but also as part of Truewit's plan to gain Dauphine the favors of the collegiate ladies, who are invited to watch the tragicomedy's catastrophe. Status's function here parallels the function of gold in *Volpone*: it is the insubstantial nothing that fixes the characters' thoughts and desires and shapes the material fictions they live, the theatrical film that transforms material objects into props and material existence into play.

When we turn to Morose, the connections between the epistemological limits of the mind and the material world it inhabits become more complex. Morose's credulity combines with other limiting factors to produce a solipsist who actively struggles to create around himself an epistemological space in which his solipsism can function as truth. Critics often have described Morose's character in terms of humors psychology, which in itself tends toward a form of materialist epistemology in its diagnoses of mental aberrations as effects of the imbalance of bodily fluids. The diagnosis is, of course, that Morose suffers from "melancholy" (4.4.51) and that his melancholia manifests itself in his extreme aversion to noise. The character sketch drawn of him by the three wits at the play's beginning presents him largely in these terms: he is plagued by a "disease" (1.1.140) whose advanced state has produced the "ridiculous" (1.1.140) symptoms that Clerimont and his boy take turns wittily describing. This diagnosis, however, takes us only so far. Morose's solipsism, which is as much a world of words as Daw and La Foole's world, is the result of a peculiar combination of thinking by tradition and "philautia" or self-love, the root of all humors according to Thomas Wright in *The Passions of the Mind in General*.[25] In act 5, scene 3, Morose gives his own etiology of his condition:

> My father, in my education, was wont to advise me that I should always collect and contain my mind, not suff'ring it to flow loosely, that I should look to what things were necessary to the carriage of my life, and what not, embracing the one and eschewing the other. In short that I should endear myself to rest and avoid turmoil, which now is grown to be another nature to me. So that I come not to your public pleadings or your places of noise, not that I neglect those things that make for the dignity of the commonwealth, but for the mere avoiding of clamours and impertinacies of orators that know not how to be silent. (45–56)

In a move reminiscent of humanist strategies of legitimation, Morose invokes his father as both the source and legitimation of his paradigm of thought, which divides things into two categories, those things that are necessary for him and those that are not. Morose here seems to be the typical oedipal son who has identified with the law of the Father, but his extreme reading of this law indicates an oedipal surplus beyond identification that is roughly the equivalent of Wright's "philautia." If Daw and La Foole have no selves to forget, Morose, at the other extreme, is unable to forget himself. Through the narcissistic "green spectacles"[26] of philautia Morose rereads necessary and not necessary as self and other. Morose's aversion to noise is a function of these green spectacles. Significantly,

Morose is not averse to all noise but merely to the "noise" of others' discourses: "all discourses but mine own afflict me, they seem harsh, impertinent, and irksome" (2.1.3–5). For Morose, the discourse of others is alien and incomprehensible, and its sources are monstrous and to be exterminated. The play makes this point emphatically by placing Truewit's noisy arrival at Morose's house immediately after Morose's lengthy discourse on the virtues of silence in others: when Truewit, come to persuade Morose not to marry, winds his horn outside Morose's doors, Morose exclaims "What prodigy of mankind is that? . . . Oh! Cut his throat, cut his throat: what murderer, hell-hound, devil can this be?" (2.1.38–40).

To borrow Bakhtinian terminology, throughout the play Morose struggles to render his world a space of "closed and deaf monoglossia";[27] for this reason he avoids markets and law courts, places in which the word is dialogic and his discourse must compete with others. (Ironically, his monologia develops into a form of monologorrhoea: Morose rivals even Truewit in prolixity.) Several recent critics, however, have commented that, paradoxically, only in London, the biggest and noisiest city in Jacobean England, could Morose achieve any measure of success in carving out his monologic epistemological space. It is at first surprising that Morose, with his fifteen hundred pounds per year, should choose to live in London rather than in the country or even a smaller town. But as Maus perceptively asks, "where else would Morose live?"[28] Maus points out that only in London would the labor pool have been large enough to find a silent barber or a builder capable of building a sound-proof house. The materials for such a house would have been more readily available in London than elsewhere. Maus also points out that by living in London Morose can acquire a degree of anonymity and independence from his neighbors not possible in a smaller setting. One can add to this the predominance of contractual over kin relations. Through contracts, which Morose manages to conclude with "fishwives and orange-women" (1.1.142), Morose transforms social relationships into impersonal, limited transactions which firmly distinguish between *meum* and *tuum*, self and other. Ayers describes Morose as "an urban solipsist who simultaneously hates the city yet chooses to live in its very centre, because it is only there that he can indulge freely his self-assertive egotism."[29] Only in the material environment created by the rapidly growing, increasingly capitalist Jacobean London could Morose create his small world, and because of these material conditions, which free Morose from the need to revise his thinking, his epistemological malady remains unchecked.

Morose's monologia or solipsism generates for him epistemological difficulties similar to those experienced by Daw and La Foole. His inability to hear others and his failure to acknowledge any sort of slippage between discourse and reality lead, ultimately, to his undoing. Morose's epistemological difficulties are perhaps most evident in one of the play's pivotal scenes, his interview with Epicoene. Here it is apparent that people exist for Morose only as either aliens with whom he is at war or transparent and subordinate objects. When Epicoene does not fall into the former category, Morose can only place "her" in the latter. To Morose's questions Epicoene returns the desired answers, and Morose accepts "her" performance of silence and subordination as the truth. Morose's either/or thinking cannot comprehend the possibility of duplicity, and Epicoene's performance gains "her" entry into Morose's world as a construction, an extension of Morose's monologic ego. To Morose, Epicoene is a doll or a puppet: he imagines that she will not compete with him linguistically, that she will resign her judgment to him, and that she will allow him completely to shape her exterior as well as mental interior. When Epicoene later proves to be neither silent nor subordinate, Morose recategorizes her as an alien, "a Penthesilea, a Semiramis" (3.5.51–52) who must be expelled from his world at any cost. To bring Morose to this point has been Dauphine's intention all along, of course. But like Truewit's tragicomedy, Dauphine's plotting does not result in a humors comedy but a "comedy of affliction" (2.6.35–36). As Donaldson puts it, the play's action is unified around "the persecution of a misanthrope."[30] Although, like Asper in *Every Man Out of His Humour*, Dauphine writes the play in which he acts, his goal is not to cure Morose's humor by exacerbating it to its breaking point but to exploit Morose for his own ends, and in the play's final scene he sends an uncured Morose back to his solitary world "till you trouble me with your funeral, which I care not how soon it come" (5.4.195–96).

Epicoene's explorations in epistemological space are not limited to the more or less learned folly that is a consequence of credulity and the material conditions that maintain and reinforce it. While the play's dramatization of fools such as Daw, La Foole and Morose renders their folly readily comprehensible in terms of a revised Baconian or Jonsonian project of learning, the interaction between the three wits and the collegiate ladies problematizes a key assumption of this revised project, the assumption of what philosophers of science call the "translatability" of discourse.[31] Baconian induction assumes, in protological positivist fashion, that experience determines knowledge, that words have stable referents against which the truth value of individual statements, taken from any discourse new or old, can be measured. But if, as Kuhn, Quine, and other philosophers of science argue, theory determines experience, constructs rather than labels the objects to which it refers, then the Baconian project is merely another instance of the cosmological poetics it claims to supersede; its reconstitution of knowledge as a discourse of the present through the sifting mechanism of induction becomes *bricolage*, not translation but appropriative redefinition. Conversely, knowledge is performative, a matter of act not fact. Discourse is true only insofar as it can be enacted as true or made to function as the truth.

The impossibility of translation, the unsettling interaction between performative knowledge and the material conditions of its performance, structures the erotic economy in which the three wits and the collegiate ladies participate. As Ovidian erotic discourse is translated from the patriarchal context of its initial articulation into the brave new world of the collegiate ladies and the wits, its ability to function as the truth is destabilized. Truewit is Ovid's spokesman in the play, and Ovid is Truewit's main authority as he throughout the play schools Clerimont and Dauphine in the finer points of the erotic economy which structures the wits' relations with the collegiates. The tutoring begins in the play's first scene, after Truewit has set aside Plutarch and Seneca to take issue with Clerimont's praise of "natural" female dress. Clerimont, whose suit to Lady Haughty is not going well, praises the woman "That makes simplicity a grace; / Robes loosely flowing, hair as free" (1.1.92–93). Truewit is "clearly o' the other side" (1.1.97) and responds with a lengthy argument in favor of female cosmetic, sartorial, and gestural artifice:

> I love a good dressing before any beauty o' the world. Oh, a woman is then like a delicate garden; nor is there one kind of it: she may vary every hour, take often counsel of her glass and choose the best. If she have good ears, shew 'em; good hair, lay it out; good legs, wear short clothes; a good hand, discover it often; practice any art to mend breath, cleanse teeth, repair eyebrows, paint, and profess it. (1.1.97–101)

Truewit continues with this sort of advice for another thirteen lines and offers another version of the argument in act 4. Implicit in his discourse is the assumption that women are objects whose appearance should be pleasing to men's tastes. Truewit's Ovidian discourse, then, reproduces Morose's distinction between self and other in the narrower terms of the binary opposition between male and female. Misogynistic as this discourse is, however, it seems to allow for a power reversal in the erotic economy. Lyons observes that the play's Ovidian erotics implements "a comic politics in which male desire temporarily endows the female with a special kind of authority."[32] The Ovidian lover is like Pygmalion in his objectification of women, but the desire he invests in his creation turns him into its servant. Or so the theory goes. The collegiate ladies are very aware of the power to be gained by submitting to male objectification: it gains them a "plurality of servants" (4.3.28–29) who are willing not only to write them poems and escort them to the theater but also to "draw their weapons for our honors"

(4.3.45). In short, it allows them to harness male physical and sexual energy to satisfy their own desires.

Nonetheless, the power with which Ovidian erotics with one hand endows women, it takes away (or attempts to take away) with the other. Here Truewit's further remarks on the art of love are revealing:

> A man should not doubt to overcome any woman. Think he can vanquish 'em and he shall; for though they deny, their desire is to be tempted. Penelope herself cannot hold out long. Ostend, you saw, was taken at last. You must persevere and hold to your purpose. They would solicit us, but that they are afraid. . . . Though they strive, they would be overcome. (4.1.67–77)

According to Truewit, rape is "to them an acceptable violence, and has ofttimes the place of the greatest courtesy. She that might have been forc'd, and you let her go free, without touching, though then she seem to thank you, will ever hate you after; and glad i' the face, is assuredly sad at the heart" (4.1.79–83). The power an objectified or constructed woman gains is negated by the lover's prerogative to construct her interior and to interpret according to his own hermeneutic her answer to his sexual advances. It is at this point, however, that the breakdown in the translatability of Ovidian discourse begins. In the patriarchal worlds of classical Rome and, perhaps less so, Jacobean England generally, men possessed the power, through conventions, institutions, and brute force, to produce as truth the answers they constructed for women. In *Epicoene*'s fictional world, however, matters are somewhat different. As Epicoene herself emphatically demonstrates, a woman's silence cannot be taken for consent: although "she says nothing" (2.3.121) initially, ultimately she is not "*videtur consentire*" (2.3.121). The collegiate ladies have the wealth and have taken advantage of the opportunities created by London's development to obtain the independence necessary to restructure the power relations in their statusphere. Consequently, Dauphine, who is in love with all the collegiate ladies and who has been given Truewit's lecture on "acceptable violence," later in the play finds himself in a position similar to the one in which Morose finds himself when Epicoene begins to speak, faced with an unexpected discrepancy between discursive construction and reality. Truewit's plan to work Dauphine into the collegiate ladies' favors meets with unexpected success: the tables are turned and Dauphine is "assaulted" (5.2.48), metamorphosed into the object of the collegiate ladies' sexual predation.

In the collegiate ladies' world, then, the erotic power the collegiate women gain by crafting their exterior according to Ovidian codes is not negated by the male lover's power to enforce as truth his constructions of their interiors. Consequently, this world's erotic economy trades on performance unconstrained by at least some of the naturalizing truth effects of the assertion of patriarchal power. A number of critics have argued that the play ultimately shuts down this space of erotic performance. Rackin, for example, argues that "In *Epicoene*, Jonson attempts to deal with the dangers of social and sexual transgression by upholding the socially sanctioned gender divisions and by resolving his play in the abolition of sexual ambiguity: the transvestite figure is finally revealed as the boy the actor who played him really was."[33] However, if sex is rendered unambiguous, through Epiocene's unwigging gender is revealed to be a performance. In the play there is no "natural" social entity to which the word "woman" might refer, and the performance of gender becomes a mode of exchange: the unnamed page boy who plays Epicoene has exchanged his performance for a half year's food and lodgings; Dauphine has exchanged the boy's performance for an annual income; the collegiate ladies exchange their performances for erotic power. The economics of gender performance extends beyond the play's fictional world: the male actors who have played the collegiate ladies have exchanged their performance for the price of admission. In the collegiate ladies' world, then, Ovidian discourse cannot be produced as knowledge; it becomes a script, a set of scenarios whose instantiations are improvised, never fully played "by the book," and subject to contestations by other performances based on other scripts. Indeed, the restructured power relations of the collegiate ladies' statusphere allow them to articulate their own counter-discourse, a body of knowledge which becomes a tradition as it is transmitted from senior to junior collegiates. One of the topics treated in this counter-discourse is the governance of husbands; the relationship between Captain Otter and Mistress Otter, who has mastered this topic though only an aspirant to college membership, clearly dramatizes the intimate relationship between discourse and power. Mistress Otter, the "rich china-woman" (1.4.27), uses her wealth and her fists to keep Captain Otter, formerly a "great man at the Bear Garden" (2.6.57), in his proper place as her "subject" (4.3.6). Although behind her back he savagely satirizes her and claims that he married her only for her "six thousand pound" (4.2.69), Captain Otter speaks to her only "under correction" (3.1.9) and it is clear that by his marriage he did not get what he had bargained for. Captain Otter is Truewit's parodic twin, reproducing standard misogynist satire and striking the familiar pose of the cynical hunter of wealthy widows in a situation in which the satire and the pose are impotent and comic.

 The breakdown in the translatability of Ovidian discourse is manifest even at the stylistic level. As Barish observes in "Ovid, Juvenal, and *The Silent Woman*," Truewit's reproduction of Ovid is rather different in tone from the original. Satirical or Juvenalian tendencies are evident in each of Truewit's adaptations of Ovid. Truewit's defenses of various forms of artifice and their uses turn Ovid's delicate advice into grotesque catalogues of natural and artificial body parts (1.1.97–104; 1.1.106–18) and physical deformities (4.1.31–42); his advice to the lover (4.1.85–120) inflates the Ovidian lover into a figure bearing more than passing resemblance to humors fools. Barish concludes that "The stern figure of the moralizing satirist glares through the elegant and polished surface [of Ovidian discourse], causing roughness of tone and uncertainty of texture."[34] According to Barish, Jonson, attempting to create an Ovidian drama to satisfy a courtly audience, "is imperfectly trying to imitate an alien spirit."[35] However, rather than conclude with Barish that Jonson has failed artistically, we can see Truewit's Juvenalian tendencies as a function of his uneasiness in the reconfigured power nexus of what Helms calls the "feminized space"[36] of the collegiate ladies' world. Ovidian authority and self-confidence have been dialogized by satire's hints of defensiveness and impotence. Several critics have felt that this also expresses Jonson's unease. Woodbridge writes that "Jonson was among many male writers in the Renaissance who recoiled in indignation from the sort of women who would leave home and meet together."[37] Howard concurs: *Epicoene* "is a play saturated with the fear of women who have moved or might move from their proper place of subordination, and it points to some of the changing social conditions that made such movement a possibility and a threat."[38] Howard argues that the play "circulates a virulent brand of antifeminist polemic."[39]

On the whole I agree with Woodbridge and Howard, but a useful distinction can be made here between Jonson's feelings and the play. However much Truewit's satirical streak is an expression of Jonson's own misogyny, the play itself is ambivalent toward the antifeminism it circulates.[40] In *The Cankered Muse* Kernan argues that the movement of satire onto the stage produced the ambivalent figure of the stage satirist (Macilente, e.g.) whose railing is largely undercut by his suspect motives and by his complicity in the targets of his attack. On stage the satirist's perspective is dialogized: the satirist is only one character, one voice, among many, and the "envy, sadism, and discontentedness [that] subtract from the satyr's moral stature" become clearly visible. Kernan writes: "the stage shifts our perspective. The shadowy face is now turned toward us and we see its full ugliness.... The satirist's various contradictions, confusions, and tensions are realized dramatically, and the dramatic perspective reveals them unambiguously."[41] Fully drawn satirist figures are absent from Jonson's major comedies, but Truewit and the other two wits are heirs to this ambivalent role. Although in the first scene he disparages artifice, later Clerimont cannot help admiring Lady Haughty's "autumnal face, her piec'd beauty" (1.1.80): "Methinks the Lady Haughty looks well today, for all my dispraise of her i' the morning" (4.1.28–30). One begins to suspect that his earlier disaffection was an instance of sour grapes over Lady Haughty's lukewarm response to his suit. Similarly, Dauphine may scorn the collegiate ladies' "ignorance" (4.5.219) for having chosen Daw and La Foole as servants, but he is nonetheless in love "with all the collegiates" (4.1.128). He does not wish to dissolve the college but to replace Daw and La Foole, and the ultimate objective of all his plotting has been to extort from his uncle an annual income that would allow him to upstage the prodigal play demise Morose has written for "it knighthood" (2.5.111) and to continue to inhabit the collegiate ladies' statusphere. If, as Lyons argues, "the community of men solidify their position"[42] at the play's end, it does so largely as a new group of competitors for the collegiate ladies' attention. Even "Epicoene" will soon be a "visitant" (5.4.227). Unlike *Every Man In His Humour*, which resembles *Epicoene* in many ways, *Epicoene* does not end in marriage but divorce and so suggests not social renewal or change but social stasis.

If the translatability of discourse is problematized by its performativity, similarly, the performativity of discourse tends to deflect discourse from its "proper" Baconian and Jonsonian end of conveying ideas to be evaluated for their truth or falsity. In *Epicoene*'s fictional world, discourses drawn from a variety of bodies of knowledge are reproduced more for their performance value than for their semantic content. In Austin's terms, the "perlocutionary" force of the reproduction of discourse frequently renders its "locutionary" content irrelevant.[43] This conversion of discourse into sheer performance is perhaps an inevitable consequence of the foundation of the statusphere in which most of the play's characters move, the institution constituted by the collegiate ladies. In their society, the collegiate ladies are the arbiters of status, the pursuit of which regulates its members' activities. They have adopted the roles of patrons and critics of scholarship and literature and consequently link learning and status through the exercise of their judgments: they "give entertainment to all the Wits and Braveries o' the time, as they call 'em, cry down or up what they like or dislike in a brain or a fashion with most masculine or rather hermaphroditical authority" (1.1.73–76). The play, however, renders the collegiate ladies' judgment rather suspect. Their choice of Daw and La Foole as servants lends some support to Truewit's assertion that "all their actions are governed by crude opinion, without reason or cause; they know not why they do anything; but as they are inform'd, believe, judge, praise, condemn, love, hate" (4.6.56–59). (What does this say about their selection of Dauphine as their new favorite, one wonders?) Here the play is clearly antifeminist: women who seize the "masculine" prerogative of judgment are incapable of judging and so trivialize learning, eliminating the distinctions between "brain" and "fashion," "religion" (2.2.116) and "bawdry" (2.2.116) and thus reducing knowledge to a chaotic competition of discourses. However, as I have argued above, the three wits, who are the collegiate ladies' severest critics (discounting Morose, their only critics), are deeply implicated in the folly they castigate. The collegiate ladies' judgments may be based on utterly groundless opinion, but, to the extent that they are groundless, the force of the collegiate ladies' performance of judgment is revealed.

Throughout the play the content of language is subordinated to its force. At its lowest level, learning is reduced to noise, whose primary function is to torment Morose. Truewit's adaptation and expansion of Juvenal's satire on the trials of marriage, the humors psychology bantered about in act 4, scene 4, and the canon law and divinity spouted by Cutbeard and Otter in the final scenes generate a level of noise whose effect on Morose is at least as significant as these discourses' contents, as the speakers of these discourses are well aware. Learning also becomes a form of status-acquiring display. Daw uses his smattering of Latin and his knowledge of authors and book titles to advertise himself, and consequently "the world reports him to be very learned" (1.2.74). Truewit's rhetorical exercises are a more sophisticated form of self-advertisement, a complex way of converting learning into status by displaying mastery of and distance from learning. From the play's beginning Truewit exercises his irony and his ability to argue *in utramque partem*, on "the other side" (1.1.97), to advertise the extent of his learning and the performative nature of his reproduction of it. Barish suggests that Truewit is always performing: Truewit "speaks through so many masks that one is not sure when, if ever, he is speaking *in propria persona*."[44] Immediately after he has entered Clerimont's rooms in the first scene, Truewit begins a lecture on the theme of *tempus fugit:* "Oh, Clerimont, this time, because it is an incorporeal thing and not subject to sense, we mock ourselves the fineliest out of it, with vanity and misery indeed" (1.1.48–51). He gains the desired response: "thou hast read Plutarch's *Morals*" (1.1.59). Shortly thereafter, rather than "spoil [his] wit utterly" (1.1.61), he takes up the *carpe diem* theme and begins his defense of cosmetics, a version of the vanity that he had moments ago attacked and perhaps the more difficult side of the Renaissance nature versus art debate. Clearly, in Truewit's case "locutionary content" is secondary to "perlocutionary force," to the impressiveness of his rhetorical ability. Even within Truewit's various reproductions of Ovidian discourse an irony is at work that privileges performance over content. Slights notes that "The wit, brilliance, sophistry, and apparent triviality of Truewit's argument are characteristic of a particular literary genre in the Renaissance, the paradox."[45] Truewit's praises of cosmetics can be seen as complex mock-encomia, praises of the trivial and defenses of the counterintuitive at once oddly compelling and ironic, generating an ambivalence about exactly how the praises or defenses are to be taken yet leaving no doubt about their author's verbal skills.[46] While attempting to dissuade Morose from marriage in act two scene two, Truewit uses another rhetorical strategy, the paradoxical dispraise of virtue, to achieve the same effect: conventional Renaissance feminine virtues—"fair"(61), "rich"(65), "noble"(66), "fruitful" (67), "learned" (70)—are recast as causes of viciousness in a wife. As Barish observes, this sort of rhetoric generates a skeptical "suspension of strong conviction" (177) while constructing a polished verbal artifice. Like cosmetics, the artifice of rhetoric becomes its own content.

In *Epicoene*'s world of performance, knowledge is replaced by wit, being-in-the-know. Knowledge as a stable, universal system of truths is replaced by provisional and improvised strategies whose aim is not truth but success. Marston's *What You Will*, a city comedy set in Venice, provides a useful commentary on the relationship between the instability of knowledge and being-in-the-know. Lampatho Doria laments to his companion Quadratus that he "was a scholar"[47] who spent seven years "in quotations / Of cross'd opinions 'bout the soul of man" (2.2.153) and yet attained no certain knowledge on the issue: "The more I learnt the more I learnt to doubt" (2.2.154). Lampatho then sums up his predicament: "I know I know naught but I naught do know. / What shall I do—what plot, what course pursue?" (2.2.193–94). Considerations of action or performance replace the quest for learning once the inadequacies and even impossibility of stable knowledge are revealed. We have already seen the Baconian response to Lampatho's question: a revised, better system of knowledge. Quadratus's response—"Why, turn a temporist, row with the tide, / Pursue the cut, the fashion of the age" (2.2.195–96)—is, however, the typical response of the Elizabethan and Jacobean intriguer, tragic or comic. More often than not, the tragic intriguer—Chapman's Bussy D'Ambois, Tourneur's D'Amville, Jonson's Sejanus—finds himself outwitted by a better conspirator: fate, divine providence whose operations are beyond mortal ken, a quasi-divine stand-in such as Tiberius. In Jacobean city comedy, however, divine providence is rarely operative, and in *Epicoene* not at all. There is no teleological absolute in *Epicoene*'s fictional world, even though Dauphine manages to pull off the plot he has been furthering for half a year. There is no supramundane plot or metanarrative to subsume all other plots and determine their truth. Consequently, plotting is improvisation and success is provisional. However much Dauphine has planned before the day on which Morose marries Epicoene, the events of the day and their direction to a successful conclusion depend largely on the wits' ability to react to the changing situation and to seize the opportunities presented them. Furthermore, in this game of plot and counterplot absolute mastery is difficult if not impossible to achieve: "That falls out often, madam, that he that thinks himself the master-wit is the master-fool" (3.6.46–47), Truewit comments to Lady Haughty. Truewit himself experiences this reversal of fortune at the play's end when he is "lurch'd . . . of the better half of the garland" (5.4.203–4) and Dauphine exchanges his cushion for the victor's crown.

Here any absolute distinction between wits and fools breaks down, and in its place we find a continuum of folly plotted along the axis of success. Everyone is potentially a fool. Benet reaches a similar conclusion from a moral perspective: "By the values and flaws the wits and fools share, Jonson suggests the universality of folly beneath the superficial distinctions of cleverness and manner."[48] An emphasis on the universality of folly, however, must be complemented by a recognition of the force that success carries in *Epicoene*'s fictional world. Dauphine's cleverness may be "superficial" in a moral sense but is extremely effective as the means by which he acquires an annual income of five hundred pounds, no superficial sum financially. The universality of folly in the play is further qualified by the antifestive, isolating, and punitive nature of the play's comic conclusion. Boehrer compares the play's action to a charivari, which was a popular but antifestive ritual: "carnivalesque arbitrariness—and with it, the universality of carnival laughter—tends to escape the charivari, which operates according to rules and for purposes [the punishment of deviation from the communal sexual norm] which render it satirical, exclusionary, and punitive."[49] At the end of Marston's *The Fawn*, a play which like *Epicoene* analyses and exposes a variety of contemporary follies, all of the play's characters but the two lovers and the formerly foolish duke are lightheartedly sentenced to join Socrates (no mean company) on the Ship of Fools. At the end of *Bartholomew Fair*, the folly of the play's authority figure, Justice Adam Overdo, is revealed by Quarlous, who himself has been mistaken for a madman; Quarlous then exhorts Overdo to "remember you are but Adam, flesh and blood! You have your frailty, forget your other name of Overdo, and invite us all to supper. There you and I will compare our discoveries; and drown the memory of all enormity in your biggest bowl at home" (5.6.89–92). *Epicoene*'s comic conclusion has none of these two play's emphasis on social leveling or the genial inclusiveness of the community of fools: the play generates clear winners and losers (as does *Bartholomew Fair*)—not in the game of love, which is a kind of folly, but in the cold, hard game of financial competition; Cutbeard, Otter, Daw, La Foole and Morose are all more or less harshly dismissed, and Daw, La Foole and Morose have been punished for their deviations from the social standards set by the three wits. The three wits are heavily implicated in the follies they satirize, but if they are fools (potentially and in moral actuality) then they are successful, unscrupulous fools bent on creating and maintaining the powerful illusion of a distinction between wits (themselves) and fools (everyone else).

Wit's orientation toward performance may supplant the project of learning as the humanists conceived of it and it may render everyone potentially a fool, but it nonetheless generates a kind of knowing which has an ironic relation to systematic knowledge. Ayers argues that wit is the mechanism by which the three friends come to terms with the protean phenomenal space engendered by London's rapidly changing urban environment: "Aware of the contradictions and irrationalities of urban life, they come to terms with them through the cultivation of irony and paradox as basic modes of apprehension and expression."[50] However, as a way of navigating an epistemological space such as the play's fictional world, wit is more than detached irony or paradox. The three wits' ironic detachment is the detachment of an actor engaged in playing a role and realizing a script. It is, furthermore, a function of their metaepistemological stance toward learning. In "Jonson's Urbane Gallants: Humanistic Contexts for *Epicoene*," Kay argues that the three wits represent an Erasmian fusion of the humanist and the courtier: they are in the world but not of it, disguise their criticisms of folly with playfulness, and wear their learning lightly. Kay admits that the three are not saints but argues that "The ideal of conduct they embody may be less charitable than that of More or Erasmus, less courtly than that of Castiglione, but it is no less an attempt to create a model which can combine gracefulness with wisdom, participation in the world and detachment from it."[51]

Throughout this chapter I have argued that the wits' engagement with their world undermines their detached stance. More importantly, though, I want to resist Kay's equation of the three wits' learning and humanist learning. The three wits' mode of knowing depends upon the humanist project's failure, the failure which plunges poor Lampatho into such perplexity. The three wits put their learning to a number of uses—display is one—but not to the humanist ends of truth or moral improvement. Roughly, they use their learning to get the upper hand on the play's other characters. The irony and paradox which characterize the wits' mode of apprehending their urban reality do not give them knowledge of that reality "in itself" but rather a knowledge of and consequent ability to exploit the conventions by which others perceive reality. Dauphine, for example, is somewhat disingenuous when he protests that Morose "shall never ha' that plea against me that I oppos'd the least fant'sy of his" (1.2.49–51). Certainly, Dauphine does not directly "oppose" his uncle's "fant'sy" until after the marriage ceremony, and even then he continues to play the friend. Rather, drawing on the same resources of wit his companions display in sketching Morose's character, Dauphine exploits his knowledge of Morose's humor and the tradition of misogyny whose conventions structure Morose's reception and subsequent rejection of Epicoene. Similarly, Truewit exploits his knowledge of revenge tragedy conventions to humiliate Daw and La Foole. Daw and La Foole know the conventions of revenge tragedy as well as Truewit, but they, like Sir Pol, believe them, allow them to structure their reality, while Truewit, of course, recognizes them as conventions and so is able to incorporate them into his own ironic tragicomic performance. And Jonson himself takes a metaepistemological stance toward his audience's knowledge by depending on the conventionality of the audience's perception of theatrical space to hide from them for five acts what they knew all along—that Epicoene is a boy.

4

The Rise of *Homo economicus* in *A Trick to Catch the Old One*

The previous chapters have outlined Jonson and Middleton's early city comedies' staging of selfhood and knowledge as at once performance and commodity. Stable, knowing selves dissolve into not entirely cohesive conglomerations of vendibles who must navigate urban spaces in which knowledge is fluid, a momentary fixing of the circulation of appearances. *Epicoene* takes the process of dissolution a degree further than *Volpone* or *Michaelmas Term*. The latter two plays more clearly than *Epicoene* distinguish between wits and gulls (although in neither play is the distinction very secure), whereas the cruel *sprezzatura* of *Epicoene*'s wits is fully immersed in the folly it attempts to overcome. *A Trick to Catch the Old One* mirrors *Epicoene*'s elimination of the boundary between wits and fools: if in *Epicoene* everyone is a fool, in *A Trick* everyone is on the make, cynically manipulating conventional selves and the discourses in which they are articulated. *A Trick* is a prodigal son play in the "satiric mode,"[1] and it dramatizes the complete disjunction between old moral paradigms and Jacobean London's complex new world. Yet the play is not, as Beck would have it, "true to the Christian assumptions inherent in the prodigal-son paradigm."[2] On the contrary, the moral vision of the prodigal son paradigm is transformed by the commercial forces that shape Middleton's Jacobean London. *A Trick* reverses the priorities of the prodigal son paradigm: spiritual narratives are subordinated to economic ends. The paradigm's dramatic conventions and the forms of relationships that constitute the fabric of its social vision are reproduced as tools, contingent and manipulable positions performed in conflicts motivated by secular and economic structures of thought and feeling. Middleton's aesthetics is one of dissociation and dissonance: old forms are inhabited—and undermined—by new sensibilities. Neither medieval complaint nor mercantilist apology, *A Trick* dramatizes the rise of *Homo economicus* as a crisis in social signification.

The fictional world of *A Trick* is not a world of which typical sixteenth- and seventeenth-century English commentators on economic matters would have approved, even if it increasingly was the world in which they found themselves living. However, these thinkers and writers ("economists" is significantly anachronistic) disapproved of emergent capitalist economic trends, which *A Trick* precipitates out in its usury-dominated world, for reasons more fundamental than a simple repugnance to lending at interest. At stake was their perception of the nature of the English commonwealth. In *Religion and the Rise of Capitalism*, Tawney states that medieval social thought's "fundamental assumptions, both of which were to leave a deep imprint on the social thought of the sixteenth and seventeenth centuries, were two: that economic interests are subordinate to the real business of life, which is salvation, and that economic conduct is one aspect of personal conduct upon which, as on other parts of it, the rules of morality are binding."[3] Working within this medieval intellectual tradition, Tudor and early Stuart writers saw the commonwealth as a fusion of church and state, of the sacred and the secular, that was threatened by the individualistic and narrowly economic ethic manifested in many of the economic changes of the period. In *The Laws of Ecclesiastical Polity* Hooker asserts the unity of state and church: "The Church and the commonwealth therefore are in this case personally one society, which society being termed a commonwealth as it liveth under whatsoever form of secular laws and regiment, a church as it hath the spiritual law of Jesus Christ; forasmuch as these two laws contain so many and so different offices, there must of necessity be appointed in it some to one charge, and some to another, yet without dividing the whole, and making it two several impaled societies."[4] Every member of the English state was automatically a member of the English church and subject to its values and discipline. This implied that in the Christian commonwealth the injunction to love one's neighbor took precedence over the impulse to accumulate capital, that the economic did not constitute an autonomous sphere of (private) activity but was—or should be—subordinated to the public good of the Christian social body (and the spiritual welfare of the commonwealth was, of course, a public good). Each coin bore the face of the monarch, head of state and church. Even Bacon, whose thought in other ways contributed to the separation of the secular and the sacred, the natural and the supernatural, seems largely to share this subordination of private to public, economic to moral. His thoughts on wealth are most striking in their unoriginality: "I cannot call riches better than the baggage of virtue. . . . For as the baggage is to an army, so is riches to virtue. It cannot be spared nor left behind, but it hindereth the march; yea and the care of it sometimes loseth or disturbeth the victory. Of great riches there is no real use, except it be in the distribution; the rest is but conceit."[5]

But even before Hooker had written his definition of the English commonwealth, this official reality had begun to show signs of its fictionality. The canon law that the Anglican church appropriated from its pre-Reformation predecessor prohibited usury, which it defined as any economic practice which produced private gain at the expense of public good and Christian morality and, as Tawney documents, church courts continued, albeit sporadically, to prosecute up to the civil war those who engaged in usurious practices.[6] Yet between 1545 and 1552 and from 1571 on, usury was in limited forms legal by parliamentary statute, and those who struggled, through the ecclesiastical judicial system, the pulpit or the press, to materialize the fiction of a Christian commonwealth in which wealth was merely a means to common material and spiritual enrichment were fighting a losing battle. *A Trick* contains traces of this battle. The play reproduces the conventions of the prodigal son parable, a parable in which economics are subordinated to the spiritual values of grace and forgiveness, in the world of capitalist Jacobean London, which refuses the parable's hierarchy of values and, ultimately, its spiritual significance. Much as the Dürer "Monument to Commemorate a Victory over the Rebellious Peasants" that Greenblatt analyses in "Murdering Peasants: Status, Genre, and the Representation of Rebellion," *A Trick* demonstrates the inapplicability of certain conventions to a particular event or world by applying them and allowing the irony full resonance.[7] The fictional world of the play is in some ways as imaginary as Hooker's Christian commonwealth, but its satire and caricature render it more of an exaggeration of than a departure from the changes restructuring early modern London. The play brings together passing and emergent worlds, and, while it is relatively clear which is the stronger of the two, the play's skepticism lies not—or not only—in the doubting of official reality but in the peculiar relationship that emerges between the old paradigms of thought and the new world. Not only is the old world passing but its moral paradigms have no place in the new world, except perhaps as irrelevant nostalgia; yet, with a few exceptions, those who operate by the ethos of the new world do not seem to be able entirely to dispense with the old paradigms, reproducing and underwriting them—in short, using them— within a pervasively economic world. In *A Trick* spiritual paradigms and narratives are not wholly abolished but are subordinated as means to entirely pecuniary ends.

As we have seen, the law in early modern England was an agent of the dissolution of the complex unity of Hooker's Christian commonwealth. The law in *A Trick* performs the same function. In the play, the law is pervasive and secularizing, reducing all relations to economic relations and rendering irrelevant all the values and obligations attached to these relations except insofar as they can be factored into a strictly economic calculus. The play's movement and energy originate in this legal reduction. In the play's first scene the penitent prodigal Witgood assesses the prospects of returning home to the "goodly uplands" and "goodly downlands" of his ancestral residence, "Long-acre."[8] He makes it clear that the return home for the Jacobean prodigal will not be as straightforward as his New Testament predecessor's: "But where's Long-acre? In my uncle's conscience, which is three years' voyage about; he that sets out upon his conscience ne'er finds the way home again; he is either swallowed in the quicksands of law-quillets or splits upon the piles of a *praemunire*" (1.1.6–10). The parable's father-son relationship, in which inhere the values of forgiveness and grace (spiritual values that, like prodigality, are economic liabilities), is supplanted by an uncle-nephew relationship defined entirely in legal and economic terms. Although aware that from a certain perspective his treatment of his nephew is "unnatural" (2.1.103), at bottom Lucre recognizes no obligations other than his own profit and no restraints other than the same restraint Witgood places on his own trickery, "the compass of the law" (1.1.24). In taking legal advantage of his "dissolute nephew" (2.1.2), Lucre the "virtuous uncle" (2.1.2) has merely had "an uncle's pen'worth" (2.1.7), which was better given to him than to one of Witgood's "aunts" (2.1.10) or bawds. Lucre's pun on aunt, which needs no explanation since "everyone knows what 'aunt' stands for in the last translation" (2.1.11), indicates that the reduction of relationships to monetary and contractual transactions is not merely Lucre's personal peculiarity but a general trend that has effected a semantic shift in language itself: in the last translation all relations are economic. Indeed, in the context of this semantic shift, the vocabulary by which the stages of the prodigals' progress are demarcated—debt, bondage, redemption, reclamation—has primarily legal and economic significance and charts not a spiritual but a legal and economic journey. In *A Trick* damnation is penury and the only saving grace is hard coin.

None of the play's relationships escapes this general trend. In *Michaelmas Term* and *Chaste Maid in Cheapside*, the sex-money calculus is an expression of the same urge to reduce all to the economic, but in these plays sexuality and sexual relations, while they may be harnessed to economic ends and always have economic significance, are a disruptive, carnivalesque force with a degree of autonomy associated with the constructed difference of the landed, fertile gentry from the wealthy but sterile citizenry. In *A Trick*, however, the sex-money calculus is present only in the background. The most explicit statement of this calculus is given by Witgood urging the Courtesan to marry Hoard: "y'ave fell upon wealth enough, and there's young gentlemen enow can help you to the rest" (3.1.241–43). However, the cuckolding of the "fox-brained and ox-browed" (1.1.10) Hoard by the young gentlemen he exploits is beyond the frame of the dramatic action, situated in one of the play's possible futures. Witgood and the Courtesan's riotous sexual life together is likewise outside the play's frame. The play brackets the disruptive potential of sexuality, and throughout the play sexual relations, and social relations, figure only as liabilities or assets entered in the balance-sheet columns of economic calculation. Thus Witgood figures his prodigality as a bad investment: "All sunk into that little pit, lechery" (1.1.3–4). Similarly, the Courtesan presents her prodigality as an economic transaction gone wrong: "Lands mortgaged may return, and more esteemed, / But honesty, once pawned, is ne'er redeemed" (1.1.35–36). In fact the Courtesan does find a way to redeem her honesty, and her distinction between the material and the spiritual, lands and honesty, proves not to hold. The sociosexual relation that dominates the play, marriage, is an exclusively economic and legal relationship. For Witgood and the Courtesan it is a method of financial recovery. It might be argued that Witgood marries Joyce as much for her "love" (1.1.19) and "virtues" (1.1.20) as for her "portion" (1.1.19). Perhaps so, but Joyce's love and virtue occupy very little of the play's time and even less of Witgood's attention. Witgood is almost entirely concerned with regaining his land and financial stability, and marriage is only one means to these ends. For Lucre and Hoard, marriage is a business merger, even a hostile take-over. Even when Hoard finds himself sexually aroused by the Courtesan, he expresses it by saying "She's worth four hundred a year in her very smock, if a man knew how to use it" (4.4.8–9). For Moneylove it is an investment whose every cost must be calculated and weighed against the expected return. And for the creditors it is merely another market in which to speculate. Love and even raw sexuality are conspicuously absent in the characters' motivations for involving themselves in a relationship that was, according to *The Book of Common Prayer*, "an honorable estate instituted of God in paradise, in the time of mannes innocencie, signifying unto us the misticall union that is betwixte Christe and his Churche,"[9] a microcosmic expression of the Christian commonwealth's fusion of the secular and the sacred.

The pervasiveness of the law and, through it, the reduction of all relationships to the economic might suggest a rigid and systematic advance of a unified capitalist power bloc. But in the play this is not the case. Rather, the insinuation of the law into social relationships generates an anarchic dispersal of power. Prison, corporal punishment, torture—in short, all the punitive prerogatives of personal sovereign power—have been made available through the functioning of impersonal law to (theoretically) anyone competing in the economic field defined by the law's compass. "Money or carcass" (4.3.44) the three creditors (small fry in comparison to Lucre, Hoard, or Dampit) can demand of Witgood. And given that the law seems to mediate all relationships, everyone is caught up in the dispersal, willingly or unwillingly. One either seizes power through the law and becomes, like Dampit, Lucre, and Hoard, a "trampler of time" (1.4.10) or one becomes one of the trampled, like Witgood and the other young heirs who are the staple with which Lucre and Hoard feed their seemingly insatiable acquisitive appetite. But, as Witgood's case shows, these power relationships are unstable, easily reversed. The play's characters play a Lyotardian game in which terror is a possible move. As Foucault puts it,

> Power's conditions of possibility . . . must not be sought in the primary existence of a central point, in a unique source of sovereignty from which secondary and descendent forms would emanate; it is the moving substrate of force relations which, by virtue of their inequality, constantly engender states of power, but the latter are always local and unstable. . . . And "Power," insofar as it is permanent, repetitious, inert, and self-reproducing, is simply the over-all effect that emerges from all these mobilities, the concatenation that rests on each of them and seeks in turn to arrest their movement.[10]

Foucault's description of power is not, of course, intended to be a description of the workings of power in a specifically capitalist social formation but an attempt to describe the workings of power on which all social formations are built. And as Norbert Elias in *The Civilizing Process* documents in his own terms, feudalism and its absolutist successors no less than the capitalist world dramatized by the play were products of the provisional alliances of local power relationships. Even so, the play's representation of the anarchic dispersal of power strikingly contrasts with the orderly and personal flow of power from a quasi-divine center envisioned by ideologues of the centralizing Elizabethan state and its absolutist Jacobean heir.

According to Tennenhouse, this contrast characterizes city comedy generally, and city comedy's representations of the dispersal of power in Jacobean London register, are implicit recognitions of, the need for the imposition of absolutist, patriarchal sovereignty: "City comedy thus stages the sinister side of comic desire, a city of night, an urban underworld run by greed and illicit desires. . . . These forces of disorder are unleashed upon the world when patriarchy is absent"; consequently, city comedy demonstrates "that the patriarch alone could bring order into a world given over to diseased forms of desire."[11] However, Tennenhouse's argument can recoup for sovereign authority city comedy's disquieting probing of the dynamics of power only by unwarrantedly assuming that absolutist ideology constitutes—for both the audience and for the plays themselves—the ultimate frame of reference in which representations of power signify. As we have seen in *Michaelmas Term*, however, city comedy often dialogizes absolutist ideology, reproducing authority's voice only to problematize it, draw it into the chaos. In *A Trick*, authority—whether that of the church, state, or of a unified social body—is almost entirely absent, and the impersonal, decentered, and provisional microdynamics of power are unchecked by the lines of power implicit in the personal and centered relationships of absolutist social formations. This can be seen in the weakness of such lines of conflict as citizen versus gentry and youth versus age. Unlike the struggle between Quomodo and Easy, the struggle between Lucre and Witgood is not primarily a struggle between citizen and gentry. That these two are blood relations diminishes the absoluteness of the birth-based status division between them, and the two are quickly reconciled when the mutual benefit of the reconciliation becomes apparent. Nor is the play's conflict structured along the lines of youth versus age (the main line of conflict in the typical New Comedy intrigue drama): the play is motivated as much by the conflict between the two old ones, Lucre and Hoard, as by the young ones' efforts to catch them, and the young ones are not as united as they seem. The play's lines of conflict are drawn in positional terms, of which the relationship between creditor and debtor is paradigmatic, and alliances are made not on the basis of stable categories such as status or age but on the basis of economic self-interest and are wholly provisional in nature.

Although the play's characters (with perhaps the exception of Dampit) seem unable to think of their social relationships except through the forms of such stable alliances as kinship, marriage, and friendship, they treat these forms as temporary combinations to obtain specific, and not necessarily mutually beneficial, ends. Thus, in act 2, scene 1, Lucre and Witgood flawlessly perform the uncle-nephew relationship, Lucre with the hope of eventually acquiring some of the rich Widow Medlar's lands and Witgood in order to gain his own mortgaged lands back from his uncle. Throughout the play Lucre continues to champion Witgood's suit and Witgood continues to play the penitent nephew only to advance these ends. (Lucre also has the motivation of scoring yet another victory over his business rival Hoard.) Similarly, the marriage between the Courtesan and Hoard is entirely a business venture. For Hoard, marriage to Widow Medlar is "not only the means laid before me extremely to cross my adversary and confound the last hopes of his nephew, but thereby to enrich my state, augment my revenues, and build mine own fortunes greater" (2.2.41–44). Ironically, Hoard's very sophistication in using the forms of social relationships to pursue his self-interest is the cause of his entrapment. When Widow Medlar confesses that "I ha' nothing, sir" (3.1.212), Hoard replies "Well said, widow, / Well said. Thy love is all I seek, before / These gentlemen" (3.1.213–15). This is the response of a consummate game-player, one who not only uses social relations strategically but knows he does and fully appreciates the strategic maneuvering of others. Unfortunately for Hoard, the Courtesan's move was deeper than he saw, and, when Witgood denounces her to Hoard as a penniless whore, she can say in all legal honesty that she did not deceive him and that consequently the marriage is still legally binding—more for her benefit than his.

More indicative of the provisionality of such alliances is the friendship between Witgood and the Courtesan. It is tempting to exempt their relationship from this provisionality. The camaraderie between these two rogues is the play's most attractive relationship, and several critics have argued for its qualitative difference from the rest of the play's relationships. Thus Rowe in *Thomas Middleton and the New Comedy Tradition* argues while the "mentality of Hoard, Lucre and most of the characters in the drama is the mentality of the Old Law. . . . The values and qualities of Witgood and the Courtesan, on the other hand, are primarily New Testament ones; they are carefully associated with mercy and forgiveness."[12] However, as Mount in "The '[Un]reclaymed forme' of Middleton's *A Trick to Catch the Old One*" argues, the forgiveness and mercy that Witgood and the Courtesan seem to show are quite frequently merely functions of underlying self-interested motivation, and their relationship does not constitute a "moral center"[13] from which a critique of the play's other relationships might proceed. In the play's opening scene Witgood does not hesitate to blame the Courtesan for his situation and to proclaim her "My loathing . . . a round-webbed tarantula / That dryest the roses in the cheeks of youth!" (1.1.27, 30–31)—until he realizes that "Fate has so cast it that all my means I must derive from thee [the Courtesan]" (1.1.46–47). From that point on the two work together to advance their interests. When, however, they have achieved their goals, when she has "become new" (4.4.134) and he has recovered the "soul of my estate" (4.2.88) and has been freed from his debts, the alliance breaks down. After her marriage to Hoard, the Courtesan begins to consider Witgood a liability and tells him, when he comes to her for help, "methinks, i'faith, you might have made some shift to discharge this yourself, having in the mortgage, and never have burdened my conscience with it" (4.4.162–64). Likewise Witgood, once on financially sound footing, discards his alliance with the Courtesan for an alliance with his uncle, which he plans to establish by publicly humiliating the Courtesan. "Uncle, let me perish in your favour" (5.1.12), Witgood tells Lucre, if Lucre finds it not the case that Hoard "is married to a whore" (5.1.9); by this colossal joke the two are reconciled and Lucre agrees to attend Hoard's wedding banquet. The play's festive conclusion does not bring about an end to the tactical provisionality of relationships, does not establish long-term stability and reconciliation. Significantly, the play's concluding festive order is not brought about by the intrusion of the voice of authority, as it is in *Michaelmas*

Term. It is, rather, an uneasy moment of stasis brought about by a temporary balance or coincidence of interests, a moment of seeming social unity that has emerged out of the play's mobile, local conflicts and whose fault lines are clearly visible. The self-interest that brings the characters together at Hoard's wedding banquet will inevitably move them apart, position them once again as competitors. The play hints that even Witgood and the Courtesan will not be exempt from this kaleidoscopic reconfiguration. It is difficult to consider Witgood and the Courtesan's concluding repentances as anything more than the latest performances of social roles for strategic ends. Lucre may, then, have the opportunity yet again to hunt after Witgood's lands and, if indeed there are, as Witgood claims, "young gentlemen enow" to help the Courtesan to what Hoard cannot give her, then mistress Jane Hoard may become a protagonist in yet another city comedy with its own provisional conflicts and alliances.

Just as social forms and lines of power are transformed by their immersion in the individualistic, competitive, and provisional world of the legal pursuit of economic ends, so also selfhood is reconfigured. The self in precapitalist social formations is social: the rights and obligations of social position are internalized as self (this accounts for the personal nature of power in these social formations); hereditary and hierarchical social status is thus naturalized as the essence of selfhood. In *Capitalism and Modernity: An excurus on Marx and Weber*, Derek Sayer states that "within precapitalist societies individuals are wholly engulfed by the social relations which define them. Their subjectivities are inseparable from their social position."[14] As we have seen, *Michaelmas Term* dramatizes the denaturalizing, corrosive effects of incipient capitalism on pre-capitalist social identity. The self, far from being a hereditary essence, is a commodity to be bought and sold. In *A Trick*, Middleton extends his exploration of this early but distinctively modern form of subjectivity. The self here is a peculiarly minimalist entity, crafted by economic calculation and relatively untouched by the drive to extravagance that renders self-fashioning in *Michaelmas Term* so spectacular. The characters in *A Trick* are no less protean than the characters in *Michaelmas Term*, but their metamorphoses are wholly functional, the necessary byproducts of the provisional, self-interested alliances that the characters form. If this form of subjectivity has a substance, this substantiality is external, materialized in possessions. Thus Witgood's opening words are "All's gone! Still thou'rt a gentleman, that's all; but a poor one, that's nothing" (1.1.1–2). These lines register the shift from a self with a social essence to a self that is nothing without possessions, nothing but possessions. Witgood regains his "soul" (4.2.88) only when he reacquires the mortgage to the lands whose loss is, in the first scene, self-annihilation. Hoard's statement that he is able "To buy three of Lucre" (2.2.49) likewise indicates the reductive equation of self and the goods one owns and also suggests that this externalization of the self renders selfhood itself one of the material stakes of economic competition. Thus, Hoard pays Witgood's debts only after Witgood has signed a legal document disclaiming "any title, right, or interest in or to the said widow [Widow Medlar]" (4.4.226–27) who is "now in the occupation of Walkadine Hoard" (4.4.228). Hoard asserts his occupation, his possession of the Widow Medlar's self through a legal document that defines the Widow primarily in terms of "her manors, manor houses, parks, groves, meadow-grounds, arable lands, barns, stacks, stables, doveholes, and coney-burrows; together with all her cattle, money, plate, jewels, borders, chains, bracelets, furnitures, hangings, moveables, or immovables" (4.4.230–34). In this light the economic competition in Jacobean London becomes a form of cannibalism: in appropriating others' possessions one is ingesting their souls, their substance.

As the legal mediation of Hoard's dealings with Witgood over the Widow's person suggests, the law is a crucial element of selfhood dramatized in *A Trick*. If the self is the sum of its possessions, then all that is left to the self intrinsically is the act of possessing or giving up possession. What the self possesses is accidental. The self, paradoxically, is emptied into the material world only to be profoundly alienated from it. Surrounded by the carapace of its possessions (Weber's "iron cage"),[15] this self is stripped down to the legal self of the contract, the positional self of legal possession shorn of all social rights and obligations. This type of selfhood is what Marx in the *Grundisse* calls "the juridical moment of the Person," the abstract individual of capitalist social formation in which

> the ties of personal dependence are in fact broken, torn asunder, as also differences of blood, educational differences, etc. . . . Thus the individuals appear to be independent (though this independence is merely a complete illusion and should rather be termed indifference); independent, that is, to collide with one another freely and to barter within the limits of this freedom.[16]

Interestingly, the play makes quite clear the gender divisions in the supposed universality of this abstract juridical individual: Witgood and Hoard are free to possess others; Jane—whether Courtesan, Widow Medlar, or mistress Jane Hoard—is free only to give herself to be possessed.

The alienation of the legal self from its possessions is not, however, limited to material possessions. The play provides several indications that intellectual ability and social status are similarly external to the self, alienated in the form of, in Bourdieu's terms, cultural capital and symbolic capital respectively. Witgood's wit is the play's most prominent example of cultural capital, which Bourdieu defines as the "forms of cultural knowledge, competences or dispositions."[17] An amalgam of practical psychology, flair in the performance of social scripts and ruthless means-ends economic calculation, wit is a tool the possession of which is necessary for survival in the play's fictional world. Almost all the play's characters possess it in some measure. Lucre, Hoard, and Dampit have amassed their fortunes by it, and Witgood and the Courtesan are in the process of doing likewise. "Why, are there not a million of men in the world that only sojourn upon their brain and make their wits their mercers" (1.1.21–23), Witgood exclaims at the play's commencement, and he may be wrong only insofar as he has overestimated the population of Jacobean London. Yet significantly the play sets wit, that body of know-how which allows the play's characters to navigate their world, at a distance from Witgood, its most outstanding possessor. Tracked down near the play's end by his creditors, Witgood represents his wit as external to himself, as an otherness to which he appeals for help: "I perceive I must crave a little more aid from my wits: do but make shift for me this once and I'll forswear ever to trouble you in like fashion hereafter; I'll have better employment for you, an I live" (4.4.49–52). Unlike force or privilege, which inhered in the aristocratic self of an earlier social formation, wit, the agent of Witgood's salvation, is precariously possessed, as much a product of converging circumstances and the opportunities they create as an intrinsic personal quality. Wit, as cultural capital, is like other forms of high-risk capital subject to the vicissitudes of the impersonal market and so is partially alienated from its possessor.

Status is similarly alienated as symbolic capital, which Bourdieu defines as the "degree of accumulated prestige, celebrity, consecration or honour."[18] Status, like other social forms, is not, as Marx argues, wholly "abolished" but is, rather, converted into a legally mediated possession whose symbolic value is as important as (and, as *Michaelmas Term* demonstrates, is translatable into) material wealth. At the play's end, Witgood is a gentleman only because he has regained possession of gentry status by regaining the legal title to his lands. The Courtesan redeems her "honesty" (1.1.36) by becoming mistress Jane Hoard, a legal fiction. Hoard is pleased with his marriage to the Widow Medlar as much for the symbolic capital it brings him as for the material possessions he imagines he has acquired, and his fantasy journey to the widow's lands is a forceful display of the symbolic value of his latest business venture:

> But the journey will be all, in troth, into the country; to ride to her lands in state and order following—my brother and other worshipful gentlemen, whose companies I ha' sent down for already to ride along with us in their goodly decorum beards, their broad velvet cassocks, and chains of gold

twice or thrice double; against which time I'll entertain some ten men of mine own into liveries, all of occupations or qualities. I will not keep an idle man about me, the sight of which will so vex my adversary, Lucre—for we'll pass by his door of purpose, make a little stand for the nonce, and have our horses curvet before the window—certainly, he will never endure it, but run up and hang himself. (4.4.9–19)

For the next fifty lines Hoard is preoccupied with his newly employed tailor, barber, huntsman, and falconer, all possessors of specialized cultural capital, directing them in various ways to use their skills to increase his own symbolic capital: "all the gentlemen o'th'country shall be beholding to us and our pastimes" (4.4.49–59), Hoard dreams.

Hoard's imaginary journey into the country indicates more than the appropriation of status as powerful symbolic capital, however. In *Michaelmas Term* Quomodo embarks on a similar imaginary trek to the lands he has just cozened from Easy, but Quomodo's fantasy is dominated by the sexualization of these lands. In contrast, Hoard's imaginary journey is saturated with anger and extreme competitiveness: Hoard intends one of the results of his display of symbolic capital to be Lucre's suicide. Hoard's anger and extreme competitiveness are symptoms of the irrationality of the subjectivity of the Jacobean *Homo economicus* formed at the intersection of economic imperatives and a legalized but anarchic field of economic competition. The differences between the structure of this economic subjectivity and that of the subjectivities that Greenblatt discusses in *Renaissance Self-Fashioning* are telling. For Greenblatt's subjects, the formation of selfhood "involves submission to an absolute power or authority situated at least partially outside the self—God, a sacred book, an institution" and "is achieved in relation to something perceived as alien, strange, or hostile. This threatening Other—heretic, savage, witch, adulteress, traitor, Antichrist—must be discovered or invented in order to be attacked and destroyed."[19] The Jacobean economic self is constructed through a similar dialectic of authority and other, but its authority is not sacred but secular, the arational or, as Weber puts it, "irrational,"[20] economic imperative to pursue wealth. Even when God is invoked, it is as a capricious, potentially malevolent natural force to be harnessed for material, secular ends: Dampit last prayed "In anno '88 when the great armada was coming; and in anno '99 when the great thunder and lightning was. I prayed heartily then, i'faith, to overthrow Poovies' new buildings" (3.4.1–4). The other of the economic self has no essential definition such as witch or savage but is purely positional, a legal and economic space whose occupants are more or less transitory. The monologic force of the irrational imperative driving the economic subject in its interaction with the plurality of its others in Jacobean London's anarchic world of economic competition propels the economic subject into a ceaseless hostility which is intensified by its need to overcome the paranoia inevitably produced by inhabiting an alien and alienated world. Hostility is the high-voltage energy that drives the play, and the irrational economic self is the dynamo by which the energy is created. As Ayers in "Plot, Subplot, and the Uses of Dramatic Discord in *A Mad World, My Masters* and *A Trick to Catch the Old One*" argues, "Intrigue here is not the relatively genial contest of 'wits at war with wits' celebrated in most Jacobean comedy, but a far grimmer battle fought to the death by rival predators who have, in their attitudes, strikingly anticipated Hobbes and Darwin."[21]

The mutually antagonistic relationship between Lucre and Hoard, if unusual in its longevity, is exemplary, in its intensity and extremity, of the irrational underpinnings of the rational, calculating, and fundamentally secular economic self. Each is intent on the other's ruin, and the desire to destroy the other at times takes precedence over what might seem to be more sober economic reasoning. Lucre virtually declares war on Hoard after Hoard runs off with the Courtesan:

> I will not bear it, 'tis in hate of me;
> That villain seeks my shame, nay thirsts my blood;
> He owes me mortal malice.
> I'll spend my wealth on this despiteful plot
> Ere he shall cross me and my nephew thus.
>
> (3.3.101–5)

Lucre's determination to spend his wealth to right what he perceives to be a wrong done to his nephew is not, of course, an indication that through the course of the play Lucre has gradually changed his attitude toward his nephew from rejection to loving acceptance. Rather, Lucre's determination represents merely an escalation in the war between the two rivals, in which Witgood has been a pawn for a long time (at the play's beginning we find Hoard twitting Lucre by reminding him of his dissolute nephew), a war in which the hostility generated by the dialectic between self and other is able, at times, to derail the economic imperative under whose authority the dialectic initially takes shape. Even Witgood and the Courtesan are caught up in the dialectic of economic self-fashioning. Messina in "The Moral Design of *A Trick to Catch the Old One*" argues that Witgood and the Courtesan's several penitent asides signal the sincerity of their repentance.[22] This, however, begs the question of what exactly the two are repenting, and it is more plausible to view their penitence as repentance of previous economic imprudence than spiritual repentance that leads to forgiveness and grace. In these asides we witness the two protagonists internalizing economic imperatives. The play's elaboration of the progress of the two prodigals in the modern economic world of Jacobean London leads not through spiritual renewal to integration into a godly society but through economic self-fashioning to integration into the atomistic society of which Lucre and Hoard are the representatives.

The reconfiguration of social formation and selfhood discussed above is also an epistemological reconfiguration: traditional moral paradigms are no longer adequate to make sense of Jacobean London's complex world. In this world of strategic and provisional alliances motivated by economic self-interest, the discourses of moral criticism are, like the social forms in which they are rooted, appropriated for purely strategic reasons and economic ends. Although the moral criticisms that various characters direct against prodigals and usurers are based upon the traditional conception of society as a fusion of the sacred and secular (Hooker's Christian commonwealth), these moral criticisms, articulated in the play's fundamentally secular world, have a merely residual moral force that is used for private rather than social and economic rather than spiritual perlocutionary ends. The criticism of Witgood's prodigality is a primary instance of this. Throughout the play Witgood is condemned for his prodigality. Yet, prodigality is an essential part of Jacobean London's economy. As a rapidly expanding center of conspicuous consumption and accumulation of capital, London inevitably encouraged and profited from the types of behavior characterized as prodigal, and the play's satiric lens brings this aspect of London's economy sharply into focus. With perhaps the exceptions of Witgood and the Courtesan, all of the play's major characters and most of its minor ones draw a considerable portion of their wealth from others' prodigality. Lucre, Hoard, and Dampit have turned prodigality into big business, accumulating wealth as quickly as, if not more quickly than (depending on the interest rates), wastethrift young heirs can spend it. The three creditors' dependence on prodigality is obvious. Even the host thrives on prodigality: "Come forfeitures to a usurer, fees to an officer, punks to an host, and pigs to a parson desiredly?" (1.2.17–18) the host responds to Witgood's "Comes my prosperity desiredly to thee?" (1.2.16). Consequently, the prodigal's moral culpability is shared if not reduced by London's complicity in prodigality. More importantly, those who morally condemn the prodigal are just those characters who profit by it. In each instance, the moral condemnation of prodigality is not made with the intention of reforming the prodigal (and given the stake these characters have in prodigality, this is understandable) but with other, self-interested intentions. Thus, Lucre, the man who conned Witgood out of his lands in the first place, uses moral discourse to defend his unscrupulous economic actions: "Why may not a virtuous uncle have a dissolute nephew? What though he be a brotheller, a wastethrift, a common surfeiter, and, to concluded, a beggar; must sin in him call up shame in me?" (2.1.2–5). Hoard denounces Witgood as "a riotous, undone man" (3.1.171) and Lucre as "a severe extortioner" (3.1.181) only in order to thwart Witgood's (supposed) suit to Widow Medlar and to advance his own. Perhaps most telling is Limber's easy dismissal of Witgood in the play's first scene: he tells Onesiphorus that Witgood is "the common rioter, take no note of him" (1.1.100). Limber and Onesiphorus then quite casually proceed to discuss Lucre and Hoard's quarrel over "fetching over a young heir" (1.1.113), a matter which they treat as a standard though somewhat trivial business transaction. The moral discourse condemning prodigality has been appropriated by those who profit from it and by "respectable" society generally in order to render invisible or to avoid confronting the social consequences of their own economic activities and so to allow these activities to continue. The play, then, reveals the characters' use of moral discourse to be "ideological" in the narrow sense of ideology as "ideas which help to legitimate a dominant political power"[23] or, as is the case here, a powerful economic structure.

Moral criticism of usury is similarly appropriated for entirely strategic reasons. Interestingly, aside from the barbs flung by Lucre and Hoard (usurers themselves) in 1.3, reproduction of moral discourse condemning usury is largely confined to the last of the three Dampit scenes, which according to Levin in "The Dampit Scenes in *A Trick to Catch the Old One*" constitute "a kind of Hogarthian 'Usurer's Progress'" and act as a sort of "lightning rod"[24] to deflect moral attention away from the usury of the main plot. According to Levin, the third Dampit scene explicitly provides the moral logic of Dampit's decline from the zenith of the festive tavern scene in which we first encounter him. Lamprey then Gulf pronounce the moral at the bedside of the erstwhile trampler of time, now a dying alcoholic who, in Lamprey's words, lies "like the devil in chains" (4.5.6). "Note but the misery of this usuring slave: here he lies like a noisome dunghill full of the poison of his drunken blasphemies, and they, to whom he bequeaths all, grudge him the very meat that feeds him, the very pillow that eases him. Here may a usurer behold his end" (4.5.55–59), Lamprey declaims in the fashion of a morality play presenter. Gulf puts it more succinctly and learnedly: "What, hung alive in chains? Oh spectacle! Bed-staffs of steel? *O monstrum horrendum, informe, ingens, cui lumen ademptum!* Oh Dampit, Dampit, here's a just judgement shown upon usury, extortion, and trampling villainy" (4.5.147–50). But not for a moment does the play allow us to take these pronouncements as serious moral criticisms. As Shershow in "The Pit of Wit: Subplot and Unity in Middleton's *A Trick to Catch the Old One*" points out, Lamprey's "explicitly moralizing passage, so clearly held out to the audience as a convenient interpretation of the scene, actually contradicts at least some aspects of Dampit's apparent theatrical reality."[25] Audrey and the boy in fact have not been bequeathed anything as far as we know, and even so they do not grudge him his meat and pillow. And the play provides a counterexample of the end of usury in Hoard's wedding feast, of which we are reminded by Hoard's entrance in the scene to invite Dampit to the festivities. More importantly, usury is as essential to Jacobean London's economy as prodigality, and Lamprey and Gulf are as much involved in usury as Dampit himself. The play provides little information about Lamprey other than his name, but if that is any indication (and names in Middleton's city comedies usually are) then his activities—preying on the weak—fall under the broad definition of usury. Gulf's involvement in usury is more certain: he is Dampit's business partner and, in Dampit's words, is "great Lucifer's little vicar" (4.5.157–58). Even Lancelot, who mocks Dampit with his improvised theater, is part of the economy of usury as a borrower. At first glance, then, Lamprey and Gulf's attacks seem unmotivated and even paradoxical given their own usury. Yet Levin's argument that Dampit is a moral "lightning rod" is suggestive. If the logic of the "Usurer's Progress" is Lamprey and Gulf's construction (rather than that of the play as a whole), then Dampit is a moral lightning rod *for them*. That is, the weak and dying Dampit is the perfect other on whom Lamprey and Gulf can vent the irrational and destructive hostility of economic subjectivity. Strangely, the fact that in Jacobean London the usurer is not a racial or class alien renders the term's application positional: whoever occupies the position of hostile other is also the morally condemnable usurer. Moral discourse is thus caught up in the dynamics of economic self-fashioning and becomes another mode of labeling and seeking to destroy the other. This is also evident in 1.3, as Lucre and Hoard vehemently accuse each other of being usurers before engaging in more physical abuse. The last Dampit scene repeats this pattern: after Gulf and Dampit have leveled moral discourse against each other, the scene descends into grotesque farce as Gulf draws his dagger and Dampit defends himself with his "close-stool" (4.5.168). In both these scenes moral discourse is a weapon of the excessive and absurd violence of the Jacobean economic individual.

In another, subtler way, the last Dampit scene dramatizes the failure of traditional moral discourses and spiritual narratives to make sense of Jacobean London's complex world. Unrepentantly "atheistical" (1.4.13) to the end, Dampit is strangely attractive. His heavy drinking and his blasphemous, earthy, and exuberant language give his character a Rabelaisian, carnivalesque nature. Consistent with this nature, he resists the monologic spiritual narratives that Lamprey and Gulf would foist upon him, refuses to be anything other than what he is (a virtue that none of the play's other main characters possesses): a dying, alcoholic trampler of time. Shershow argues that Dampit "refuses quite to be, as so many critics have found him, a mere emblem, a convenient focus of authorial didacticism."[26] And in fact the play seems to accept Dampit's refusal, accept his decision to live and die in an entirely material and secular world. The play's most moving moments are perhaps Dampit's final moments. The tableau created by Dampit with his head in the lap of Audrey, the maid whom he has incessantly verbally abused, is the play's only scene of unconditional love. As Shershow observes, the scene evokes the image of the Virgin and Child.[27] But though the form and the tenderness of the scene conjure up this staple of Christian iconography, the icon remains completely inapplicable to the tableau's contents, hauntingly hovering over a dying usurer and a supposed maid but irrelevant to the moment's meaning. Dampit's refusal reverberates throughout the play. His secularity lays bare the secularity of the play's fictional world; his final moment is paradigmatic of the irrelevance of spiritual narratives in capitalist Jacobean London. The play's morality play structure, used by Tudor dramatists to present a moral lesson through the contrasting fates of good and bad protagonists, thus becomes merely a way to organize the presentation of two contrasting secular progressions: Witgood's "prosocial" integration into an individualistic, competitive, and economically motivated society, and Dampit's "antisocial"[28] withdrawal through drink and his decline through the material consequences of his alcoholism. But "merely" is not the right word, for the spiritual echoes of the morality play framework, like the echoes of the image of the Virgin and Child, register by their inapplicability the epistemological transformation generated by the breakdown of the Christian commonwealth, the need for new modes of thought to map the new modes of social and economic organization emerging in Jacobean London. As Audrey's song at the beginning of Dampit's final scene indicates, the London of *A Trick* is its own—material, secular—heaven and hell: "There's pits enow to damn him [the usurer] before he comes to hell; / In Holborn some, in Fleet Street some" (4.5.2–3).

5

Play and Plague in *The Alchemist*

> If the essential theater is like the plague, it is not because it is contagious but because like the plague it is the revelation, the bringing forth, the exteriorization of a depth of latent cruelty by means of which all the perverse possibilities of the mind, whether of an individual or a people, are localized.
> —Antonin Artaud, "The Theater and the Plague"

Set during the 1610 plague in London, *The Alchemist* is Jonson's meditation on the epistemological complexities of the intersections of plague and theater. The two are causally related: the plague closed London's regular, licensed theaters and turned London into a space of extreme, unlicensed theater, not necessarily a theater of cruelty but certainly a theater in which "the perverse possibilities of the mind" find room for expansion. The play localizes this extreme theater in the alchemical laboratory operated by Face, Subtle, and Dol, not to valorize it as what theater should be but skeptically to interrogate the false epistemologies it constructs and exploits. As in *Volpone* and *Epicoene*, Jonson here dramatizes a small space of intense illusion to examine the relations of desire, knowledge, and power that structure the existence of material minds in a material world. Indeed, Jonson's Cartesian view of essential theater seems to be exactly the opposite of Artaud's. Through his theatrical interrogation of theater, Jonson insists on the distinction between the dangerous delusiveness of plague-time and plaguelike theater and his own true, essential theater which provides "wholesome remedies"[1] for spiritual diseases whose relation to biological plague was considered to be both metaphorical and causal by the medical and theological discourses of the period.[2] The theater, though, shows itself to have the dangerous ambiguities of the *pharmakon*, and the play's skepticism—perversely—turns in on its own poetics to interrogate the precarious position of the doubting self. Skepticism here is truly Montaigne's dangerous, double-edged weapon. In Derrida's formulation, "there is no such thing as a harmless remedy. The *pharmakon* can never be simply beneficial";[3] plague or remedy, illusion violates the play's cordon sanitaire to establish itself as an elusive but ineradicable constituent of reality.

In medieval and early modern Europe the plague traveled with socially transformative force. In urban centers like London, whose stability at the best of times was precarious, the plague corroded normal social bonds and structures to inaugurate a world of extremes, extreme disorder countered by the extraordinary regimes of plague orders. Although it did not experience the popular uprisings, the scapegoat hunting, or the massive millennial fever generated by the plague in other European cities, and was unwilling or unable to implement the comprehensive plague policies established in most other European urban centers, during the plague London was shaped by pressures it was ill-equipped to meet. Many (but not all) major public officials fled: mayors, aldermen, doctors, the clergy, and the rich quickly abandoned the city. Those officials who remained to implement the plague orders, the primary feature of which was the confinement of the afflicted and their households in their homes until the disease had run its course, faced the problems of insufficient funds to relieve those confined, inadequate and often corrupt minor officials with which to enforce the orders, and the general unpopularity of and resistance to the orders. At the height of the severe plagues of 1603 and 1625 the machinery of enforcement broke down entirely.[4] At these times living in London must have been hellish: in *The Wonderfull Yeare* (1603) Dekker compares it to being "bard up every night in a vast silent Charnell-house."[5]

There was no single response to the plague and its terrifying effects. The plague's origins and modes of transmission remained matters of diverse speculation leading to a variety of behavioral responses. By 1603 the government's position, articulated in the "Exhortation" attached to the special form of prayer issued in 1603, was fairly clear: the plague was divine punishment for sin, but, as God works through nature, it had entirely natural secondary causes and effects against which medical and public hygiene measures could be taken.[6] The plague orders and the special *Fourme to be used in Common prayer twyse aweke . . . duryng this time of mortalitie* (1563; reissued 1593 and 1603) were the complementary outcomes of this position, attempts to impose on the community a common interpretation of the plague that circumscribed individual action, spiritual and secular, within the hierarchical framework of church and state control. As Foucault argues in relation to plague orders in seventeenth-century France, the disorder of the plague perversely opened up utopian possibilities in the imaginations of those in authority, and the plagued city provided the theater in which those possibilities could be enacted: "The plague-stricken town, traversed throughout with hierarchy, surveillance, observation, writing; the town immobilized by the functioning of an extensive power that bears in a distinct way over all individual bodies—this is the utopia of the perfectly governed city."[7] Foucault is of course aware that what he is describing is a "political dream," a totalitarian fantasy of "omnipresent and omniscient power" that certainly could not be fully realized in early modern Europe (or, arguably, ever).[8] And indeed, in early modern England other interpretations of the plague circulated and were put into action, all the more easily as the plague progressed and the machinery of public authority weakened or broke down. At the extremes were responses of intense sensuality and intense spirituality. The grim conditions of London during the peak periods of mortality provided a macabre setting and motivation for carnivalesque behavior. According to contemporaries, drunkenness, dancing in graveyards and infected houses, promiscuous sexual behavior, and looting the abandoned houses of the rich were common.[9] The flagrant denial of spiritual and secular order in the ludic, anarchic, and carnal pursuit of life in the fleeting moment is understandable: death was imminent, public plague policy and Galenic medicine were ineffective, the plague appeared to distinguish not between just and unjust but between rich and poor, and many had little left to lose.

Intensely spiritual responses could be equally disruptive. Even those who recognized the role of natural causes in the plague could interpret Galenic medicine's failure to pinpoint the plague's material cause as an indication that the plague had primarily immaterial, divine causes and must, therefore, have primarily spiritual significance and remedies. Robert Lerner argues that one of the primary responses to the first outbreak of the plague in Europe in 1347–50 was to fit it into current eschatological paradigms as a sign of the imminence of the millennium: "Europeans tried to comprehend the fury of the plague with the aid of what might be called a prophetic 'deep structure,'" and prophecies "foresaw contemporary storms being succeeded by wondrous times of peace and Christian triumph."[10] By the seventeenth century, the plague had a history; its terror had lost the singularity and surprise that rendered it such an unambiguous sign of the imminent fulfillment of apocalyptic prophecy, and Europeans had formulated other medical and theological responses. Still, as Katharine Firth documents in *The Apocalyptic Tradition in Reformation Britain, 1530–1645*, the millenarian thought of continental Reformation theologians had widespread influence in late-sixteenth- and early-seventeenth-century England,[11] and its influence can be detected in the numerous interpretations of the plague as a sign of direct divine intervention in human affairs, providing a typological framework in which plague-stricken London could enter divine history as Jerusalem, city of God's chosen people being punished for their sins.

Alexander Nowell's *An Homily Concerning the Justice of God*, affixed to the 1563 and 1593 editions of the *Fourme to be used in Common prayer*, presents London in precisely these terms. God "hath dealt with his people of all ages" by "menaces" as well as "fair promises," through which "he laboureth to bring [his people] to due obedience of his law,"[12] and England should therefore "learn by this affliction to mourn for our sins, to hate and forsake sin, for the which God doth thus shew his anger and displeasure."[13] Donne's sermon on the 1625 plague is fully within this tradition, presenting London during the plague as the "Holy City" in which God's judgment was revealed: its unrepentant inhabitants had cried out "let us eat and drink, and take our pleasure, and make our profits, for tomorrow we shall die, and so were cut off by the hand of God, some even in their robberies, in half-empty houses, and in their lusts and wantonness in licentious houses."[14] Plague-stricken London inhabited a more or less apocalyptic space and time.

This interpretation could lead to the denial that the plague had any natural causes whatsoever and consequently to behavior implicitly or explicitly opposed to the government's efforts to regulate the plague through the plague orders. If the plague had no natural causes and was the expression of God's judgment, then to those with faith enough in their own election it was logical to believe that they were immune to the plague, as God's wrath was directed not at them but at the unregenerate. This position was held primarily by Puritans, and many Puritan ministers refused to abandon their ministries in London during the plague, they and others violating the plague orders by continuing to visit the sick and to gather in large assemblies for worship, prayer, and preaching. In 1603 the government reacted strongly against this position: Nowell's homily was replaced by the naturalistic "Exhortation," and one of the most outspoken advocates of the extreme spiritualist view, Henoch Clapman, was imprisoned until he qualified his opinion.[15]

During the plague, then, London became contested epistemological space. Through the church and the administrative apparatus of the plague orders, the state attempted to impose its epistemology. The official discourse on the plague defined the plague as a particular medical and theological object of knowledge and articulated behavioral rules—rules for preventing, detecting, and containing the consequences of the plague in oneself and in one's neighbors—governed by this definition; various church and state apparatuses were coordinated to enforce behavioral compliance to official discourse, to create an environment in which the discourse *functioned* as the truth. By stressing the functionality of official discourse I do not intend to argue that the alternative, apocalyptic, and carnivalesque discourses, were in any sense truer than the official discourse. Until the real causes of the plague were discovered in the late nineteenth century (that is, until modern scientific discourse produced a definition of the plague that was substantially more effective than the definitions of other discourses), the "truth" about the plague could remain multiple and contradictory. Rather, we can see early modern discourses on the plague as components of competing epistemologies, of what Wittgenstein in *Philosophical Investigations* calls "language-games" in which knowledge is grounded entirely in the functionality of language, in the complex of discourse and action that constitutes a "form of life."[16]

Other less-than-orthodox language games also flourished in London during the plague, particularly those that exploited the failure of Galenic medicine by selling magical or semimagical plague remedies. "*Galen* could do no more good, than Sir Giles Goosecap,"[17] Dekker recounts, and

> Only a band of Desper-vewes, some fewe Empiricall madcaps . . . turned themselves into Bees (or more properlie into Drones) and went humming up and down, with hony-brags in their mouthes, sucking the sweetnes of Silver, (and now and then of *Aurum Potabile*) out of the poison of Blaines and Carbuncles: and these jolly Mountibanks clapt up their bills upon every post (like a Fencers Challenge) threatning to canvas the Plague and to fight with him at all his own severall weapons.[18]

The wise women, alchemists, and quack doctors who set up shop in London during the plague were not merely hucksters peddling their wares, though. Charms and other magical items were accompanied by rituals—perhaps trivial, perhaps elaborate—for the proper manipulation of the charm and by hermeneutic rules to explain failure and success. As Keith Thomas explains in *Religion and the Decline of Magic*, charms and other magical objects were embedded in a popular, magical worldview in which the universe was crisscrossed by occult lines of force.[19] Various adepts professed to possess the knowledge necessary to produce the magical objects and prescribe the attendant rituals that together constituted a cure for or, more likely, a prophylactic against the plague; those who sought out these adepts, purchased their services, and performed the rituals enacted the adepts' knowledge, participated in and extended their language games. As the tone of Dekker's description of the "Empiricall madcaps" who hung out their shingles during the plague indicates, it was possible to perceive these language games as con games, rogue epistemologies established to transmute the "poison" of the plague into the "sweetness of Silver"[20] by exploiting the epistemologically malleable circumstances created by the plague, by playing on the fear and desire that propelled people to believe and the uncertainty that rendered magical beliefs and actions as plausible as anything else.

The laboratory set up by Dol, Subtle, and Face is just this kind of rogue epistemology. Enabled by the plague and exploiting the fertile and perverse imaginations of those remaining in London's heterogeneous epistemological space, the three rogues convert Lovewit's empty house into an alchemical theater and "begin to act" (Argument 8). Like the "statusphere" inhabited by *Epicoene*'s characters, the alchemical theater is a space in which desire governs the processes of knowledge; like *Volpone*'s bedchambers, it is a small and fragile world, as brittle as Subtle's glassware and as ephemeral as the smoke of his furnaces, constantly threatened by internal and external pressures with collapse into the realm of clouded memories and bad dreams or, worse, with the compulsory relocation of its principal performers onto other stages to perform others' scripts, to perform the criminal—whore, cozener, sorcerer—on the cart, pillory, or scaffold. Yet, while living in the borrowed time and space defined by play and delimited by plague, the three rogues create perhaps the most fascinating of the small spaces of intense illusion that throughout Jonson's work serve as laboratories for his analysis of the difficulties of knowing faced by material beings in a material but theatrical world.

One of the key aspects of Jonson's treatment of city space in his four major city comedies is the dramatic centrality of private or otherwise marginal space. Volpone's bedchambers dominate *Volpone*, *Epicoene* shifts between Morose's house and the various interior spaces in which the private lives of London's fashionable society are played out, and *Bartholomew Fair* is set in the temporary and exotic space of the fair. *The Alchemist*, likewise, is set in the private and marginal space of a house in Blackfriars. Yet, all of London seems to converge on the three rogues' temporary residence. The rapid-fire report Lovewit receives from his neighbors upon his return conveys the impression of a highly unusual volume of traffic having arrived at and departed from his doors during his absence, an around-the-clock train of "ladies and gentlemen" (5.1.3), "citizens' wives" (5.1.3), "Knights" (5.1.4), "coaches" (5.1.4), "oyster-women" (5.1.4), "gallants" (5.1.5), "sailors' wives" (5.1.5) and "Tobacco-men" (5.1.5). Throughout the play, the increasingly frequent knocks on the door, the progressively frantic entrances and exits, and the references to other of the rogues' customers who do not actually appear in the play convincingly establish the feeling that the three rogues have attracted a barely controllable torrent of people.

This crowd is, significantly, socially heterogeneous, a collection of characters from all walks and stations of life. Arguing that *The Alchemist* is an updated version of the estates morality play, Alan Dessen sees the play's characters as types, each a representative of a different social estate and illustrating that estate's corruptness: Jonson "has transformed the traditional conflict between a Vice or set of Vices and a group of representative 'estates' into a 'literal' conflict between a group of business-like rogues and a panoramic cross section of figures from English society."[21] Middletonian city comedy, however, employs a similarly typical cast of characters, and *The Alchemist*'s crowd of customers is constituted by much the same figures that populate Middleton's city comedies but in significantly reconfigured relationships. Middleton's merchants, gentry, prodigal young heirs, marketable young heiresses, and social climbers are locked together in a sexual, economic, and social struggle whose terrains are the public ideologies and forms of life that the dramatic action reveals to be hollow but powerful fictions. In *The Alchemist*, more so than in even the humors plays, the customers are isolated from each other, connected only by the fact that they all have found their way to the house in Blackfriars, whose space allows the frictionless expression and expansion of desires that meet resistance in the daily struggles of public life. As Jonathan Haynes observes, these desires are social, and "the victims' relations with the conycatchers are all based on unsettled ambitions within the social order and/ or dreams which would explode it."[22] This is the pursuit of social mobility and symbolic capital so characteristic of Middleton's city comedies rather than simply the greed of the estates play, but its shortcut is not Middletonian wit, a mode of engagement with social reality, but the magic of the philosopher's stone, a form of flight into fictions in which all impediments to social mobility and the acquisition of symbolic capital vanish. Dapper will "blow up gamester after gamester, / As they do crackers, in a puppet play" (1.2.78–79); Drugger will encounter no opposition to his meteoric rise through the ranks of his company; the stone will instantaneously establish the Brethren as "lords" (3.2.52) of "a faction / And party in the realm" (3.2.25–26); and in Mammon's fantasies the entire world unquestioningly acquiesces to its priapic god's every impulse. The three rogues' theater is truly alchemical in the transformative possibilities it promises.

Theater is more than a metaphor for the goings-on in this house in Blackfriars. The play's argument presents the three rogues' alliance as a joint-stock acting company: Face supplies the "House to set up in" (7), and Dol and Subtle with him "contract, / Each for a share, and all begin to act" (7–8). "Cheater" (4) and "Cozeners" (6), terms Jonson applies to Dol, Subtle, and Face, were familiar terms in Puritan invective against the theater. As R. L. Smallwood demonstrates, the play goes beyond similarity to construct, through its specification of dramatic time and space, an "absolute topicality and simultaneity" between the rogues' temporary theater and the venue of *The Alchemist*'s first performances: "An audience in a theater in the autumn of 1610 pays money to pass what the Prologue promises will be two hours (and an interval), to watch three masters of pretense, in the autumn of 1610, take two hours (and an interval) to deprive a number of representative gulls of their money";[23] both theaters—Lovewit's residence and the private theater used by the King's Men from 1608—are located in Blackfriars. The identity extends even to the response each theater receives from its neighbors. As Smallwood notes, Blackfriars residents several times complained against the commotion caused by the King's Men's performances, as do Lovewit's neighbors at the play's end.

This theatrical equation is not merely a sly metadramatic joke at the expense of Jonson's audience. Nor is it part of an elaborate and paradoxically theatrical antitheatrical gesture dismissing theater in toto as a scam. Rather, the play conflates the two theaters to attack a particular, contagious kind of theater, to explore and expose its modes of transmission and its dangerous effects. R. N. Watson remarks that the alchemist's customers' fantasies—and the rogues' repertoire—are "full of tales of the sort that packed Elizabethan theaters and bookstalls: not only coney-catching stories, but also versions of Marlowe's dramas of extravagant riches and supernatural pleasures, Sidney's and Middleton's stories of dynastic marriage, Shakespeare's and Spenser's adult fairy tales, even Deloney's chronicles of triumphant middle-class commercial diligence."[24] To this one can add the New World narratives on which Mammon patterns much of his golden age fantasies. If the rogues' theater is, in Ian Donaldson's phrase, "a sounding-board for the imagination,"[25] then it is a sounding board for an imagination deeply saturated and decisively shaped by Elizabethan and Jacobean England's most popular cultural products, including the dramatic styles and genres against which Jonson protests throughout the prefaces and dedications to his plays. Created by literary hacks and luminaries of various stripes and broadcast by the printing press and the commercial stage, the scripts of the miniplays in which each customer plays a leading part are, like the scenarios of commedia dell'arte, theatrical commonplaces all the more powerful for their commonness, the narrative structures of everyday fantasy life that provide the three rogues the means to perpetrate what William Slights calls "epistemological fraud,"[26] the deliberate confusion of fiction and reality through which the rogues fill their money chest. Indeed the rogues' theater draws its customers into a circulation between life and art much more direct than that established by the regular theaters for which it is the plague-time substitute, theaters in which the boundary between life and art is visible if not stable. The rogues' customers frequent the house in Blackfriars precisely because they do not think its magic to be illusion, *deceptio visus*. They live their parts, while Dol, Subtle, and Face for the most part merely perform theirs.

As a result, the customers participate in a series of language games that give a peculiar reality to their imaginings, possibilities of the mind at once individual and deeply cultural. Dr. Subtle's plague-time magic offers Dapper his fly, Drugger his sign, and promises Mammon and the Brethren the philosopher's stone. These items exist within discourses—popular superstition, astrology, alchemy, and apocalyptic thought—that dictate how the catalytic agent is to be produced, approached, and handled and are able to transform apparent failure into further confirmation of their truth. To receive his familiar spirit Dapper must pass through "a world of ceremonies" (1.2.144). When he finally receives it in act 5, it comes with a number of rules setting out when he must feed it, when he can look at it, and how he should wear it (5.4.35–40). In the unlikely case that Dapper does become the gambler he hopes to be, all credit is due the fly; if not, then he has failed to perform the rituals properly, has violated a rule concerning the fly's handling, or has otherwise offended his venerable aunt, the Queen of Fairies. Astrology and alchemy repeat this structure in more complex ways, and the very complexity of these discourses provides a way to recoup failure: the smallest miscalculation, mismeasurement, or misbehavior (as Mammon discovers) within these complex amalgams of mathematics, philosophy, astronomy, theology, experimentation, and religious ritual can account for disappointed expectations. The rogues' schemes depend on this. Similarly, the Brethren's apocalyptic thinking contains no exit. As Frank Kermode remarks, "apocalypse can be disconfirmed without being discredited":[27] the failure of the kingdom of the Saints to materialize on schedule can be attributed to calculation errors or a change in God's plan, and the setbacks suffered by the elect can be explained as a part of the necessary and purifying "last patience of the Saints" (5.5.105). So the Brethren come to the house in Blackfriars well fortified against failure. Although the philosopher's stone is central to their plans—the "restoring of the silenced Saints" will "ne'er be, but by the philosopher's stone" (3.1.38-39), Tribulation tells Ananias—they show not the tiniest flicker of doubt about their beliefs even when they realize that they have been had. Rather, they curse Lovewit and retreat to exile in Amsterdam, where presumably they will continue the search for the alchemical key to their millennial triumph. The exposure of the three rogues' game has no impact on Dapper, Drugger, or the Brethren, and merely propels Mammon from one "dream" (5.5.83) to the next, from visions of the *"novo orbe"* (2.1.2) to a "turnip-cart" upon which he will "preach / The end o'the world, within these two months" (5.5.81–82). These characters go beyond the humors characters of Jonson's early plays: they are incurable.

The skeptical Surly might remark that any epistemology that can explain away failure so well is for that very reason not wholly compelling, and he at least is proof that Subtle's "stone / Cannot transmute" (2.1.78–79) everyone. Still, Subtle does transmute his customers' social desires into a willingness to believe that sucks them into the self-contained language games he plays and to varying degrees allows the rogues to reshape their customers' perceptions and even memories. Drugger suffers perhaps the least transmutation: the social ambitions excited by Subtle's prediction of his rapid advancement lead Drugger to a fairly expensive but relatively harmless overvaluation of Subtle's astrological services. The Brethren are Subtle's most recalcitrant project. Upon his first appearance in the play, Ananias, the Brethren's representative, displays some skepticism about Subtle's alchemical endeavors: the Brethren, Ananias tells Subtle, "will not venture any more, / Till they may see projection" (2.5.65–66). Subtle calls their bluff, threatening that if the Brethren do not meet his demands "out goes / The fire: and down the alembics and the furnace" (2.5.78.79), and with them "All hope of rooting out the Bishops, / Or the Antichristian Hierarchy shall perish" (2.5.82–83). After Ananias leaves, Subtle predicts that "This will fetch 'em, / And make 'em haste towards their gulling more" (2.5.87–88), and he is right. When Ananias returns with Tribulation they are humbled and contrite, willing to "lend their willing hands to any project / The spirit and you direct" (3.2.13–14). The millenarian hopes of the Saints, and the centrality of the stone to those hopes, produce in the Brethren a willingness to believe that overrules their initial doubts. In this scene Subtle shrewdly switches from accepting the Brethren's apologies to talking about the stone and "the good that it shall bring your [the Brethren's] cause" (3.2.21), and the importance of the stone and the Brethren's need to believe in its possibility increase as Subtle inflates their fantasies to the point where they "may be anything" (3.2.53) through the stone. Dapper is the play's best example of the process involved in reshaping, reeducating memory and perception. He must be cajoled into remembering that he was "born with a caul o' your head" (1.2.128) by the same combination of threats and fantasy expansion that brought the Brethren into line. Face intimates that Dapper may well leave empty-handed, without any sort of gaming fly, if he continues to demonstrate his untrustworthiness by denying "a thing so known / Unto the Doctor" (1.2.131–32); at the same time, Face raises the sum of Dapper's fantasy winnings to "six thousand pound" (1.2.134). Mammon's memory, in contrast, needs no coaching: as if on cue he fabricates a memory of "my lord Whats'hum's sister" (2.4.6) in an attempt to allay Surly's suspicions that the alchemist's laboratory is moonlighting as "a bawdy house" (2.3.226). Dapper and Mammon compare interestingly on another point: Dapper must be blindfolded while meeting Dol masquerading as the Queen of Fairies; Mammon, however, needs no blindfold and with eyes wide open transforms Dol with hyperbolic ease into the paragon of European nobility. One suspects that Mammon has been so well trained by Subtle and Face over the ten months (2.1.5) of their acquaintance that he quite reflexively shapes his memories and perceptions to preempt his own potential doubts.

In other fictional worlds—a play by Calderón, perhaps, or Pirandello—the rogues' victims, especially Mammon, might have been quixotic figures, deluded but noble and even tragic. Of course, the play's gulls are no such creatures: they are the comic and base objects of savage Jonsonian satire. Yet Jonson's satire is primarily concerned not with the gulls' hypocrisy, extensive though it is, but with the logic of the rogues' epistemological fraud, the logic of the cultural scripts that the gulls inhabit, a logic that prohibits their escape from the world of material self-interest even as they ostensibly anticipate and work toward its future transformation. This is the logic of the in-between, the logic that structures the gulls' behavior in the time between hope and fulfillment. It is the logic of romance and alchemy. As Geraldo de Sousa argues, the gulls' fantasies share with romance an "open-endedness or non-closure."[28] The fulfillment of their dreams is constantly deferred but never lost sight of. The hopeful gulls cannot be discouraged by the delays and setbacks by which the rogues postpone delivering on their promises and advance their own schemes. Consequently, the rogues draw their customers into analogues of alchemy's logic of destroying matter in order to create it anew radically transformed. Thus Face tells Kastril that he must "spend" (3.4.50) himself through gambling to recreate himself as a witty gallant: gambling "will repair you, when you are spent. / How do they live by their wits, then, that have vented / Six times your fortune?" (3.4.51–53). Likewise, the Brethren must immerse themselves in sin to transcend it. "[W]e must bend unto all means, / That may give furtherance to the holy cause" (3.1.11–12), Tribulation tells Ananias, for "The children of perdition are, oft-times, / Made instruments even of the greatest works" (3.1.15–16). Significantly, it is in the logic of capitalist speculation that the dupes' peculiar logic is most concretely realized—and exploited. "[S]pend what thou canst" (1.3.83) Face urges Drugger, and the rogues' customers do just that, throwing away their money in hopes of recovering it in the future in the form of realized wishes (in Mammon and the Brethren's cases, utopian wishes.)

Capitalism appears to be the antithesis of Mammon and the Brethren's ideal societies. By linking the Brethren with the infamous Münster Anabaptists the play places them firmly in the tradition of millenarian communism.[29] Similarly, although Mammon's utopian visions only vaguely hint at economic and political organization, they contain echoes of the classical myth of the golden age, an age free from disease, labor, and sexual constraints.[30] Yet their hopes for the future fully immerse Mammon and the Brethren in capitalism's ethos. The metaphysics of ownership underpin Mammon's involvement with Subtle's alchemical endeavors. After being subjected to Mammon's erotic fantasies, Surly comments that the one with the stone must be "A pious, holy and religious man, / One free from mortal sin, a very virgin" (2.2.98–99). In reply Mammon makes a critical distinction: "That makes it, sir, he is so. But I buy it" (2.2.100). Likewise, the Brethren turn the distinction between the elect and non-elect into the distinction between those with whom they must bargain fairly and those whom they can cheat (2.5.56–60); they attempt to bargain hard with Subtle by mentioning the rumored success of his competition (2.5.70); the agent of their millennium is not Christ but money, which they are willing to acquire by counterfeiting and will employ without scruple on bribing officials (3.1.42–44) and hiring mercenaries (3.2.22). Even their visions of the future do not escape the ethos of capitalism, and in Mammon and the Brethren Jonson dramatizes the failure of the utopian imagination to be more than counterfeit gold: Mammon carries the metaphysics of ownership over into his golden age, which at root is prostitution and conspicuous consumption on a large scale; the distinction between the elect and nonelect, mine and thine, with all its implications, structures the Kingdom of the Saints.

The capitalist logic of the rogue's alchemical theater has ontological as well as epistemological effects. The logic of capital privileges appearance over being—something has value not because it *is* valuable but because it appears to be valuable—and transforms the gulls' imaginations with its reverse alchemy. Mammon's fantasies present the most extreme evidence of the perversity of capital's Midas touch: his erotic, epicurean imaginings, the "substance" of his fantasies, create a world of pure surface in which appetite and selfhood exist only as part of the play of appearances. Mammon is obsessed with food, not for its nutritive value but for its value as exotica, its differential value as appearance within a system of appearances. "The tongues of carps, dormice, and camels' heels" (2.2.75), "The beards of barbels" (2.2.82), and shrimp swimming in "a rare butter, made of dolphins' milk" (4.1.160) are a few of the morsels that grace the tables of Mammon's culinary paradise, appropriately served in "Dishes of agate, set in gold, and studded / With emeralds, sapphires, hyacinths, and rubies" (2.2.74). Mammon's various lists of exotic items resemble Subtle's alchemical jargon in their lack of obvious referentiality: like Subtle's alchemical terminology, camels' heels, barbel beards, and dolphin butter signify primarily an exotic difference and only vaguely if at all have a real referential function. Anything that appears to be exotic—from shirts of "taffeta-sarsnet" (2.2.89) to Lady Dol—provokes Mammon's appetite. Thus he proclaims to Surly that he will rescue London gallants from their "thirst of satin" (2.1.15) and "hunger / Of velvet entrails" (2.1.15–16); yet his own clothing "shall be such as might provoke the Persian; / Were he to teach the world riot anew" (2.3.91–92). The objects of desire in Mammon's world of appearance—objects desired for their appearance—simultaneously satisfy and provoke appetite, and Mammon's golden world is designed continually to agitate a restless desire whose pleasure depends on its incompleteness.

Even Mammon's sexual appetite depends upon the play of appearances. He fantasizes that when he makes love to Dol "She shall feel gold, taste gold, hear gold, sleep gold: / Nay we will *concumbere* gold" (4.1.29–30). Yet, this desire can be sustained only through perpetual permutation in costume: Dol's wardrobe must be "Richer than Nature's, still, to change thyself, / And vary oftener, for thy pride, than she" (4.1.167–68). And just as Mammon here constructs Dol's self as the sum of her appearances, so too he constructs his own self, whose greatest pleasure seems to be multiplication, fragmentation, and dispersal. At the heart of Mammon's erotic universe is his "oval room" (2.2.42) in which he will have

> my glasses,
> Cut in more subtle angles, to disperse
> And multiply the figures, as I walk
> Naked between my *succubae*. My mists
> I'll have of perfume, vapoured 'bout the room,
> To loose ourselves in; and my baths like pits
> To fall into.
>
> (2.2.45–51)

Mammon is like Volpone in the utter artificiality of his desires. Paradoxically, were he in possession of the philosopher's stone, were he able to transmute the being of substances, he would transmute the substance of being out of existence.

If, however, in the alchemical theater the material world appears to surrender itself, to shape itself frictionlessly to desire, Jonson's theater allows the material its revenge by associating gulls and rogues alike with physical pollution. The play is permeated with references to stinks, excrement, the lower bodily stratum and diseases that surround the characters like a bad smell that won't go away. The play's first scene sets the tone as Face and Subtle hurl back and forth numerous scatological insults. Dapper spends much of the play in a vile-smelling privy, and to complete his ceremonies he must kiss Dol's "departing part" (5.4.57). Drugger "has the worms" (2.6.82). Mammon intends "to fright the plague / Out o'the kingdom, in three months" (2.1.69–70), along with pox, leprosy, and venereal diseases (1.4.19–23); his choice of poets is "The same that writ so subtly of the fart, / Whom I will entertain, still, for that subject" (2.2.63–64). Ananias's curse on Lovewit is "may dogs defile thy walls" (5.5.113). The foregrounding of the muckiness of existence is particularly appropriate to the play's plague-time setting: the "sickness hot" (The Argument 1), with its odors, oozes, and orifices, cannot be cured or sublimated by the feverish imaginings it has excited. Furthermore, as Cheryl Lynn Ross argues in connection with Subtle, the play's use of images of physical pollution has a social valence: "When Subtle, the waste product that effaces boundaries, and his smokes, stinks and fumes that spread and swirl incontinently, enter the social body by invading Lovewit's house in Blackfriars . . . he eclipses the strong borders that lend a society its symbolic identity, integrity and strength. The effect is the social equivalent of putrefaction and plague."[31] This social valence is not limited to Subtle. All the play's characters are motivated by the desire to transgress social boundaries, transgressions as disruptive as Subtle's: Dapper would engross "all the treasure in the realm" (1.2.102), Mammon dreams of "wealth unfit / For any private subject" (4.1.149–50), and the Brethren's goal to be a "faction" (3.2.25) will bring with it the worst of all social plagues, civil war.

The obnoxious recalcitrance of the material epitomizes *The Alchemist*'s poetics. In contrast to Marlowe's *Dr. Faustus*, whose fictional reality is magical, from the beginning *The Alchemist* attempts to separate the realm of magic from the realm of the real, attempting to confine the former to the rogues' alchemical theater, which takes place within the ironic, "realist" drama of the play as a whole. Pointed and pungent, the critical thrust enabled by the framework of theater-within-theater moves beyond the particularities of satire to become a forceful statement about theater. By establishing from the outset the framework of theater-within-theater, Jonson links the literary distinction between kinds of theater and the distinction between illusion and reality. Both alchemy and the popular literary genres that shape the customers' fantasies imply a radically transformative perspective on the world, a perspective to which Jonson was opposed. Both "run away from Nature and [are] afraid of her" (To the Reader 6). Alchemy exalts art over nature: through Subtle's alchemy Mammon will make

> Nature ashamed of her long sleep: when art,
> Who's but a stepdame, shall do more than she,
> In her best love to mankind, ever could.
>
> (1.4.26–28)

Popular literary and dramatic works, according to Jonson, ignore nature and the natural laws of art: making nature afraid "is the only point of art that tickles the spectators" (To the Reader 6–7), and those who write the works that tickle the spectators "are deriders of all diligence" (To the Reader 10) who dismiss as waste the effort required to learn art's principles. Like Ananias, they scorn tradition and are "presumers on their own naturals" (To the Reader 9). Both fabricate substitute worlds for nature according to their own desires. By linking alchemy and popular cultural production within the rogues' epistemological con game, Jonson anatomizes their dangerous illusory potential and exposes them as frauds. The alchemical theater is presented as object of analysis and exposure within the play's own antitransformative poetics, a poetics deeply embedded in tradition and whose adherence to the classical unities of time, space, and action creates a causal universe that leaves no room for magic, for the transformative imposition of human desires upon the world.

Only after the alchemical theater has served its critical function within the play's skeptical, ironic drama does Lovewit return to disperse the rogues' magic and the gulls' fantasies. The plague has ended (or at least dropped to mortality levels with which Lovewit feels comfortable), and with it ends the extreme, unlicensed theater of which it was the enabling precondition. Strikingly little evidence remains of the theater's multiple worlds, their occupants, and the sense of excitement and even danger they generated, and when Lovewit invites the constables in to search for the vanished Doctor and Captain all he finds are

> The empty walls, worse than I left 'em, smoked,
> A few cracked pots, and glasses, and a furnace,
> The ceiling filled with poesies of the candle:
> And Madam, with a dildo, writ o' the walls.
>
> (5.5.39–42)

The gulls, like Descartes's madmen, lived their dreams in fragile bodies of glass broken by Lovewit's return. Private property and law, both enforced by officers of the crown, replace social fantasy and self-contained hermeneutics as the bases of knowledge. Lovewit refuses to allow Mammon to retrieve his pots and pans from his cellar because, he tells Mammon, "I can take no knowledge, / That they are yours, but by public means" (5.5.66–67). If, however, Mammon

> can bring certificate, that you were gulled of 'em,
> Or any formal writ, out of a court,
> That you did cozen yourself: I will not hold them.
>
> (5.5.68–70)

Lovewit's return seems to set a period to the time of play, illusion, and transformative possibilities and to reestablish everyday society and everyday, public organs of knowledge.

Yet illusion is not so easily contained. Münster hovers in the background of the play as proof that apocalyptic fantasies have been lived on stages much larger than Lovewit's house, with devastating consequences.

Dol and Subtle slip over the back wall to establish other rogue epistemologies elsewhere, while Face takes on the "new Face" (5.3.21) of Jeremy the butler. The three rogues have constituted the internal frame or boundary between the alchemical theater and the ironic drama of the play as a whole: the gulls have accepted them as what they appeared to be, while the audience has been entertained by their flawless performances. With the rogues' dispersal this comforting boundary between illusion and reality, a boundary that was porous even when in place, vanishes. Subtle at times seems to have forgotten that he is a charlatan: his rhetoric in the opening scene, in which he threatens to "thunder you [Face] in pieces" (1.1.60) and to teach Face "How to beware to tempt a fury again / That carries tempest in his hand and voice" (1.1.61–62), betrays the extent to which the self Subtle has fashioned through the performances of alchemy—its modes of utterance, its paraphernalia, its rituals and practices—has become his self, despite the consciousness he displays throughout the rest of the play of the con game he, Dol and Face are playing. Dol and Face might not get lost in the roles they play, but they have no "real" selves to which to return after performing. They are always performing, both before and after the collapse of the alchemical theater, and, as Jonathan Haynes remarks, "all traces of origins are effaced by their constant and impeccable role-playing. . . . [I]t is hard to imagine them falling back on their 'real' social identities."[32] Like Andrew Lethe and the Country Wench in Middleton's *Michaelmas Term*, the rogues live in and by appearances, through self-fashionings that supplant "natural" origins.

Lovewit too is not immune from the theatricality of existence. Judd Arnold has argued that Lovewit's return is "the personal triumph of the cavalierly aloof, intellectual aristocrat over the hopeless and helpless mass of fools,"[33] and certainly Lovewit possesses enough wit and ironic detachment quickly to guess the nature of what has gone on in his house during his absence to be suspicious of Face's ghost stories, and to take advantage of Mammon's foolishness. It is therefore a measure of illusion's power and pervasiveness that, as Wayne Rebhorn argues, "although Lovewit thinks he triumphs as a sharper, his values and self-perception, action and language, all are those of the sharpers' victims. By the end of act 5 in *The Alchemist*, Lovewit has made himself into nothing less than Face's final dupe."[34] Lovewit has his own desires and susceptibilities, which Face manipulates to pull off his last and greatest scam. He persuades Lovewit to play the role of the Spanish Don and so suckers him into a January-May match with a young woman seemingly open to any suggestion and in whom Face has previously expressed sexual interest. Lovewit, however, considers himself transformed and, like Face's previous gulls, "will be ruled by thee in anything, Jeremy" (5.5.143). Dame Pliant is Lovewit's philosopher's stone; like the elixir the rogues promise Mammon, she promises happiness, wealth and even to "stretch age's truth sometimes, and crack it too" (5.5.156). The similarities between the purported powers of Mammon's elixir and Dame Pliant lead one to suspect that those who base their hopes on either of these catalytic agents will come to similar ends. Lovewit returns to end one fantasy-expanding theater and begin living himself in another—in the same house in Blackfriars.

If by the play's end the distinction between illusion and reality breaks down, so too does the distinction between true and false theater, Jonson's skeptical, realist drama and the romantic, transformative dramas Jonson satirizes through the rogues' alchemical theater. To understand this breakdown, it is worthwhile glancing back at an earlier moment in the play, for in Surly's resistance to epistemological entrapment in act 2 the play lays bare and probes the difficulties of its own skeptical poetics, in relation to alchemy and apocalypse and ultimately to theatricality generally. It is a critical commonplace that the play denies coherent representation to alchemical and apocalyptic thought, and for the most part this is true. Dol's reproduction of scraps of Hugh Broughton's apocalyptic works in act 4, scene 5, is not only, as Ian Donaldson puts it, "a parody of the Pentecostal miracle,"[35] as unintelligible as it is erudite, but also part of the rogues' plot to delay completion of the stone and so to continue to fleece Mammon. Likewise, the alchemical catechism that Subtle and Face perform for Ananias in act 2, scene 5, involving the elaborate and esoteric symbolic expression of a complicated alchemical procedure, would have been "Heathen Greek" (2.5.16) to most of Jonson's audience as well as to Ananias, and its sole purpose is to make Ananias "admire" (2.4.32) Subtle as the possessor of secret knowledge rivaling the Brethren's own. "Subtle's jargon exists solely to confound, mystify, and impress his listeners," Ross argues, and "rather than presenting such a language as a tool with which to construct and describe the world from another viewpoint, providing an alternative to the dominant perspective, the play shows private languages in service of greed, immorality, and self-aggrandizement. Such tongues have no meaning, only force."[36] Indeed, the play refuses directly to confront the truth-claims of millenarianism and alchemy, choosing rather, as we have seen, to focus attention on the ways in which the rogues use the epistemological structures of these discourses to manipulate the social desires and pick the pockets of their customers. Surly, a con artist himself, is an expert at this sort of skeptical bracketing of the truth. He mocks Mammon's golden dreams. He remains "incredulous" (2.1.77) even after Mammon presents the orthodox alchemical decryption of works ranging from Moses to Boccaccio as "abstract riddles of our stone" (2.1.104). (Mammon's allegoresis is another aspect of the self-confirming nature of his alchemical beliefs: having accepted the truth of alchemy, Mammon sees ciphers of it everywhere.) He refuses to see the language of alchemy as anything other than deliberate and deceitful obfuscation (2.3.182–98). Surly's asides during the exchanges between Mammon, Subtle and Face—"Oh, I looked for this. / The hay is a-pitching" (2.3.69–70) and "Oh, this ferret / Is rank as any polecat" (2.3.80–81)—show that he is struck far more by the uses than the promises of alchemy, not surprisingly so given that he of all the play's characters should recognize a con game when he sees one.

Nonetheless, at one point Surly finds himself on the defensive: he allows himself to be drawn into a debate with Subtle about the possibility of alchemy—and he loses. Throughout act 2, scene 3, Surly suffers epistemological temptation. Mammon tells Subtle that Surly is "An heretic, that I did bring along, / In hope, sir, to convert him" (2.3.3–4), and Subtle accepts the challenge. Crucially, Surly does not share the audience's privileged position: he has not seen the opening quarrel between Face, Subtle, and Dol, and he has not heard Subtle's cynical rhapsody on Mammon. His doubts have less support than the audience's, and the possibility that he might be persuaded is correspondingly greater. Yet, Surly remains unconverted, and this scene explores the difficulties and disturbing epistemological implications of Surly's resistance by allowing alchemy a coherence it is denied elsewhere in the play. The scene wastes no time unsettling not only Surly but also the audience. Subtle's first effort to convince Surly is quite simply to offer the completed philosopher's stone as proof: "All that I can convince him in, is this / The work is done: bright Sol is in his robe" (2.3.28–29). Any audience members who do not know what comes next must at this point wonder if they have completely misunderstood the play so far, and it comes almost as a relief that Subtle in fact does not produce the finished product. Still, after the delays in producing ocular proof have provoked further skeptical remarks by Surly, Subtle confronts him: "what have you observed, sir, in our art, / Seems so impossible?" (2.3.125–26). In the ensuing debate Surly finds himself intellectually overmatched. Not only does he lose the debate, but he loses it on his own ground. He chooses the debate's analogy: "that you should hatch gold in a furnace, sir, / As they do eggs, in Egypt!" (2.3.127–28). He chooses the Aristotelian terms in which the debate proceeds, attempting to distinguish between eggs and metals on the ground that "The egg's ordained by nature to that end: / And is a chicken in *potentia*" (2.3.133–34). Both of Surly's choices seem calculated by Jonson to lead to Surly's defeat. Although Mammon elsewhere labels Subtle a "Paracelsian" (2.3.230), Subtle's impeccably Aristotelian reply converts Surly's analogy into a strong argument for alchemy: "The same we say of lead, and other metals, / Which would be gold, if they had time" (2.3.135–36). As David Lindberg discusses in *The Beginnings of Western Science*, the theory of alchemy as it developed through the Middle Ages was firmly grounded in the basic principles of Aristotelian natural philosophy, which held that all matter is transformative and that transformations proceeded naturally from an entity's potential being to its perfection in the end dictated by the entity's "final cause" or teleological end. Thus all metals naturally strive for the perfection of gold, just as an embryo grows into a fully developed organism, and alchemy merely attempts to provide an incubator for metals to hasten the process.[37] Subtle's speech from line 142 to line 176 is a condensed but fairly coherent statement and elaboration of the theory of alchemy within the framework of Aristotelian natural philosophy.[38] Aristotle's philosophical system still provided educated Europeans with a common reference point, a default, "common sense" world view, and Subtle here has seductively built his argument for alchemy on the theoretical underpinnings of his opponent's "common sense" thinking.

Tellingly, Surly has no adequate philosophical reply. The intellectual sophistication required, say, to distinguish between the final causes of animate and inanimate matter is beyond him. All he can do is reiterate his belief:

> Rather, then I'll be brayed, sir, I'll believe,
> That Alchemy is a pretty kind of game,
> Somewhat like tricks o' the cards, to cheat a man,
> With charming.
>
> (2.3.179–82)

In an earlier scene Surly has indicated the lengths to which he is prepared to go to prevent himself from being charmed. Mammon tells Surly that "when you see the effects of the great medicine" (2.1.37), then "You will believe me" (2.1.42). Surly replies:

> Yes, when I see't, I will.
> But if my eyes do cozen me so (and I
> Giving 'em no occasion) sure, I'll have
> A whore, shall piss 'em out, next day.
>
> (2.1.42–45)

Like the Brethren, Surly has beforehand determined the structure and meaning of the events he later witnesses; as much as Mammon's, his desire governs his perception and reason. He shuts his eyes and ears to the Siren-like suasion of alchemy, but only because "I have a humour, / I would not willingly be gulled" (2.1.77–78). Surly's later exploits as the Spanish Don prove him right, but to get to that point he must cling to his disbelief as dogmatically as the alchemist's customers cling to their beliefs. Jonson makes it clear, then, that while Surly's skepticism has its gains it comes at a price: an epistemological groundlessness resulting from the selective denial of perceptual and rational bases of knowledge.

The epistemological groundlessness of Surly's perspective is also the play's groundlessness. The audience has been watching Jonson's antitransformative, ironic drama, but no curtain falls at the play's end to cover over the theatricality, the constructedness of the perspective Jonson has offered on alchemy, its practitioners, and its customers. On the contrary, Jeremy, or Face, or the actor playing both steps forward to address the audience with an epilogue that underscores the play's status as illusion. By engaging in metadramatic commentary upon his role, the actor foregrounds the fact that his role, and with it the entire debunking of alchemy to which his role is so pivotal, was scripted beforehand in accordance with a classical poetics: "My part a little fell in this last scene, / Yet 'twas decorum" (5.5.158–59). *The Alchemist*'s ironic drama is the product of Jonson's skeptical imagination, his humor, an a priori epistemological grid that cannot be supported, only sold. The rest of the epilogue makes explicit the parallels between Jonson's theater and the rogues' theater:

> And though I am clean
> Got off, from Subtle, Surly, Mammon, Dol,
> Hot Ananias, Dapper, Drugger, all
> With whom I traded; yet I put myself
> On you, that are my country: and this pelf,
> Which I have got, if you do quit me, rests
> To feast you often, and invite new guests.
>
> (5.5.159–65)

The actor steps from one theater to another, but it is business as usual: in the same small, dark, smoky room he coins appearance into gold. If the audience claps, it has like the gulls willingly traded good money for fiction; if it doesn't, it is surly but it has paid its money nonetheless. Those who reply that Jonson's drama is worth applause for its corrective, medicinal properties assume the transformational logic that the play satirizes, accepting Jonson's claim to be the true alchemist and his realist poetics the true philosopher's stone without considering that all alchemists make such claims. The theatricality of reality is a Renaissance commonplace, but Jonson here is not repeating it in its usual form in which "Heaven the Judicious sharpe spectator is."[39] Jonson offers no eternal, stable vantage point from which illusory existence might be distinguished from a higher reality, only equally illusory and groundless epistemologies competing in the theatrical marketplace. The price of Jonson's skepticism is the price of admission to the Blackfriars playhouse.

6

Paradox, Wonder, and the Reproduction of Patriarchy in *A Chaste Maid in Cheapside*

Although written approximately six years after *Michaelmas Term* and *Volpone*, *A Chaste Maid in Cheapside* has much in common with these earlier city comedies. In *A Chaste Maid* Middleton continues to explore the micropolitics of conflicting desires and the performative production of truth in a resolutely secular world. But the emphasis has shifted. In *A Chaste Maid* Middleton is less concerned with self-fashioning than with the fashioning of social order. The play's skeptical dramaturgy deconstructs idealist, monolithic notions of social order to expose the intensely paradoxical nature of social order's imposition and reproduction. This chapter, and the following chapter on *Bartholomew Fair*, shift their focus to examine Middleton and Jonson's skeptical interrogations of the impossible epistemological fantasies of power.

The fundamental comic principles that organize the play and drive its conflicts and final resolutions are paradoxes. Several other critics—most extensively, Covatta and Rowe—have remarked on the play's paradoxical aesthetics before. Against Covatta and Rowe's considerations of the play's paradoxes as complications of universal comic paradigms, however, I want to explore the implications of their crucial specificity, the fact that these paradoxes are, in one way or another, patriarchal paradoxes, paradoxes that structure the reproduction of a specifically patriarchal social order.[1] In *The Political Unconscious*, Frederic Jameson argues that, as a socially symbolic act, each text must be read as "the imaginary resolution to a real contradiction."[2] *A Chaste Maid* opens up other possibilities, even if only partially. Rather than resolving contradictions, the play dramatizes patriarchal social order's tenuous, imaginary reproduction through inescapable paradox.

In the first two acts the play establishes as one of its main comic principles the paradox that patriarchal order is subverted by the sexualities of just those males most concerned to maintain it. This paradox structures the dramatic careers of the two characters singled out by Levin as the linchpins of the play's tightly interconnected multiple plots, Touchwood Senior and Sir Walter Whorehound. Touchwood Senior and Mistress Touchwood first take the stage at the beginning of act 2. The two are temporarily breaking up their household because "our desires / Are both too fruitful for our barren fortunes."³ The dissolution of the household, patriarchy's central institution, frees Touchwood Senior for comic intrigue with the Kixes: after the two express their affection for each other and acknowledge that their sexual appetites must be ruled by necessity, Mistress Touchwood departs to her uncle, and Touchwood Senior is left to find, by means however dubious, the resources necessary to reestablish his household. A number of critics have argued that the scene in which the Touchwoods first appear establishes Touchwood Senior as a kindhearted, basically decent figure who represents the forces of fertility and love in a harsh world. But the scene is deeply ironic, eroding favorable first impressions to expose the paradox that Touchwood Senior embodies. After Mistress Touchwood departs, Touchwood Senior praises her:

> I hold that wife a most unmatched treasure
> That can unto her fortunes fix her pleasure,
> And not unto her blood: this is like wedlock;
> The feast of marriage is not lust but love,
> And care of the estate.
>
> (2.1.47–51)

Mistress Touchwood's ability to govern her sexual appetite "in care of the estate" has been the theme of Touchwood Senior's praise from the scene's beginning; her reply to Touchwood Senior's renunciation of sexual relations with her—"Your will be mine, sir" (2.1.42)—clearly indicates that he as head of his household determines what is necessary for the care of the Touchwood estate and that his wife's sexuality is considered to be part of that estate. Yet, as the scene unfolds, Touchwood Senior's care of his estate, his concern for the maintenance of patriarchal order, is ironically contrasted with the destructive consequences of his own ungovernable sexual appetite. Arthur Marotti calls Touchwood Senior a "benevolent fertility god."⁴ Certainly, the staggering potency of Touchwood Senior's "fatal finger" (2.1.59) borders on the magical, but the overall effect of his unbridled sex drive is far from benevolent. His country adventures have been economically disastrous to the rural population, disabling a significant part of the labor force during harvest. In his encounter with the Country Wench, sex is associated with disease, specifically syphilis, and deformity.

More indicative of the paradoxical nature of Touchwood Senior's position, however, are his appetite's effects on the institution about which he claims to care so much, the household. His appetite destroys others' households. The Country Wench complains to him that "Nothing grieves me but Ellen, my poor cousin in Derbyshire, thou hast crack'd her marriage quite; she'll have a bout with thee" (2.1.74–76). Touchwood Senior's response to the threat of legal action reveals that this situation is not new to him:

> I'll tender her a husband;
> I keep of purpose two or three gulls in pickle
> To eat such mutton with, and she shall choose one.
> (2.1.80–82)

Touchwood Senior plays a game of brinkmanship, pitting his fatal finger against his wit and his resources, fantastically undermining patriarchal sexual and social order then frantically undertaking to patch it up again. The intensity of the game takes its toll. The food imagery—pickled gulls eating mutton—suggests the purely appetitive nature of these marriages of expediency, feasts not of love but lust, far from the restrained, well-governed relationship praised by Touchwood Senior at the scene's beginning. It takes its toll on the Touchwood household itself, and the scene seems to indicate that Touchwood Senior's appetite has destroyed his own household also. Later in the scene Touchwood Senior employs a telling mercantile metaphor: "would I were rid of all the ware i'the shop so" (2.1.100), he comments as he pays the Country Wench to dispose of their child herself. Touchwood Senior's store is overstocked and he must pay people to take his wares off his hands; his inexhaustible sexual appetite has exhausted his own financial resources and destroyed his ability to care for his estate.

As I will argue later, the paradox of which Touchwood Senior is one instance generates further paradoxes on the discursive level, but in itself Touchwood Senior's position at the play's beginning can be roughly defined in terms of an opposition between words and actions. The paradoxical nature of Sir Walter Whorehound's position is more complex. Stephen Wigler insightfully observes that Whorehound "is the spirit of care."[5] As a worried prodigal figure Whorehound is indeed an oxymoron, a paradox that plays itself out in a number of areas whose ordering is of strong patriarchal concern. Like Touchwood Senior's, Whorehound's concerns are with the management of his sociosexual estate, but that estate is complicated by his long-standing arrangement with the Allwits. One of Whorehound's main concerns is the purity of bloodlines, which his own profligate sexuality threatens to confuse. In act 1, scene 2, at the sight of his children by Mistress Allwit, Whorehound comments:

> How shall I dispose of these two brats now
> When I am married? For they must not mingle
> Amongst my children that I get in wedlock,
> 'Twill make foul work that, and raise many storms.
>
> (1.2.126–29)

As Touchwood Senior is not, Whorehound is concerned about the fate of his offspring, but this concern is not evidence of a tender heart. Rather, Whorehound's anxiety is generated by the threat his illegitimate children might pose to the transmission of power, privilege, and wealth through the established patriarchal institution of the family. He is concerned about not only the "foul work" that might result from the incestuous union of his children from his various sexual relationships but also the "many storms"—legal, social, economic—that might be raised by their mingling in other ways, by the confusions of status that would result if Whorehound does not maintain rigid social and economic distinctions between his legitimate and illegitimate offspring. With the need to create firm distinctions in mind, Whorehound decides to bind Wat and Nick as apprentices, locating them as citizens not gentry, outside the main lines of patriarchal inheritance.

Whorehound's management of his estate has an immediate urgency in the play. Whorehound is locked with Sir Oliver Kix in a competition whose rules are those governing proper patriarchal sociosexual management: whichever of the two men first produces a legitimate heir will inherit "goodly lands and livings" (2.1.156). Whorehound has borrowed heavily on his expected success and is in the end destroyed by Kix's unexpected, borrowed potency. Fundamentally, however, Whorehound is destroyed by his own miscalculation, specifically by underestimating the consequences of his transgressive relationship with the Allwits. While fully aware of the trouble his illegitimate children by Mistress Allwit might cause, he seems not to understand that his arrangement with the Allwits has established a socioeconomic institution with interests not altogether coincident with his own desire to consolidate his position in patriarchal society. Although he has completely financed the Allwit household for ten years, Whorehound's goal is marriage; he seems to view his arrangement with the Allwits as a temporary indulgence whose dissolution upon his marriage will be inevitable and relatively unproblematic. Allwit, however, views the arrangement rather differently. His paradoxical encomium on the life of a wittol is as outrageously utopian as Volpone's praise of his own golden world. Allwit considers his arrangement with Whorehound to be "[t]he happiest state that ever man was born to" (1.2.21) and has done what he can to preserve his happy estate, primarily by ruining Whorehound's various marriage plans (1.2.110–12). Whorehound funds the Allwits in order to retain complete control over this part of his sociosexual estate, to dictate its terms and direct its consequences. He assumes the father's responsibility for choosing his sons' careers; he expects to be treated as the head of the Allwit household and uses the threat of marriage to enforce this expectation; he considers Mistress Allwit's sexuality to be his exclusive property. Yet, paradoxically, the steps he has taken to control his estate have led him to establish an institution that opposes that estate's patriarchal consolidation and that rejects him when he becomes unprofitable.

The dramatic paradox that drives Touchwood Senior and Whorehound in their respective comic plots also, but less prominently, structures the positions of several other major male characters: Touchwood Junior, whose desire to marry Moll causes him to subvert her father's authority to determine her husband; Sir Oliver Kix, whose impotence only raises his anxiety about producing, by any means, an heir; and Allwit, whose sexual passivity defeats his half-hearted attempt in act one to assert his authority as master over his servants. The dramatic paradox is, though, significant for more than just considerations of plot. It creates a number of discursive responses that are themselves paradoxical. In *The Body Embarrassed: Drama and the Disciplines of Shame in Early Modern England*, Gail Kern Paster observes that the play's male characters, and the play as a whole, reproduce a common Renaissance patriarchal discursive strategy to contain and to capitalize on the paradoxical, not to mention hypocritical, position of men like Touchwood Senior. Paster's detailed reading of the play argues that the imagery by which the sexual and excretory openness of the humoral body is represented is gender-differentiated: "water, when it is male water, has changed, now representing power, not leaking or loss of control. Male water, unlike female leaking, has economic value and under the right circumstances can even be shared in order to preserve or enlarge dynastic claims."[6] The greedy, drunk, lecherous, and incontinent women in the christening scene are only the most extreme examples of the figuration of the open, female body as out of control, while Touchwood Senior is the primary example of the figuration of the open, male body as fertile and potent, his "water" (2.1.189) a "certain remedy" (2.1.184) for the Kixes' sexual and social ills. Paster points out that the distinction between male potency and female incontinence not only obscures male sexual hypocrisy but also authorizes patriarchal control of women's sexuality: "Like the daughters of Danaus in Whitney's emblem, the leaky women of Middleton's Cheapside cannot by themselves keep their barrels full or their holes plugged. Attempting such impossible tasks becomes the self-imposed responsibility of the patriarchal order."[7] As Maudline Yellowhammer tells her daughter Moll in the play's first scene, "'tis a husband sowders up all cracks" (1.1.27). The incontinent bodies of women must be governed, must have their cracks filled by potent men.

The play, however, represents this discursive strategy as highly unstable, dramatizing ways in which the discursive strategy designed to contain anxiety about the paradoxical nature of male sociosexual management paradoxically increases that anxiety. The discursive strategy that justifies patriarchal control by representing women as incontinent produces representations of women as voracious, grotesque bodies who threaten to overwhelm patriarchal control. This paradox lies behind Touchwood Senior's praise of his wife. Mistress Touchwood is a "perfect treasure" (2.1.22) because she, unlike most women, subjects her sexuality to her husband's will. Touchwood Senior praises her by imagining the destructive consequences of having married what he considers to be the typical gentlewoman:

> had I married
> A sensual fool now, as 'tis hard to 'scape it
> 'Mongst gentlewomen of our time, she would ha' hang'd
> About my neck, and never left her hold
> Till she had kiss'd me into wanton businesses
> Which at the waking of my better judgement
> I should have curs'd most bitterly.
>
> (2.1.25–31)

Mistress Touchwood shines against the background of the majority of women, whose sexuality Touchwood Senior represents as aggressively seductive, an appetite that threatens to destroy the "better judgement" of the potent patriarchal male. Similarly, Touchwood Senior, upon first encountering the quarreling Kixes, imagines the cause of the dispute to be Lady Kix's desire for meat prohibited during Lent, a desire quickly transformed by Touchwood Senior's imagination into a cannibalistic appetite threatening literally to devour the head of the Kix household: Lady Kix "weeps for some calf's head now; / Methinks her husband's head might serve, with bacon" (2.1.123–24).

In the same fashion this discursive paradox generates Whorehound's jealousy for Mistress Allwit. Mistress Allwit is pregnant, has been "sowdered up" by Whorehound, yet according to Allwit this has only increased her appetite—for goods, food, and (Whorehound suspects) sex—to gargantuan proportions. She lies in "with all the gaudy shops / In Gresham's Burse around her" (1.2.33–34), consumes her "sugar by whole loaves, her wines by rundlets" (1.2.37), and "longs for nothing but pickled cucumbers and his [Whorehound's] coming" (1.2.6). The phallic connotations of edible pickled cucumbers and their association with Whorehound's "coming" suggest that Mistress Allwit's sexual appetite is perceived to be a direct threat to patriarchal order, devouring the symbol of its power and instrument of its potency. Whorehound's jealousy shows that he too fears that his "pickled cucumber" is not enough to fill Mistress Allwit. Significantly, Whorehound's response is to set spies on Mistress Allwit. The discursive strategy intended to contain the difficulties of patriarchal sociosexual management generates an epistemological crisis for Whorehound: to protect his exclusive claim to Mistress Allwit's sexuality, he needs to know the extent of her appetite, yet his suspicions, generated by representations of female appetite as unruly and insatiable, can never be satisfied. In *Anxious Masculinity in Early Modern England*, Mark Breitenberg elaborates on this paradox: "men scurry about trying to contain a threat to their authority that they have themselves constructed in the first place. They possess an anxious 'need to know' women that is fed by their construction of women as essentially incapable of self-government."[8] Yet, as Breitenberg argues throughout his book, this paradox and others like it do not derail patriarchal order but add (anxious) impetus to further attempts to reproduce it.

Allwit seems to be a major exception to this paradoxical dialectic of anxiety and control. His passivity, sexual and otherwise, seems to remove him from any sort of participation in the reproduction of patriarchal order. Yet, quite the opposite is the case. This can best be seen through a close reading of Allwit's justification of his mode of life, his paradoxical encomium on the life of a wittol. As justification, the encomium is Allwit's response to the contradictions of his dramatic position. As head and not head of his household, Allwit is caught in what would seem to be an uncomfortable contradiction, but his encomium transforms his position into the best of patriarchal worlds. At first glance, Allwit's happy estate appears to be far from patriarchal. Ingrid Hotz-Davies notes that Allwit seems to be "ignoring exactly those requirements demanded of men in a patriarchal system of values: he refuses to fully assume his position as head of the family or indeed as 'head' of his wife; he openly gives over his rights to a monogamous marriage; he will not accept his role as the family's provider, and he will not sleep with his wife."[9] Yet although it reaches unconventional conclusions, the encomium's argument shares fundamental assumptions about women with the compensatory discursive strategies already discussed and depends on patriarchal order even while seeming to reject it. The paradox of Allwit's paradoxical defense of his lifestyle is not simply that it defends the conventionally indefensible but that it does so using the patriarchal assumptions that have rendered that lifestyle conventionally indefensible.[10] As Ronald Huebert in "Middleton's Nameless Art" argues, Allwit is no feminist: he "secretly hates women,"[11] and his defense of the life of a wittol, someone who has resigned his patriarchal prerogatives, proceeds from the same assumptions about women used to defend patriarchal order as necessary. Allwit's paradoxical encomium reproduces the standard patriarchal representations of women as voraciously appetitive—for goods, for food, for sex—not to urge the necessity of patriarchal control over women but to refigure that control as slavery. For Allwit, marriage and other similar arrangements place the male/ husband as a slave to an endlessly consuming female appetite and produces a misogynistic uxoriousness that destroys both body and soul:

> some merchants would in soul kiss hell
> To buy a paradise for their wives, and dye
> Their conscience in the bloods of prodigal heirs
> To deck their night-piece, yet all this being done,
> Eaten with jealousy to the inmost bone-
> As what affliction nature more constrains
> Than feed the wife plump for another's veins?
>
> (1.2.41–47)

Allwit considers Whorehound to be thus enslaved. Indeed, in the process of buying a paradise for Mistress Allwit and Allwit himself, Whorehound embraces a number of hells: financial ruin, jealousy, and possibly eternal damnation. Thanks to his arrangement with Whorehound, however, Allwit is a free man: "I live at ease, / He has both the cost and the torment" (1.2.54–59). Yet, Allwit's freedom is not freedom from patriarchy. His paradoxical encomium reproduces the assumptions that enable patriarchal order while seeming to subvert it. His position is logically and materially parasitic upon the patriarchal order it claims to abandon. Wittolry, even complaisant wittolry, is a meaningless category outside the system of patriarchal sociosexual management, and someone—in this case, Whorehound—must occupy the position that Allwit refuses in order for Allwit's position to be materially tenable. Indeed, Allwit is as kept as Mistress Allwit, and his freedom is merely another form of slavery.

If representations of women's bodies as grotesque both create patriarchal anxiety and add impetus to efforts to impose patriarchal control, they are also in the play a cause of male homosocial bonding. The female grotesque body becomes the foundation of alliances between males to govern that body. As Paster argues, the tasks of governing the female body "offer patriarchy the distinct advantage of promoting unusually stable male alliances—between Master Allwit and Sir Walter; between Touchwood Senior and the Kixes; between the Touchwood brothers themselves—to get the job done."[12] Paster, however, overstates the stability of these cooperative male relationships. Patriarchy is not a monolith: if, as Heidi Hartmann argues, patriarchy can be defined as "relations between men . . . that enable them to dominate women,"[13] relations between men constructed through women, then these relations are competitive as well as cooperative. The play derives much of its comic energy from the tension between these two aspects of male relationships. In "The Four Plots of *A Chaste Maid in Cheapside*," Levin observes that the relationships that define the play's plots are triangular, each involving two men and a woman.[14] These triangular relationships are relatively straightforward examples of the triangular nature of male homosocial relationships in patriarchal society explored by Eve Kosofsky Sedgwick in *Between Men: English Literature and Male Homosocial Desire*: the woman mediates relationships between men that are economic as well as social, potentially deadly as well as occasionally unifying.[15] In fact, nearly all of the play's male homosocial bonds are unstable compounds of cooperation and conflict, the centripetal impulse to govern women's sexualities opposed by the centrifugal pull of competition for women as more or less valuable commodities. The play's comic dynamics emphasize that patriarchal order is not a matter of course but a matter of game. Patriarchy defines the rules, and patriarchal order is reproduced as a field of contestation as well as collaboration.

The Whorehound-Allwit relationship presents the best example of the tension in male bonds. Fear of and the desire to control the female body, particularly Mistress Allwit's, draws the two men together. As Paster comments, the two men are "partners in arms, banding together to conserve for themselves and the variously fathered offspring whom they feel obliged to support an economic and sexual substance that the appetite of woman and her conspicuous lack of self-control threaten to destroy."[16] Yet this unifying bond mediated by Mistress Allwit is fragile, threatened by and ultimately disintegrating under economic pressure. For ten years Allwit has profitably traded his wife's sexuality—Whorehound has quite lavishly footed the Allwit household's bills—and when at the play's end he realizes that trade with Whorehound will no longer be profitable he abruptly ends their relationship. Significantly, these economic considerations take precedence over the gynophobia that was a source of unity between the two men. Content for most of the play to let Whorehound service and police his wife's appetite, at the play's end Allwit, in a sudden and hilarious reversal, takes back the position of household head and recasts his wife's sexuality as a source of contention between himself and Whorehound:

> I must tell you, sir,
> You have been somewhat bolder in my house
> Than I could well like of; I suff'red you
> Till it stuck here at my heart; I tell you truly
> I thought you had been familiar with my wife once.
> (5.1.151–55)

As we have seen, the Whorehound-Allwit bond is under similar economic pressure from Whorehound's various attempts to construct more lucrative male-male relationships through marriage. Whorehound's marriage plans, of course, involve him in the play's most obviously competitive male homosocial relationship, his rivalry with Touchwood Junior for Moll and her dowry. The contestatory and strategic nature of alliances between men is emphasized at key points in the play by the troping of the field of patriarchal relations as game. After preventing Moll and Touchwood Junior's first marriage attempt, Whorehound calls the Touchwood brothers (but not Moll) "both losers" (3.1.62). More prominently, at the end of act 5, scene 1, a repentant but rejected Whorehound concedes defeat to the Allwits in the same vocabulary in which he figured his temporary victory over the two Touchwoods: "Gamesters, farewell, I have nothing left to play" (5.1.158). Allwit continues the metaphor in his self-congratulations: "There's no gamester like a politic sinner" (5.1.179), he crows.

Even the relationship between Touchwood Senior and Sir Oliver Kix contains sources of conflict under its seemingly placid, cooperative surface. The two are brought together in a relationship that furthers both their sociosexual estates by the unusual expedient of combining them: Kix provides Touchwood Senior with "purse, and bed, and board" (5.4.80), and Touchwood Senior provides Kix with the heir necessary to beat Whorehound in the inheritance derby. Yet the mutuality of this unifying relationship is based on potentially divisive power asymmetries. Like Allwit on Whorehound, Touchwood Senior will be economically dependent on Sir Oliver, who is more than senior partner in the arrangement. "Get children, and I'll keep them" (5.4.82), Kix tells Touchwood Senior, thus assuming paternal responsibility for both men's estates. On the other hand, Kix is, after all, a cuckold. As cuckold he is the subordinate in a clearly hierarchical power relationship. The bond of cuckoldry is, Sedgwick argues,

> *necessarily* hierarchical in structure, with an "active" participant who is clearly in the ascendancy over the "passive" one. Most characteristically, the difference of power occurs in the form of a difference of knowledge: the cuckold is not even supposed to know that he is in such a relationship. Thus, cuckoldry inscribes and institutionalizes . . . an impoverishment of horizontal or mutual ties in favor of an asymmetrical relation of cognitive transcendence.[17]

The final dialogue between the two men stresses the tension between the horizontal and vertical in their relationship, pointing at the potential for conflict in these power asymmetries. Kix commands then dares Touchwood Senior to "Get children, and I'll keep them" (5.4.82). His imperative indicates Touchwood Senior's economic dependence. Touchwood Senior's response is to counter Kix's assertion of economic authority with his own cognitive transcendence: "Take heed how you dare a man, while you live, sir, / That has good skill at his weapon" (5.4.84–85). This ironic response is a threat that gains force by the very fact that Kix cannot understand it (the play gives no indication that Kix knows the exact nature of the method used by Touchwood Senior to administer his fertility drug to Lady Kix). Touchwood Senior threatens to continue his secret usurpation of Kix's authority by obeying his imperative to an extent that Kix most likely did not intend. The dueling metaphor in these lines is highly appropriate: the relationship between the two men balances a temporary coincidence of interests against the pressures of economic and sexual power asymmetries in a (potentially dangerous) game.

Yet in spite of, or because of, its emphasis on the paradoxical and gamelike nature of patriarchal order, *A Chaste Maid* is not a feminist play. Unlike in *The Roaring Girl*, in *A Chaste Maid* Middleton seems uninterested in articulating a feminist position, even though the play seems to provide ample opportunity to do so. As Hotz-Davies argues, although the play raises a number of issues about the oppression of women, its interests lie elsewhere. In order to maintain the tight, complex plotting that Levin so admired and that is essential to the play's comic analysis of patriarchy's paradoxical reproduction, Middleton flattens the play's pivotal female characters—Mistress Allwit, Lady Kix, and Moll Yellowhammer—into little more than media for relations between men. Mistress Allwit and Lady Kix are represented as completely acquiescent in the transactions between men that occur through them. Moll is slightly more complex. She makes a decision, but it is a decision between two men and is undermined by Touchwood Junior's suggestion that it is motivated primarily by appetite: "her blood's mine," he comments, "and that's the surest" (1.1.134–35). Hotz-Davies observes that Moll, unlike her namesake in *The Roaring Girl*, "is incapable of analysing her own situation or even articulating her own cause."[18] Moll's volition may make her a player as well as a prize in patriarchy's game (although the play continually displaces the controlling agency behind Moll's escape attempts away from her onto others—the Touchwood brothers, Susan the chambermaid, and even the abstraction "love," which finds "strange hidden ways" [3.3.32]), but the play does not give her the voice to critique the game.

A Chaste Maid dramatizes patriarchy's paradoxical reproduction not only as game but also as play. As game, patriarchy is a set of rules defining a field of contestation and collaboration. As play, it involves the performative interplay between restraint and liberty or license. This interplay constitutes the play's second main comic principle, the paradox that restraint not only opposes but also in various ways generates license. The central instance of this is the escalating intensity of the comic dynamics of confinement and escape which determine Moll's dramatic progression through the play. As her confinement becomes more severe, Moll's escape attempts become more desperate. Moll "made hard shift" (3.1.12) to escape the first time; to effect her second escape, "she's led through gutters, / Strange hidden ways which none but love could find" (3.3.31–32); her last escape is through (faked) death and resurrection. The subterranean trajectories of Moll's flight—sewers, death—link her to the grotesque, whose basic movement is, according to Bakhtin, "a transfer to the material level, to the sphere of earth and body in their indissoluble unity."[19] Because Moll is the play's heroine the grotesque is displaced: she is not grotesque (as Mistress Allwit is) but passes through the grotesque to a different form of order. Nonetheless, the porousness of the grotesque, its hostility to order and restraint, renders it the ineradicable location of the "strange hidden ways" by which restraint is evaded. The relationship between restraint and license is not, however, simply oppositional. As the Yellowhammers' treatment of their daughter illustrates, restraint can be a violent form of liberty-taking or abuse. Conversely, Moll's liberty seeks the restraint or order of marriage. Here, restraint and liberty mark a merely positional difference within a fundamental sameness.

The play's dramatization of the relationship between restraint and license complicates their condition of opposition in other ways. Throughout the play, the performance of order provides the occasion for misrule. The play seems to generalize this into a comic law of its fictional world. London's "religious, wholesome laws" (2.1.113) are exploited by "promoters / And other poisonous officers" (2.1.116–17). The promoters have been using their position as enforcers of Lent's "carnal strictness" (2.2.77) to "fat" themselves "with sweetbreads / And lard their whores with lamb-stones" (2.2.68–69). The gathering of drunken women at Mistress Allwit's christening is perhaps the most prominent instance of the performance of order providing an occasion for misrule (an instance whose carnivalesque subversiveness is seriously qualified by the function of representations of women as grotesque in patriarchal discourse). The hypocrisy of the performance of the christening ritual is also in a sense subversive, not by overturning order but by hollowing it out into a mask or cover for license. The ritual of christening is intended to initiate the infant into an order that is both metaphysical and, in its incarnations, patriarchal. The infant is catechized and baptized into a mystical community whose head is Christ, from whom descends the series of analogous material power relations by which early modern English patriarchal society is ordered: king and subject, husband and wife, parent and child, master and servant.[20] The christening of the Allwit infant, however, does not mark her entrance into social order as metaphysical incarnation but rather her first performance in social order as charade. The ceremony is a formal exercise, in several ways "unhappy,"[21] to borrow Austin's term: Whorehound and the Allwits cannot sincerely intend to fulfill the spiritual obligations that they must promise to undertake in the ceremony; the ceremony is not, substantially, performed correctly, given that Allwit plays the father and Whorehound stands as a godparent. At the ceremony Allwit is dressed, in fine Middletonian style, in Whorehound's suit, ironically heightening the perception that Allwit is not Whorehound, is not the newborn's father, while at the same time emphasizing the costume-like nature of the ceremony which permits such formal interchangeability of bodies. This is not to say that the performance of the ceremony is trivial. On the contrary, Whorehound at least feels that it is important, but only to establish the appearance of orthodox patriarchal order in order to protect his unorthodox arrangement. Thus, we find a strange inversion: long-standing license provides the occasion for particular reiterations of patriarchal order. Here and also, as we shall see, in Moll and Touchwood Junior's deaths and resurrections, order is epiphenomenal, precariously produced by the dialectic between game and play. Robbed of its metaphysical moorings, patriarchal order must performatively enact and re-enact itself on the stage of intersecting desires.

Like the first of the play's structuring paradoxes discussed, the second is echoed on a discursive level. Particularly in the main plot, language and the subjectivities it constructs are subject to what Chakravorty calls "linguistic policing."[22] At the very least, this policing, through its insistence on discursive boundaries, foregrounds the plurality of discourses and so discloses other discourses as alternatives to itself. The play in fact opens with a scene of linguistic policing, as Yellowhammer rebukes Maudline for telling Moll of her "errors" (1.1.19):

> Errors? Nay, the City cannot hold you, wife, but you must needs fetch words from Westminster; I ha' done, i'faith. Has no attorney's clerk been here a' late and changed his half-crown-piece his mother sent him, or rather cozen'd you with a gilded twopence, to bring the word in fashion for her faults or cracks in duty and obedience? Term 'em e'en so, sweet wife. As there is no woman made without a flaw, your purest lawns have frays, and cambrics bracks.
>
> (1.1.20–26)

Yellowhammer objects to the Westminster provenance of "error" not because he is a proponent of a plain, citizen style—his concluding simile indicates that he has no aversion to rhetorical ornamentation—but because "error" is a law term that grants Moll a degree of volition with which he is uncomfortable. Yellowhammer's translation denies Moll subjectivity and agency: Moll is a commodity, like lawns and cambrics, and her "errors" are frays and bracks and cracks to be mended by others, through the application of external force. Persuasion is not an option in Yellowhammer's commodifying discourse. The Yellowhammers, of course, are seeking to trade Moll and her enormous dowry to Whorehound in return for the symbolic capital that accompanies his gentry status. To ensure the transaction's success, Yellowhammer enforces Moll's commodity status, physically by "lock[ing] up this baggage / As carefully as my gold" (3.1.42–43) and discursively by objecting to the terms of courtly love with which Whorehound addresses Moll. Whorehound addresses Moll twice in the play, in both instances positioning Moll in courtly love terms as an active participant in the relationship that he is attempting to establish: he first greets Moll with "Why, how now, pretty mistress, now I have caught you. What, can you injure so your time to stray thus from your faithful servant?" (1.1.113–15); in response to her second escape attempt, he asks her "Why have you us'd me thus, unkind mistress? Wherein have I deserved?" (4.3.40–41). Significantly, the second instance comes immediately after Whorehound has stopped the Yellowhammers from beating Moll, from brutally degrading her into an object, thus illustrating the differences in material practice entailed by the differing discourses employed by Yellowhammer and Whorehound. Persuasion is at least a rhetorical possibility in the discourse of courtly love.

The scene in which Moll's recapture occurs leaves no doubt that Whorehound is only playing Moll's knight in shining armor and can do so only because the Yellowhammers so willingly play the villains. Before Maudline enters dragging Moll by the hair, Whorehound berates Yellowhammer for not guarding Moll closely enough, and although he puts on a good show for Moll he does not object to but secretly approves Yellowhammer's plan to hurry Moll into a forced marriage with him. Yet even Whorehound's rhetorical artifice makes Yellowhammer nervous because, by addressing Moll in terms that Yellowhammer feels are properly reserved for aristocratic women, his social superiors, it muddies the clear lines of paternal authority summed up in "duty and obedience." Consequently, Yellowhammer immediately polices the first words Whorehound speaks to Moll: "Pish, stop your words, good knight, 'twill make her blush else, which wound too high for the daughters of the Freedom. 'Honour', and 'faithful servant', they are compliments for the worthies of Whitehall or Greenwich. E'en plain, sufficient, subsidy words serves us, sir" (1.1.116–20). Ultimately, however, Yellowhammer's efforts to confine Moll to the small room of his own discourse are frustrated. The education that he gives Moll, no doubt intending to make her a more marketable commodity, also in the process makes her literate, and literacy is the key to her freedom. Moll's literacy enables her to read Touchwood Junior's crucial letter in act 5, scene 2. More importantly, through literacy Moll has had access to alternative worlds and subject positions, from which she chooses one—the world of tragicomedy, with its imperiled but eternally true lovers—in which to couch her resistance to her father's coercion and through which finally to escape his tyranny.

The play's comic conclusion continues the dramatization of patriarchy's reproduction through paradox. The conclusion consolidates patriarchal order by establishing three households: Touchwood Senior and his wife are reunited under the Kixes' roof; Tim and the Welsh Gentlewoman, and Touchwood Junior and Moll, are married. Each of these households, however, embodies patriarchal order only paradoxically. The Touchwood Senior-Kix arrangement provides Kix with the heir necessary to inherit a substantial estate and Touchwood Senior with the solution to the sex-money calculus that caused the breakup of his household at the play's beginning. Yet, of course, this consolidation of patriarchal order is possible only through Touchwood Senior's usurpation of Kix's patriarchal authority. Tim's marriage to the Welsh Gentlewoman also involves paradox. Tim is reconciled to his fate—"Come from the university, / To marry a whore in London" (5.4.89–90)—only when he can prove by logic that the whore he has married is not a whore. A past master of the specious syllogism who has earlier boasted that "By logic I'll prove anything" (4.1.37), Tim does not find this task too difficult: *"Uxor non est meretrix"* (5.4.113); but the Welsh Gentlewoman is his wife; *ergo*, she is not a whore but an honest woman. Tim's argument reaches its contradictory conclusion—the whore is not a whore—by rigorously applying the law of non-contradiction to patriarchy's classification of women as maids, wives, widows, or whores. Tim's paradox is essentially comic, mirroring in logic the Welsh Gentlewoman's promised social transformation through marriage into an honest wife: "Sir, if your logic cannot prove me honest, / There's a thing call'd marriage, and that makes me honest" (5.4.114–15).

Moll, however, is caught in a potentially tragic reversal of the paradox that enables the Welsh Gentlewoman's integration into patriarchal order. In his discussion of the play, Covatta argues that "the dilemma of the title story is whether Moll will be married off profitably, or romantically and chastely."[23] Yet Moll's dilemma is not so simple. If the Welsh Gentlewoman can be a whore yet an honest woman, Moll is a chaste maid who cannot, it seems, escape classification as a whore. On the one hand, were Moll to marry Whorehound, she would enter into a form of legalized prostitution. Whorehound is after not only Moll's "two thousand pound in gold" (4.3.58) but also her "maidenhead / Worth forty" (4.3.59), the going price for a virgin prostitute. Furthermore, Moll seems to have some sort of precontract, legal or merely emotional, with Touchwood Junior. Thus, Moll can say about the possibility of marriage to Whorehound what William Scarborrow says in Wilkin's *Miseries of Inforst Marriage*: "My marriage makes me an

Adulterer."²⁴ On the other hand, clandestine marriage to Touchwood Junior would also lead to Moll's classification as a whore. Although common law in the period grudgingly acknowledged the validity of such marriages, there was little doubt in the minds of the writers of books on household governance and marriage that these marriages were fundamentally wrong. Even while urging parents to consult their children's wishes when arranging marriages for them and depicting the evils of forced marriage, these writers stated that parents must ultimately be obeyed. Just as there was no room for legitimate rebellion in divine-right monarchy theories of the state such as James I's, so too there was no room for filial disobedience in patriarchal theories of the family, which conceived parents, especially fathers, to be, like monarchs, God's representatives on earth.²⁵ Moll's disobedience, her defiance of her father's authority over her sexuality, is, then, the equivalent of unchastity or whoredom. Yellowhammer makes this explicit when he calls Moll an "impudent strumpet" (4.3.38) for attempting to escape. Furthermore, as Desdemona's case in *Othello* illustrates, disobedience to a father may be perceived in a patriarchal society to be a prelude to unfaithfulness to a husband: "Look to her, Moor, if thou hast eyes to see: / She has deceived her father, and may thee" are Brabantio's last words to Othello.²⁶ Like the provocative poesy Touchwood Junior has inscribed on the wedding ring, Moll's unruliness will be engraved on her marriage bonds, as both necessary precondition and sign of possible future behavior. Moll's position, then, seems utterly hopeless: whichever man she marries (and the play presents her no other option), she will become unchaste. The chaste/chased maid/Moll of Cheapside must become a strumpet to avoid becoming Whorehound's whore.

The play's conclusion finds a way for Moll to escape from her dilemma into patriarchal order through marriage to Touchwood Junior, but only at the cost of rendering truth itself paradoxical. This paradox is generated by Moll's choice of romantic love as the discourse in which to express her resistance to her father and the narrative vehicle through which finally to escape his plans for her. The discourse of romantic love offers Moll a way to transvalue her disobedience into chaste, true love even against parental opposition: "Though violence keep me, thou canst lose me never; / I am ever thine although we part for ever" (3.1.49–50), Moll tells Touchwood Junior after pleading with her father to pity her "for love's sake" (3.1.45). Until the play's final act, of course, this alternative set of values carries little weight and is ignored if not burlesqued. Romantic love is no match for the cynicism and greed that motivate the players of the play's patriarchal game. The helplessness and futility of romantic love in a harsh, materialistic world are what render it potentially so tragic, and it is precisely at its tragic extreme that Moll and Touchwood Junior establish romantic love's truth and alternative validity. Death is the lovers' trump card. By the end of act 5, scene 2, Touchwood Junior has died from wounds received in a duel with Whorehound, and Moll has died of a broken heart, providing irrefutable testimony of the strength and truth of her love. Her death gives life to her swan song:

> Weep eyes, break heart,
> My love and I must part;
> Cruel fates true love do soonest sever
>
> (5.2.41–43)

Touchwood Senior's funeral oration hammers home the connections between love, death, and truth. Death, by capturing the two lovers as his richest trophy, confirms the truth and value of their love:

> Never could death boast of a richer prize
> From the first parent, let the world bring forth
> A pair of truer hearts.
>
> (5.4.1–3)

Death transvalues Moll's disobedience: the dead maid leaves to posterity "The true, chaste monument of her living name, / Which no time can deface" (5.4.12–13). Death, and only death, brings the community together to affirm the values of romantic love. Even the Yellowhammers feel the force death gives to the values on which Moll acted. Significantly, although they themselves do not appear much affected by Moll's death, it causes them to feel shame, the product of community disapproval of their treatment of Moll as mere commodity: "All the whole street will hate us and the world / Point me out cruel" (5.2.107–8), Yellowhammer comments to his wife, implicitly recognizing the validity of values other than those of his own authoritarian, commodifying discourse. Most importantly, only death establishes the desirability of the seemingly impossible fulfillment of the contrary to fact conditional with which Touchwood Senior concludes his funeral oration:

> I cannot think there's any one amongst you
> In this full fair assembly, maid, man, or wife,
> Whose heart would not have sprung with joy and gladness
> To have seen their marriage day.
>
> (5.4.22–25)

Death creates the fantasy of its own defeat by love through the lovers' marriage.

The play, then, accomplishes what Susan Wells in "Jacobean City Comedy and the Ideology of the City" calls "an audacious redirection of its tone"[27] through death's rapid marshaling of community support for the values of romantic love. This community includes the audience, who are as unaware as the play-world audience of Touchwood Senior's funeral oration that the two lovers are not really dead but actually performing a script. The lengths to which the play goes to build up this community suggest, though, that this performance is more than a burlesque. Certainly, the play quickly robs the resurrections of their miraculousness: the audience is allowed only a moment to marvel before Touchwood Senior reveals that it was all a plot, and the speed and tone of the subsequent performance of the marriage ceremony are comic not solemn. Yet the death-trick, a standard theatrical device used to savagely ironic effect in *Volpone* and *Michaelmas Term*, is here redeployed for more complex ends. The concealment of the fact that the lovers are actually alive and the elaborate, visually spectacular and emotionally evocative stage settings at the beginning of the final, funeral scene project the play, albeit momentarily, into the worlds of *Romeo and Juliet* then *The Winter's Tale*. Touchwood Senior's solemn eulogy is a tale of woe, and the lovers' resurrections, like Hermione's, evoke "joy and wonder" (5.4.54). The sentimentality of these moments is not gratuitous. Rather, the creation of joy and wonder is necessary to transform mere performance into saving paradox. (Tellingly, Puttenham in *The Arte of English Poesie* glosses paradox as "the Wondrer.")[28] As mere performance, Moll's sham death and resurrection, part of a plan to defeat her father's will, is a further sign of her unruliness. The performative nature of the funeral should negate the truths it seeks to establish. Only if Moll is dead can the truth and chastity of her love and the desirability of her union with Touchwood Junior be established. And, obviously, she is not. Yet, joy and wonder mark a paradoxical suspension of the law of noncontradiction. The elaborate performance of death seems to have created a fantasy of love's triumph over death too compelling to be dismissed as mere sleight of hand. Although the resurrections are robbed of their miraculousness, the effects of miracle as sign of truth remain: no one challenges Moll's chastity or the truth of her love; no one questions the appropriateness of her marriage to Touchwood Junior. The stage, then, becomes a space of multiple ontologies, breaking performance's subordination to "reality" and enabling the paradox that fulfills the fantasy and resolves Moll's dilemma: the truth of the matter is that Moll was and was not dead.

7

Skeptical Laughter in the Brave New World of *Bartholomew Fair*

> Nor, is the moving of laughter always the end of comedy, that is rather a fooling for the people's delight, or their fooling. For, as Aristotle says rightly, the moving of laughter is a fault in comedy, a kind of turpitude, that depraves some part of man's nature without a disease.
> —Jonson, *Discoveries*

Jonson's sentiments were a commonplace of Renaissance literary theory.[1] In his *Defence of Poesy* Sidney had expressed them as part of a critique of the comic drama of his time: after having distinguished between true delight and laughter, which "hath only a scornful tickling," Sidney states "I speak to this purpose that all the end of the comical part be not upon such scornful matters as stir laughter only, but, mixed with it, that delightful teaching which is the end of poesy."[2] Good comedy, according to Sidney, must obey the rules of decorum and instruct as well as move to laughter. Throughout his career Jonson professed such good intentions, however much his plays subverted them. One recalls the prologues to *Volpone* and *The Alchemist*: "In all his poems, still, hath been this measure, / To mix profit with your pleasure" (*Volpone* 7–8); "He hopes to find no spirit so much diseased, / But will, with such fair correctives, be pleased" (*The Alchemist* 17–18). *Bartholomew Fair* is prefaced by no such claims, and it is difficult to see how it could be. In this play laughter is thoroughly skeptical, directed at all sources of authority that might sanction notions of decorum and standards of instruction. The Fair is a fitting place for this kind of skeptical laughter, which is of the Fair in two ways. The play uses the carnivalesque techniques associated with the festivity of the fair to travesty authority and judgment. Yet, as I will argue, the play is ultimately not a festive comedy ending with the renewal and reassertion of community. Rather, *Bartholomew Fair*, like the fairs of Jonson's day, is a space in which boundaries of community are asserted only to be distorted, reversed, and disintegrated in a process of exchange that creates the laughter not of the pedagogue but of the con artist. The play is a fooling, both for people's laughter and their fooling.

The skepticism of *Bartholomew Fair* is inseparable from its aesthetics of carnivalesque travesty. Its pungent physicality, bringing the high low and reducing the spiritual to the material, equates authority and judgment (two key concepts in Jonson's own ethics and aesthetics) with folly and flatulence. The play appropriates the strategies of what Bakhtin labels "grotesque realism," whose essential principle is "degradation; that is, the lowering of all that is high, spiritual, abstract; it is the transfer to the material level, to the sphere of earth and the body."[3] Thus, the representatives of legal, religious, and educational authority are propelled by their humors through the muck of the Fair like Bergsonian automata set to self-destruct. Overdo's self-aggrandizement, Busy's gluttonous zeal, and Wasp's inexplicable but ever-present belligerence strip them of their pretensions to authority, first landing them in the stocks and then reducing them to the level of Cokes, the play's paradigmatic fool, and ultimately the wooden, mechanical puppets whose performance they watch at the play's conclusion. "He that will correct another, must want fault in himself,"[4] Wasp says in resignation after Cokes twits him about being in the stocks, and none of the play's authority figures are able to meet this requirement. They are "flesh and blood" (5.6.89), and as Jonas Barish puts it, "who is so disinfected of flesh and blood as to qualify as a legislator?"[5] Overdo tosses off one last Latin tag before he leaves the stage at the play's end: "*Ad correctionem, non ad destructionem*" (5.6.102–3). Among the play's characters, however, no one remains who could plausibly provide such correction.

The raw materiality of flesh and blood levels not only figures of authority but also the sources from which they claim to derive their authority. The Spirit which inspires Busy's "visions" (1.3.105) and zeal becomes in Littlewit's parodic description mere breath: "Sometime the spirit is so strong with him, it gets quite out of him, and then my mother, or Win, are fain to fetch it again with malmsey, or *Aqua coelestis*" (1.2.59–61). Later, as Busy rails against the Fair on a belly full of roast pig, it is lowered to the level of a belch or a fart issuing not in the gift of tongues but in sheer noise: his speech is "a sanctified noise. I will make a loud and most strong noise, till I have daunted the profane enemy" (3.6.92–93). Cokes's soul suffers a comparable diminution: Edgeworth declares Cokes's soul to be "a thing given him instead of salt, only to keep him from stinking" (4.2.48). Similarly, Bristle and Haggis figure Overdo's justice not as the expression of a metaphysical ideal but as the eruption of his "bile" (4.1.67). As in *Volpone*, in *Bartholomew Fair* there is no transcendent realm of the spirit or metaphysical ideals. As Barish observes, the play reduces "first the brain and then the soul itself to the level of physicality."[6] Significantly, Wasp, who as Cokes's tutor is most closely associated with reason, is also most closely associated with reason's reduction to the material—in Cokes and in himself. In a parody of the notion that the mind is a mirror of nature, he describes Cokes's brain as a vast space littered with trivial objects of the sort that most engage Cokes's attention in the Fair: "he that had the means to travel your head, now, should meet finer sights than any are i'the Fair; and make a finer voyage on't; to see it all hung with cockleshells, pebbles, fine wheat-straws, and here and there a chicken feather, and a cobweb" (1.5.84–88). Later, out of frustration Wasp reduces his own brain to the same physical level: "Would I had been set i' the ground, all but the head on me, and had my brains bowled at, or threshed out, when I first under went this plague of a charge" (3.4.40–42).

Accompanying the lowering of the mind to the material is the lowering of thought and language. As Neil Rhodes remarks, "verbal excess is used, vainly, as a means of defence against physical excess"[7] and becomes in the process merely another form of physical excess, the vaporous product of humors, ale, and tobacco. The game of vapors takes the travesty of reason to its absurd extreme. A parody of academic disputation in which "Every man [is] to oppose the last man that spoke: whether it concerned him, or no" (side note after 4.4.22), the game dramatizes the arbitrariness of argument, the role of desire in discourse, and the thinglike nature of the words thrown at each other by the game's participants. In *The World Upside-Down*, Ian Donaldson observes that the game, and the play generally, mock one of Jonson's own most cherished ideals, that "Speech is the only benefit man hath to express his excellency of mind above other creatures. It is the instrument of society."[8] Indeed, in *Bartholomew Fair*, language only adds layers to human bestiality and aggression. Even the authority of high art—the classical tales of Hero and Leander and Damon and Pythias—is travestied in the noise, violence, and obscenity of Littlewit and Leatherhead's modernized puppet-play versions of the stories, in which Leander is "a dyer's son" (5.3.102), Hero "a wench o' the Bankside" (5.3.104), Cupid "a drawer" who "strikes Hero in love with a pint of sherry" (5.3.106), and Damon and Pythias "whore-masters both" (5.4.219). In Jonson's own words, "This is truly leaping from the stage to the tumbril again, reducing all wit to the original dungcart."[9]

The play's reduction of high art to the knockabout farce of the puppet play signals the antihumanist quality of the play's carnivalesque travesty. Like *Epicoene*, but far more savagely, *Bartholomew Fair* dramatizes the absurdity of attempting to transport classical and Christian idioms and models of behavior into the present. The characters in *Bartholomew Fair* are not dwarfs on the shoulders of giants but dwarfs dressed up in giants' clothing. Although Busy, like Ananias, "derides all antiquity" and "defies any other learning than inspiration" (1.3.126), he and the other members of his congregation model their "beauteous discipline" (1.6.1) on the early church. Hooker in *The Laws of Ecclesiastical Polity* had argued against the necessity of such strict modeling, but the play dramatizes its impossibility and the ridiculousness of those who make the attempt. Busy's elevated quasi-biblical rhetoric cannot mask his "most arrogant and invincible dullness" (1.3.129), and his and Dame Purecraft's manipulation of the organizational structures of their congregation have turned it into a glorified extortion racket. Similarly, following George Whetstone's injunctions in *A Mirour for Magestrates of Cyties* (1584), Overdo consciously models his behavior and rhetoric on classical exempla of disguised magistrates and, of course, on their updated versions, the disguised duke plays so popular on the Elizabethan and Jacobean stage.[10] Yet, the play repeatedly exposes undersized Overdo's inability to fill these shoes.

Busy and Overdo, like the Puritan Brethren and Mammon in *The Alchemist*, are trapped in the roles they adopt, caught in hermeneutics that insulate them from the rough knocks of reality until the play's end. Like silkworms they spin their realities out of themselves. Thus, wherever they turn in the Fair, Overdo detects enormities and Busy sees elements of Protestant apocalyptic narrative—relics of popery, signs of the beast. Even the stocks do not daunt them. Busy "rejoiceth in his affliction" (4.6.75) because it is "for my better standing, my surer standing, hereafter" (4.6.105–6). Overdo adopts the pose of a Stoic: "I do not feel it, I do not think it, it is a thing without me. Adam, thou art above these batteries, these contumelies. *In te manca ruit fortuna*, as thy friend Horace says" (4.6.80–83). R. N. Watson considers Busy and Overdo to be quixotic, but the differences between Quixote and Busy and Overdo are equally revealing: Quixote, like the fictions he attempts to live, is too good for the world that defeats him, but Busy and Overdo, like the deluded characters in *The Alchemist*, are allowed none of Quixote's tragic pathos. They are merely sententious fools, serious asses. Thomas Cartelli has characterized the Fair as a "gray world,"[11] Jonson's urban version of Shakespeare's various green, Arcadian worlds, but there is no room for romance or miracles, the golden age or the age of the early church, in the mechanical world of the Fair, except as parody. Even Quarlous and Winwife do not make convincing pastoral figures: their attempt to write their quarrel over Grace into the Sidneyan tradition of pastoral romance by choosing pastoral names—Argalus and Palemon—for Grace's proposed lottery is merely comic, as Grace dryly points out, given the location and circumstances of the two combatants. The play's conclusion, in which Busy and Overdo's release from their self-confirming hermeneutics leads to an inclusive invitation to dinner at Overdo's, has prompted critics to describe *Bartholomew Fair* as one of Jonson's more genial plays, the triumph of festivity over the judgmental endings that conclude Jonson's earlier plays. Barish states that "Not only will no punishment be inflicted other than what has come about of its own accord in the course of the day, but all the people will repair to a feast at the home of justice.... All will partake of the promised supper, its festive nature emphasized by the presence of the little actors who have helped tame the disciplinarians, who will be brought along to resume their interrupted disports."[12] Yet the release from parody is not as complete as such festivity might seem to require. Quarlous urges Overdo to "drown the memory of all enormity in your biggest bowl at home" (5.6.91–92). In the untransubstantiatable world of the Fair the sacrament that washes away enormity is not Christ's blood but alcohol.

Despite its use of carnivalesque strategies, then, the play does not end on an unequivocally festive note. The parodic nature of the concluding feast marks Jonson's inability to endorse wholeheartedly the collective renewal of carnival. Michael McCanles argues that in the Fair's festivity Jonson presents the audience with a perverted festivity that it should reject: "unlike the description of Renaissance festival given by Mikhail Bakhtin, for Jonson, to equate festival with the reduction of all human motivations to bodily appetite is to pervert it."[13] Jonson's model of true festivity is, according to McCanles, the relaxed humanist, who even while feasting will "manifest in his gestures and speech the inner qualities of self-control, self-knowledge, and considered judgment of his relations with others."[14] Similarly, Rhodes locates the play's critical distance from the festivity it represents in a controlling satirical and moral purpose: "Although it uses saturnalian motifs, *Bartholomew Fair* is not a festive comedy; its moral vision is sceptical in a way which admits the frailty of the flesh, which satirises those who would repress its urges, but which takes no positive delight in the celebration of the flesh."[15] The satirical and moral intentions that Jonson expresses throughout the prefatory material of his plays are fundamentally inimical to the spirit of carnival. Carnival laughter, as Bakhtin remarks, "is not an individual reaction to some isolated 'comic' event. Carnival laughter is the laughter of all the people."[16] Carnival laughter engulfs those who participate in it and forges a collective identity. Jonsonian satire seeks to dissolve collective identity and produce individual, judging spectators. The Induction to *Bartholomew Fair* to some degree mocks the moral seriousness of this intention, but it nonetheless figures carnival's collective identity as a disease and seeks to disintegrate this identity by binding each and every spectator in a legal and commercial contract that forbids judging "by contagion" (87). This tension between carnival and satire is characteristic of what Bakhtin calls "Renaissance realism," in which "Two types of imagery reflecting the conception of the world here meet at the crossroads; one of them ascends to the folk culture of humor, while the other is the bourgeois conception of the completed atomized being."[17]

As Bakhtin's analysis suggests, the change in mode of festivity is closely related to changes in socioeconomic environment, not only temporal changes but also changes in location. Michael Bristol states that "A fair may contain many surface features of carnival—feasting, eroticism, noisy crowds—but its substance is strictly commodity exchange."[18] The commercial nature of fairs has important social implications that further distance their festivity from that of carnival. Bristol argues that the purpose of carnival festivity was to assert plebeian community and its social norms against the interference from higher, centralizing authorities, to construct through symbolic inversion the boundaries between plebeian communities and its others:

> Although it [Carnival] is a festive and primarily symbolic activity, it has immediate pragmatic aims, most immediately that of objectifying a collective determination to conserve the authority of the community to set its own standards of behavior and social discipline, and to enforce those standards by appropriate means. At the same time Carnival is a form of resistance to arbitrarily imposed forms of domination, especially when the constraints imposed are perceived as an aggression against the customary norms of surveillance and control.[19]

In contrast, fairs and markets were, like Renaissance realism, intersections, agents of the dissolution as well as the affirmation of the boundaries of community. Arguing against Bakhtin's idealization of the marketplace as a utopian space of plebeian solidarity, Peter Stallybrass and Allon White state that

> At the market centre of the polis we discover a commingling of categories usually kept separate and opposed: centre and periphery, inside and outside, stranger and local, commerce and festivity, high and low. . . . Thus in the marketplace "inside" and "outside" (and hence identity itself) are persistently mystified. It is a place where limit, centre and boundary are confirmed and yet also put in jeopardy.[20]

As Stallybrass and White later remark, the crossing and blurring of boundaries in the fair and marketplace substantially altered the festive excitement they generated:

> Part of the transgressive excitement of the fair for the subordinate classes was *not* its "otherness" to official discourse, but rather the disruption of provincial habits and local tradition by the introduction of a certain cosmo-

politanism, arousing desires and excitements for exotic and strange commodities. The fair "turned the world inside out" in its mercantilist aspect just as much, if not more, than it "turned the world upside down" in its popular rituals.[21]

Turning the world inside out: this strategy, just as much as the strategies of carnivalesque inversion, is exploited by *Bartholomew Fair* for its skeptical potential. As I will argue in the rest of this chapter, Jonson represents the Fair as a space that demands but defeats the assertion of boundaries, a space of the exotic and strange but not entirely other.

Jonson's representation of the Fair as a place in which boundaries of community are problematized depends on two other, related developments. Jonathan Haynes observes that "the Fair's history is the history of the specialization and fragmentation of the religious, commercial, and recreational aspects of what was originally one indivisible event."[22] The play registers the process of fragmentation: its action takes place exclusively in the pleasure grounds of the Fair. Haynes remarks that "The consequence of this separation of business and pleasure was that pleasure became a business."[23] Festivity, at least on the part of its suppliers, is subordinated to acquisitiveness, and does not assert boundaries but dissolves them through a process of exchange. More importantly, the play registers a shift in the perspective from which festivity is represented. The business of pleasure is represented from the perspective of authority as criminal activity. All the Fair's denizens are rogues, their witty but shady activities ranging from selling goods of questionable quality to outright theft and prostitution. The process of festive exchange is recast as an antagonistic relationship between sharpers and gulls, a relationship that is both symbiotic and incapable of creating a sense of inclusive community. As Haynes puts it, "The world of carnival is being restructured into the world of coney-catching pamphlets."[24] The fair is relocated to the underworld, and consequently it attracts both those who desire to participate in it and those who desire to police and destroy it, Overdo and Busy as well as Cokes and Littlewit.

As part of the underworld, the Fair becomes an exotic colonial space inhabited by aliens not plebeians, a space in which the symbolic boundaries of the communities of those surveilling and policing the Fair are threatened rather than a space in which plebeian community is asserted. Several critics have noted the connection between the underworld and colonialism. The rogue and coney-catching pamphlets that represented the underworld are, according to Haynes, "a species of ethnological literature, describing an alien and exotic population."[25] Rebecca Ann Bach, in a recent essay on "Ben Jonson's 'Civil Savages'," elaborates in detail the connections made by Jonson's contemporaries between colonial space and the underworld:

> [T]he city posited an equivalence between London's underworld inhabitants and the dangerous presences in the colonies—both Indians and "corrupted" Englishmen. Rumors identified London and the colonies but only by incorporating the wildness of the colony, its dangerous presences, into representations of the metropolis and the wildness of the metropolis into representations of the colony. Likewise, that which cannot be domesticated in Jonson's fair resembles the wild and dangerous colonial otherness.[26]

But Jonson's phrase—"civil savages" (3.4.29-30)—suggests a potentially disruptive ambivalence in representations of the underworld as colonial space, a sameness in alterity capable of generating what Jonathan Dollimore describes as the "perverse" logic of the proximate: "the proximate is often constructed as the other, and in a process that facilitates displacement. But the proximate is also what enables a tracking-back of the 'other' into the 'same.'"[27] Rogue pamphlets and associated literature discursively construct the underworld as "normal," legitimate society's paradoxical proximate, as a space of all that is alien and even antithetical to society—ungodliness, lawlessness—and yet as a fascinating and familiar space.

Glancing briefly at one of the earliest examples of rogue pamphlets, Thomas Harman's *A Caveat for Common Cursitors* (1566), we find Harman, a justice of the peace, presenting himself as an explorer who has "rigged up the ship of knowledge" to explore a previously unknown world.[28] He has, ostensibly, two purposes: the extension of God's kingdom and the queen's in England by either eliminating rogues or correcting and converting them. Like Overdo, he adopts a disguise, that of an invalid. Harman oscillates between figuring the underworld as chaos, a "rowsey, ragged rabblement of rakehells" and a "pestilent" counternation, a cancerous alien body within the commonwealth.[29] Similarly, he oscillates between asserting that rogues speak their own language ("canting") that marks them out as belonging to an other-than-English race (he suggests Egyptian at one point) and vehemently insisting and demonstrating that these people know English even when they pretend otherwise. The proximity of the alien often breaks down the antitheses that such writers as Harman would construct between the godly and the godless, the law-abiding and the lawless. As Haynes points out, the underworld can function both "as Other and as model for the rest of society."[30] Underworld activity can be seen as merely another business or trade, and supposedly legitimate activity can be represented as just another racket, thus performing locally the operation that Montaigne in "Of cannibals" effects by reversing the places of the New World cannibal and the Old World colonizer as civilized and savage.[31] The logic of the proximate wobbles even Harman's moral, punitive purpose: for the second edition of his pamphlet he has added "five or six more tales" to keep the reader interested. Desire for the Other inhabits Harman's desire to eliminate it.[32]

In *Bartholomew Fair*'s induction Jonson explicitly connects the world of the Fair and colonial space. "When it comes to the Fair," the stage-keeper states, "you were e'en as good go to Virginia, for anything there is of Smithfield" (Induction 9–10). The charge of mimetic infidelity or running away from Nature is an unusual one to level at a playwright who made a critical axiom of doing just the opposite, and Jonson through his mouthpiece the scrivener quickly contradicts it. The stage-keeper's version of the Fair is a memory of "the sword and bucklerage of Smithfield" (Induction 103); Jonson's Fair is firmly situated in "the present" (Induction 104). Yet although Jonson denies the charge of mimetic infidelity, the play maintains the connection between its world and colonial space. There may not be a "servant monster i'the fair" (Induction 112), but as substitutes the Fair's brave new world offers the exotic figures of the underworld: "the Author doth promise a strutting horse-courser, with a leer drunkard. . . . [A] fine oily pig woman with her tapster. . . . A civil cutpurse searchant . . . [and] a sweet singer of new ballads allurant" (Induction 104–11). With its catalogue of characters to be found in the Fair, then, the induction promises a space that is and is not Virginia, a space of contact and exchange between communities and the Others they desire and desire to eliminate. The play's staging of this colonial encounter focuses on its exchanges and the interplay of desires. As representatives of various communities—the Puritans, Justice Overdo, and the gentry—are drawn into the Fair one after another, it becomes less and less clear who is the colonizer and who the colonized. *Bartholomew Fair* dramatizes the perverse logic of the proximate: the Fair's visitors struggle to trope the Fair as alien, but as they are drawn into the Fair through desire and revulsion, the alien reveals itself to be very familiar while the visitors themselves become part of its strangeness. The play represents the Fair as a heterocosm constantly blurring, resisting and reversing the lines of demarcation between nation and alien.

The logic of the proximate plays itself out fairly straightforwardly in the adventures of the group of Puritans who visit the Fair. Given their hostility to such godless places, Puritans in the Fair are themselves an oddity, and indeed it takes the infernal powers of Satan himself and a remarkable display of casuistry by Busy to get them there. In the play's first act, Win is beset by the desire to eat roast pig in the Fair. Dame Purecraft figures Win's carnal desire as an invading, penetrating, and polluting alien force. She urges Win to "suffer not the enemy to enter you at this door, remember that your education has been with the purest, what polluted one was it, that named first the unclean beast, pig, to you, child?" (1.6.5–8). Win replies: "A profane black thing with a beard" (1.6.12), whom Dame Purecraft immediately identifies as "the wicked Tempter" (1.6.13–14). Win seems unable to resist the invasion, but in any event Busy's casuistry renders resistance unnecessary. In fact, Busy transforms Win's potentially polluting desire into an opportunity for the "sanctified assembly" (1.6.41) to assert their radical separation from the nonelect: "[W]e may be religious in the midst of the profane" (1.6.65) Busy concludes, later adding that "by the public eating of swine's flesh" the Puritans will "profess our hate and loathing of Judaism" (1.6.84). Having eaten his fill of roast pig in Ursula's booth, Busy abandons casuistry for a more aggressive, prophetic assertion of the antithesis between the elect and the world of the Fair. He denounces Ursula as "above all to be avoided, having the marks upon her of the three enemies of man, the world, as being in the fair; the devil, as being in the fire; and the flesh, as being herself" (3.6.30–33). Smithfield, the site of the Fair, is "the seat of the Beast" (3.6.39).

The play, of course, gleefully exposes the Puritans' hypocrisy, and in so doing it converts the Other of the Puritans' imaginary community into its mirror image. Both Dame Purecraft and Busy locate the source of carnal desire in threatening, alien figures: Satan and Ursula. Yet the alien turns out to be a projection and denial of carnal desire originating within the Puritan body. Win's longing for roast pig is provoked not by Satan but by her husband as a ruse to satisfy his sensual desire to "see sights i' the Fair" (3.6.4). And Busy's spiritual zeal is provoked only after his appetite for flesh has been satisfied. Also, through Busy the play shows that law and discipline at their extreme create their own lawlessness and chaos: at the extreme of their assertion they become what they construct as their antithesis. Thus after denouncing Ursula and the Fair Busy begins to destroy the trinkets sold at booths surrounding Ursula's, trinkets he takes to be idols, relics of anti-Christian popery. For his efforts he is arrested and put in the stocks. Dame Purecraft more fully reveals the extent to which the Puritan project of constituting an imaginary community radically separate from the heathen world disintegrates under pressure from the proximate. She confesses to Quarlous that for the past seven years she has been a "holy widow" only to gain gifts from suitors; that she devours rather than distributes the alms she has been put in charge of; that she arranges marriages between rich and poor members of the Puritan community only in order to extort a percentage—and if she does not get her percentage she does not "leave pronouncing reprobation, and damnation" (5.2.57–58) upon the offending parties. She would have married Busy, but he is her competitor: she "know[s] him to be the capital knave of the land" (5.2.59). Discipline, the process of surveillance and correction by which the subject's interiority is constituted as an extension of the kingdom of God, is motivated by the carnal desires it seeks to expel. The organization of the Brethren is a fraternity of thieves, no longer representative of an elect English nation but, like the underworld of the Fair, an alien body within society: "the second part of the society of canters, outlaws to order and discipline, and the only privileged church-robbers in Christendom" (5.2.39–41), according to Quarlous.

Justice Overdo's engagement with the Fair is more complex than the Puritans' and more clearly illustrates the treatment of the world of the Fair as colonial space. Overdo is the presiding judge of the court of Pie Powders, the court set up annually to administer justice in the Fair. He enters the Fair in act 2 "in justice's name, and the King's; and for the commonwealth" (2.1.1–2), in the name of an imaginary community divided into those in authority and those who obey, those who rule and those to be ruled. This division structures Thomas Smith's exposition of the commonwealth in *De Republica Anglorum* (1583), a work that aims at both categorical precision—positions in the commonwealth are clearly defined, even inherent—and completeness: Smith claims to represent all members of the commonwealth. Smith admits that his commonwealth does not include everyone inhabiting England: bondsmen and women are excluded, but only because their obedience to those who are included in the commonwealth can be assumed beforehand. Yet the model's categorical precision begins to break down in this realm of the excluded: the category of those who do not rule and yet are not obedient is predictably absent from Smith's commonwealth, absent even from the list of those who are absent. Overdo's project is to recover this doubly absent space for the commonwealth, first by rendering that space visible by documenting and categorizing in his black book the "enormities" he observes in the Fair, and then by using his judicial powers to establish the lawbreakers in their categorical identities (as criminals, aliens), to mark these identities on their very bodies through punishment and even destruction. Even more so than Harman, Overdo conceives his project in explicitly colonial terms: he is a "Columbus; Magellan; or . . . Drake" (5.6.33–34) extending England's empire into hitherto uncharted territory for the good of the commonwealth and his own private glory.

The relationship that Overdo intends to establish with the Fair is not only juridical and colonial but also, and fundamentally, epistemological. As Edward Said argues in *Orientalism*, colonialism *is* an epistemological relationship.[33] Only by fixing people in certain categories as objects of knowledge through the exercise of power—judicial, military, scientific—can imaginary communities such as the commonwealth define the boundaries between self and other, nation and alien. This epistemological relationship, however, is frictionless only in the imaginations of those who are at—or those who think they are at—the center of power. No one has yet suggested Francis Bacon as a model for Overdo (although Keith Sturgess suggests that Overdo may be a "playful" caricature of James I),[34] but the epistemological relationship that Overdo intends to establish with the Fair is Baconian. More precisely, Overdo attempts to play the Baconian subject of knowledge, and the disastrous results betray the impossibility of the Baconian epistemological project achieving its intended results.

Bacon's project is radically opposed to the skepticism from which *Bartholomew Fair* derives its comic energies. Bacon could not be numbered among those whom Thomas Browne considered "the wisest heads [who] prove at last, almost all Sceptics, and stand like Janus in the field of knowledge."[35] As I have already discussed in connection with *Epicoene*, Bacon recognizes the power of the skeptical challenge but, like Descartes after him, sets out to overcome that challenge. As Bacon sees it, the gap which skepticism exploits is that between discourse and reality. In *The Advancement of Learning* Bacon states that "the mind of man is far from the nature of a clear and equal glass, wherein the beams of things should reflect according to their true incidence; nay, it is rather like an enchanted glass, full of superstition and imposture, if it be not delivered and reduced."[36] Bacon's task is to deliver and reduce the enchanted glass, to restore the "commerce between the mind of man and the nature of things" and "[build] in the human understanding a true model of the world, such as it is in fact, not such as man's own reason would have it be."[37] To do this Bacon depends on a curious epistemological maneuver in which reason is split into the knowing subject and the known object—reason is both subject and object of Bacon's antiskeptical discourse. Bacon argues that, with the aid of the right method and instruments (reason's "helps"), reason can know its own faults and correct them. Reason as knowing subject becomes the distanced spectator of and corrector of the corruptions and follies of reason as object. Thus, in the naturalistic epistemology Bacon outlines in *The Advancement of Learning*, knowledge of the human faculty of reason is a subsection of natural philosophy, just one of natural philosophy's many objects. The bulk of *The New Organon* develops the inductive method by which Bacon will correct reason as object, delivering it from the theatrical world of phenomena and providing it access to the world "as it is in fact," the world of being.

There are obvious problems with the epistemological sleight of hand by which Bacon seems to overcome skepticism. Henry Van Leeuwen notes the fatally regressive movement of Bacon's solution to the skeptical problem: "One must be on constant guard against deception, but if it is the very nature of the faculties to be deceived, the hope to compensate for deceit is one that by its very nature is likely to be unfulfilled."[38] Even so, Bacon's maneuver controls the development of his politics of centralized authority. Bacon's premise that reason can know objects as they are in themselves with the help of the proper method and instruments leads him to articulate knowledge in terms of control and power. If the only way to know objects is through controlled observation and manipulation, through "nature vexed," then the knowledge so gained will be useful primarily for further manipulation. For Bacon, to know something is to know how to control it: "those twin objects, human knowledge and human power, do really meet in one."[39] Bacon's plans for an institution to generate this type of knowledge are too vast, and the power of this knowledge too dangerous, to be left in the hands of a private individual, and consequently throughout his works Bacon appeals to James I for both financial support and state supervision. Here we find that the structure of Bacon's epistemological maneuver—a single spectator knowing and controlling a multiplicity of objects—is repeated on the level of political theory. In *The Advancement of Learning* Bacon states that "Concerning Government, it is a part of knowledge secret and retired . . . [and] all governments [God's government over the world and the prince's government over the state] are obscure and invisible." Accompanying inscrutability is omniscience: "But contrawise, in governors toward the governed, all things ought, as far as the frailty of man permitteth, to be manifest and revealed," especially "the natures and dispositions of the people" (206).[40] Likewise, in Bacon's Utopian *New Atlantis*, the mission of House of Solomon is to gather and produce knowledge for the good of the state, yet it itself is shrouded in secrecy, at times revealing and at times concealing its knowledge as it deems best. Significantly, in this scheme of political organization people function as instruments just as the instruments Bacon attempts to devise in *The New Organon* function as spies and torturers of nature.[41] But *New Atlantis* goes further than *The Advancement of Learning*, for it suggests what was becoming historically evident by Bacon's time, not that the state is supplemented by the institutionalization of Bacon's *New Organon*, but that the state depends for its existence on such institutions, without whose knowledge-gathering services centralized control would be impossible.

Overdo is well aware of the problems inherent in projects such as Bacon's, projects that in their desire to weld together knowledge and power in the realm of the social gloss over the dispersal of power and distortion of knowledge attendant upon the resistance of the human "instruments" who mediate the knowledge-producing process:

> For (alas) as we are public persons, what do we know? Nay, what can we know? We hear with other men's ears; we see with other men's eyes; a foolish constable, or a sleepy watchman, is all our information, he slanders a gentleman by the virtue of his place (as he calls it) and we by the vice of ours, must believe him. As a while agone, they made me, yea me, to mistake an honest zealous pursuivant, for a seminary: and a proper young Bachelor of Music, for a bawd. This we are subject to, that live high place,

all our intelligence is idle, and most of our intelligencers, knaves; and by
your leave, ourselves, thought little better, if not arrant fools, for believing
'em. (2.1.24–34)

The public status of those who operate the commonwealth's knowledge-producing institutions, their necessary impersonality or representativeness, forces them to depend on fallible and corrupt instruments of knowledge, generating a gap between the knowing subject of authority and its objects, a gap whose manipulation blurs the boundary between the imaginary community and its others in the very process by which it seeks to define that boundary. The law court established to subordinate private desire to the order of the commonwealth becomes an instrument of private desire, an unwitting participant in the playing out of rackets and schemes; the judge becomes a knave or a fool.

This epistemological gap is only fully overcome in the ideal, godlike subject of authority, envisioned by Bacon as James, whose transcendence and immanence affords it an impersonal omniscience on which to base its judgments. It is this godlike ideal that Overdo attempts to imitate in his effort to close the epistemological gap and reaffirm the boundary between judge and knave, nation and alien. Determined "to spare spy-money hereafter, and make mine own discoveries" (2.1.35–36), Overdo enters the Fair in "the habit of a fool" (2.1.8). He invokes a number of classical and contemporary precedents for his stratagem, but as Jackson Cope has pointed out, his ultimate model is God: while disguised he is the unseen but all-seeing *deus absconditus*, and when at the play's conclusion he reveals himself to "cloud-like . . . break out rain and hail, lightning and thunder, upon the head of enormity" (5.2.4–5), he has adopted the role of *deus ex machina* in the fullest sense of the phrase.[42]

Despite his best efforts, however, Overdo fails to solidify the boundaries he sets out to create. His failure is a direct consequence of his failure to be the ideal knowing subject of his colonial discourse, of his inability to control the process of knowledge production. Having judged the reports made by others about the Fair's enormities to be unreliable, Overdo naively depends upon his own judgment to discover the truth about the Fair; in doing so, however, he shows his judgment to be a greater source of error than those reports he hopes to correct. The play repeatedly exposes Overdo's epistemological limitations: time after time Overdo fails to recognize enormities and their perpetrators; his credulity matches his shortsightedness, and he willingly believes the tapster Mooncalf's misleading reports on the Fair's various denizens. A true Baconian, Overdo supplements his reasoning with method, but this only adds to Overdo's ignorance. Disguised as Arthur Bradley and settled in Ursula's booth, Overdo overhears the vapors between Ursula and newly entered Dan Knockem. Ursula accuses Knockem of "cutting halfpenny purses" (2.3.7) and Overdo notes "Another special enormity. A cutpurse of the sword!" (2.3.11). But Overdo is careful and questions Mooncalf the tapster about the veracity of Ursula's accusation. Mooncalf denies that Knockem is a cutpurse (he is, rather, "the ranger of Turnbull . . . a horse-courser" [2.3.29]) and explains Ursula's accusation away as a result of her unreliability as a source of information: "she'll do forty such things in an hour (an you listen to her) for her recreation" (2.3.31–32). Overdo accepts Mooncalf's statement and is pleased that his comparative method has provided him with the truth: "Here might I ha' been deceived now: and ha' put a fool's blot upon myself, if I had not played an after game o' discretion" (2.3.34–36). In this particular instance Overdo's game of discretion might have been successful (if he understood what Mooncalf meant by "horse-courser," which is not likely given that he later on fails to understand what Mooncalf implies when he says that Edgeworth has "a very quick hand" [2.4.30]). But Overdo's method is obviously deeply flawed: he checks the veracity of one report by another but has no means of checking the veracity of that report except by a third, and so on. Through the comparison of observations Overdo moves across the phenomenal surface of the enchanted glass rather than reducing and delivering it. Strangely enough, even though he has come to distrust the information of knavish intelligencers, he still trusts the stories of the denizens of the fair, the very people whose enormities he has come to investigate. In the end, Overdo's method merely amounts to believing the last report he hears.

Particularly significant for Overdo's course through the play is Mooncalf's description of the young cutpurse Ezekiel Edgeworth as a "civil young gentleman . . . that keeps company with the roarers, and disburses all still" (2.4.21–22). Overdo misses the double entendre of Mooncalf's descriptions and makes it his mission to rescue this civil young man from bad company and turn him into a "commonwealth's-man" (3.5.7). However, Overdo's rescue attempts—in one instance preaching to Edgeworth on the evils of ale, tobacco and bad company, in another attempting to watch over him from a distance like the disguised fathers or uncles of prodigal son plays—turn him into an unknowing accomplice in Edgeworth's purse-cutting activities, an enabling distraction in the first instance and a convenient scapegoat in the second. For his efforts Overdo is beaten, arrested, and placed in the stocks as a "rogue" (2.6.127), "the patriarch of the cut-purses" (2.6.134–35) and a "pernicious enormity" (3.5.197), a member of the underworld he set out to colonize.

Because of his fallibility, then, Overdo is unable to reconcile the contradictory imperatives of transcendence and immanence. In order to know, Overdo must participate in the world of the Fair, but because he cannot fully control the production of knowledge he cannot preserve the distance between himself and the Fair necessary to constitute himself as a representative of an imaginary community seeking to judge those it considers antithetical, alien. In fact, Overdo's disguised duke ploy splits him in two: into the absent presence Mad Arthur Bradley who wanders the Fair misrecognized and misrecognizing, and the present absence Justice Overdo, who for some reason has not shown up in court on this day but whose name is still potent enough to be hurled as a weapon, to be appropriated as an instrument, in a quarrel between the two booth-vendors Lantern Leatherhead and Joan Trash. Neither role by itself allows Overdo to close the epistemological gap and to secure his project, and a very Beckettian moment at the heart of the play dramatizes the impossibility of these roles' coincidence: in a nonencounter with himself, a disguised Overdo is taken from the stocks to the Court of Pie Powders to be sentenced—by Justice Overdo; because the officers cannot find Justice Overdo, Overdo is taken back to the stocks, there to remain until Overdo can be found to determine his fate. He does in fact escape and in the final scene makes one last attempt to combine the contradictory demands of the role he is attempting to play. With all the main characters on stage to watch the puppet play, Overdo abandons his disguise and proceeds, on the basis of the knowledge he has acquired through his disguise, to divide the characters morality-play-like into the sheep and the goats.[43] As Quarlous quietly informs him, however, one of the prostitutes he has placed among the goats is his own wife, the lamblike Edgeworth is a cutpurse, and he is "but Adam, flesh and blood" (5.6.89). Adam: father, king, masculine subject of authority whose flesh and blood bonds it to the dripping and flaming flesh of Ursula, "the first woman" (2.2.47) and the "womb and bed of enormity" (2.2.95), the unknown territory and grotesque body politic Adam has sought to know and conquer. In Overdo, the play has explored the contradictions and subversive possibilities created by the conflict between the colonial project's impossible epistemology and its material limits.

The gentry visiting the Fair contrast interestingly with the Puritans and Overdo. Neither Cokes nor Quarlous and Winwife enter the Fair with colonizing intentions. Cokes fully immerses himself in the Fair. As Cokes buys trinket after trinket, ultimately purchasing the entire stocks of the hobbyhorse vendor and the gingerbread seller, Wasp in a fit of exasperation exclaims "An' I were you, I'd buy for all my tenants, too, they are a kind o' civil savages, that will part with their children for rattles, pipes, and knives. You were best buy a hatchet or two, and truck with 'em" (3.4.28–31). As Jeffrey Knapp documents in *An Empire Nowhere*, it was a commonplace of English writing on the inhabitants of the New World that they were willing to trade things of substance—gold, humans, food—for trifles such as rattles, pipes, and knives,[44] but here the play reverses the commonplace. Wasp casts Cokes as a potential colonizer but the "civil savage" in this instance is Cokes himself. Cokes is thoroughly colonized by the Fair, trading all his money for, ultimately, nothing at all. Significantly, part of the trifles for which Cokes pays so dearly are physical monstrosities, domesticated exotica: "the Eagle, and the Black Wolf, and the Bull with five legs, and two pizzles" (5.4.75-76). The underworld trades on its status as the exotic to perform its own countercolonizing operations.

If Cokes fully immerses himself in the Fair, Quarlous and Winwife tend to aloofness. They go to the Fair as tourists, to observe "excellent creeping sport" (1.5.126). The sport of which the two are thinking, however, is not the sport provided by the Fair itself so much as the sport that the other fairgoers provide in their interactions with the Fair: they lament having missed seeing Cokes robbed, "the prologue o' the purse" (3.2.1) but they anticipate a full "five acts" (3.2.2) of such spectacle before night. Their perspective places the other fairgoers as exotica, indicating the Fair's power to confuse the distinctions between those who are visiting the Fair and those who are part of it, colonizer and colonized. Even Quarlous and Winwife are subject to this power. Their aloofness takes the form of aristocratic condescension, an attempt to separate themselves from others on the basis of the manners of their class rather than an explicit ideology of community. And they find themselves frequently asserting their aristocratic superiority in the face of their obvious familiarity and involvement with the Fair and the underworld generally. As soon as they enter the Fair they are recognized by one of the Fair's pimps, Jordan Knockem. Winwife pretends not to notice Knockem's greetings, but Quarlous confronts them with an assertion of distance: "you'll pardon us, if we knew not of such familiarity between us afore" (2.5.31–32). Quarlous and Winwife must repeat this strategy several times in the play, as they are recognized by underworld characters who assume that they have come to the Fair in search of "punk and . . . pig" (2.5.36–37). The two gallants, however, are able to cope with their proximity to the Fair in a way that the Puritans and Overdo are not. They do not enter the Fair in the name of any imaginary community seeking to contain a threatening alien presence: "we are no catchpoles nor constables" (3.5.229–30) they tell Edgeworth. They are there for themselves and find it profitable to exploit, not eliminate, the logic of their proximity. Quarlous especially treats his aristocratic manners as a performative marker of difference to be assumed or dropped as his private interest dictates. And his, and Winwife's, private interest throughout the play is marrying money. The rich heir Grace Wellborn, who is in the Fair as part of Cokes's party and has been betrothed to Cokes by Overdo, her ward and Cokes's uncle, is of particular interest to the two gallants, and when wooing her their manners are (nearly) impeccable and their choral comments on the activities of the other fairgoers particularly condescending. To obtain and doctor the marriage license by which Cokes's marriage to Grace has been made official, however, the two exploit their familiarity with the world of the Fair, catching out Edgeworth while he is cutting Cokes's purse, setting him the task of stealing the license from Wasp and disowning him once in possession of the license. The two gallants, like cutpurses or privateers, exploit the confusion created by the interaction of the colonizer and colonized in the space of the Fair, having no real allegiance to any imaginary community but only to their own private good.

Bartholomew Fair is a heterocosm, a site that resists charting and appropriation by any imaginary community. New World, Old World, underworld, the commonwealth and the Kingdom of the Saints here collide in the production and dissolution of boundaries between communities and their others. What holds the fair together is an economy of exchange. The booth-vendors pay the authorities for the right to set up their booths in the fair. In return, the booth-vendors sell to all comers, authorities included, the trifles, the flesh, the ballads, the bull with the two pizzles, the representations of otherness that they desire. The king's stamped face endlessly circulates in this economy and knows no frontiers, traversing and blurring the borders established in its or any other name. The play *Bartholomew Fair* is a part of this economy, trading on theatergoers' well-established habit of paying to see representations of exotic, alien places while remaining firmly at home. The play, though, unsettles this tradition by providing its audience with a representation of home that troubles the very processes by which home and abroad, nation and alien, are constructed.

This brings us back to the status of Jonson's art. Throughout this study I have argued that Jonson's dramatic skepticism is Pyrrhonian, turning in on its own foundations, and this is the case in *Bartholomew Fair* no less than in *Volpone* or *The Alchemist*. Earlier in this chapter I suggested that Jonson travesties the authority of high art, reducing it to the level of Leatherhead's puppet play. In *The Place of the Stage*, Steven Mullaney argues that the Elizabethan and Jacobean stage bore a number of resemblances to popular festivities and pastimes, in its location, in the ambiguous social status of its practitioners, and not least in the negative moral effects attributed to it by its opponents. Jonson wryly acknowledges the kinship in his comment that "the Author hath observed a special decorum, the place [the Hope, which doubled as a bear-baiting arena] being as dirty as Smithfield, and stinking every whit" (Induction 139–40). Barish concludes that the play abandons all search for criteria of aesthetic value in order to defend the theater in whatever form, at whatever level, from its opponents: "Jonson

... having waged the war of the theaters at the turn of the century, and having spent fifteen years denouncing popular taste and the usual fare of the public playhouses, now closes ranks with them to present a united front against the enemies of all the theaters."[45] But, I would argue, the play's skepticism about the source of artistic authority is not so simple. Jonson's claim to please "the understanding gentlemen o' the ground" (Induction 43)—"if the puppets will please anybody, they shall be entreated to come in" (Induction 117–18)—is part of the Induction's mockery of popular taste as well as, if not more than, an expression of resignation in the face of its demands. If Jonson is defending popular art in *Bartholomew Fair*, he as one of the "Master-Poets" (Induction 23) is defending something for which he has little respect and against which he repeatedly struggled in order to fashion his own dramaturgy. Bristol argues that "The theater in its 'mature' or 'developed' form is an institution 'invented' by Jonson and by many others to oppose and displace a theater already practiced and appreciated throughout plebeian culture."[46] Jonsonian theater is the theater of the text, not the improvisatory theater of popular culture.[47] Despite its chaotic surface, *Bartholomew Fair* is no exception. Keith Sturgess's analysis of the play's staging outlines the extent to which the performance is pre-scripted, from the actual identities and physical appearances of the actors down to the details of costuming: "The actors of the play are given little autonomy, small opportunity to interpret their roles, and the language they are given is precise verbal costuming."[48] Even the improvisation of the induction is a scripted illusion. Yet the authority of the text is also burlesqued: the first mention of the "Master Poet" places him in a farcical minidrama, kicking the stage-keeper around the tiring-house.

If not in the understanding gentlemen of the ground or in the text, then where does the play locate the source of artistic legitimation? Sturgess suggests James as "final arbiter."[49] Indeed, in *The Essayes of a Prentise* James figures himself as a source of poetic as well as political authority. Jonson in *Epigram* IV, "To King James," seconds James's pretensions:

> How, best of kings, dost thou a sceptre bear!
> How, best of poets, dost thou laurel wear!
> But two things, rare, the Fates had in their store,
> And gave thee both, to show they could no more.
> For such a poet, while thy days were green,
> Thou wert, as chief of them are said t'have been.
> And such a prince thou art, we daily see,
> As chief of those still promise they will be.
> Whom should my muse then fly to, but the best
> Of kings for grace; of poets for my test?[50]

The prologue and epilogue to the play's performance at court the day after its first performance at the Hope seem to echo these sentiments, as Sturgess argues. Sturgess, however, makes a revealing assumption: he argues that the prologue's first line—"Your Majesty is welcome to a Fair"—is an alienating device because "in life such demotic pursuits as fair-going would be anathema to the upper class."[51] While it may be true that James would never wander into Smithfield during the Fair, it is also true that by 1614 his green days and tastes were long past, leaving him with artistic preferences that, as Jonson knew from his masque-writing experiences, were not all that Jonson might desire in a poet-monarch. James enjoyed hunting and bearbaiting as much as he enjoyed plays; the moralizing—what Jonson called the "spirit"—of masques bored James as much as their "carcasses," their dancing and spectacle, delighted him.[52]

Consequently, offering James "sport" (Prologue 8) and "a fairing" (12) is a deeply ironic comment on James' supposed status as arbiter of artistic value. In an attempt to locate artistic authority, Jonson's epilogue plays on the two senses of "licence"—royal approval and licentiousness:

> Your Majesty hath seen the play, and you
>   can best allow it from your ear, and view.
> You know the scope of writers, and what store
>   of leave is given them, if they take not more,
> And turn it into licence: you can tell
>   if we have used that leave you gave us well:
> Or whether we to rage, or licence break.
>
> (1–7)

Susan Wells in "Jacobean City Comedy and the Ideology of the City" concludes that these lines firmly establish James as a source of artistic authority: "The king's presence and implied permission is an assurance that the liberties taken in the play have been placed within a limited context.... Royal permission licences licence."[53] Yet, given James's tastes, the punning is equivocal: all that distinguishes between the two senses of licence is royal power. James determines aesthetic value in much the same way the avocatori in *Volpone* determine the truth. Jonathan Goldberg writes: "The king's retired mysteries clothe royal pleasures; beneath his assertions of the inscrutability of the royal will are secret desires and delights. The arcana provide a rhetoric of virtue—and virtue is power—a rhetoric of power that covers the secret pleasures and shrouds the body in the image of the state."[54] But the body and its pleasures are precisely what the play insistently thrusts into the view of even the royal beholder. Like justice, religion, and education, then, the play provides art with no uncontested source of authority.

Only its commercial nature can be affirmed with any certainty: the play, like the festivity it represents, is articulated in a process of exchange between those who pay for the images they desire and those who supply those images, between sharpers and gulls.

Conclusion

The theater stages a potentially skeptical space, on its boards materializing a world of creative nonbeing. This paradox of performance, with its troubling social and philosophical implications, generates the skeptical dynamics of the seven plays on which this study has focused. Jonson and Middleton forcefully rework the world as stage equation into a paradigm of cultural analysis that proceeds from the perspective not of God but the actor, positing a reality dizzying in its ontological groundlessness. Not heaven but the theater—embedded in material relations, ludic, illusory, and ephemeral—is these two playwrights' ultimate reference point. To theatricality are linked other concepts—appearance, power, knowledge, exchange—whose shifting configurations extend the space of skeptical suspension into the urban reality of which Jonson and Middleton were so much a part. For the two playwrights, London (or in *Volpone*'s case, Venice) is a theater; conversely, theater is a marketplace, "your poets' Royal Exchange."[1] Their plays trace the complex entanglements of theater and exchange—the theatricality of exchange, the transactional nature of all performance—in the production and reproduction of a variety of cultural scripts, ways of making sense of the world that are never fully present or entirely adequate.

The problematic relationship between theatricality and exchange emerges as a central aesthetic problem, especially for Jonson, and around this problem the differences between Jonson and Middleton can be most clearly seen. Like Jonson's plays, *Michaelmas Term*, *A Trick to Catch the Old One*, and *A Chaste Maid in Cheapside* dramatize social existence as a process of theatrical exchange. *Michaelmas Term* is concerned with the troubling ideological consequences of this process as a process of corrosive commodification within capitalist London's economy of accumulation and consumption. Similarly, *A Trick to Catch the Old One* examines the peculiar emptiness of moral social dramas, specifically the conventions and roles of the prodigal play, when reproduced as positions in the anarchic game of cut-throat economic competition. *A Chaste Maid in Cheapside* deploys its skeptical comic energies to dramatize the improvisational and paradoxical reproduction of patriarchal sociosymbolic structures, its ending suspending the law of noncontradiction to stage a spectacularly theatrical tragicomic resolution to an otherwise insoluble patriarchal dilemma. But although these three plays are fraught with philosophical and aesthetic implications, Middleton's skeptical focus remains primarily social. Jonson's plays, however, treat more fully and explicitly the philosophical and aesthetic dimensions of the intersections of theater and exchange.

Each of the four Jonson comedies I have discussed creates spaces of illusion embedded in various relations of exchange and explores the epistemological malleability of the material mind within these spaces, only to find that any "real" in comparison with which illusion might be dismissed as distortion remains beyond its grasp. The avocatori, Dauphine and his two companions, Lovewit and Overdo all succumb to the problems of knowledge they claim to be outside of and capable of judging. And more forcefully than Middleton's, Jonson's skepticism is self-consuming. Most powerfully in *Volpone* and *The Alchemist*, the problem of theater and exchange turns in on Jonson's own art. In *Volpone* Jonson's comic project of imitating justice undergoes a double deformation: the just self and society can be realized only as parodic performances constrained by power; the art by which the imitation of justice is revealed to be inevitably dystopian is itself, by its very nature as commercial theater, as an exchange of appearances for other tokens of exchange, caught in the dystopian economy it would reject. In *The Alchemist* skepticism itself is Jonson's commodity. The play's tightly unified classical poetics enables the debunking of alchemy, apocalypse, and the popular narrative structures of the cultural imagination only at the expense of its own epistemological insecurity. The play— perversely, self-reflexively— reveals its "mirror-of-nature" comic poetics to be merely one more commodity up for sale in a house in Blackfriars.

Of course, the comic skepticism of these seven plays marks only a phase in these two playwrights' dramatic careers. Middleton moved on to write Fletcherian tragicomedies and tragedies that anticipate Ford in their unflinching representations of psychological and moral disintegration within the framework of implacable and unattainable moral law. Jonson, on the other hand, moved away from cynicism to the idealism of the masque (he had, of course, been writing masques for some time) and the romantic tone that characterizes *The New Inn* and the uncompleted *The Sad Shepherd*. Significantly, this shift can be detected in Jonson's last city comedy, *The Devil Is An Ass* (1616), which for all its metadramatic mockery of morality plays and their simplistic binary constructions of virtue and vice ends by subordinating deceit and appetite to chastity and idealized courtly love. The two playwrights, like all Pyrrhonists perhaps, could not maintain their detached, ironic pose indefinitely. Nonetheless, as I have argued throughout this study, the products of the two playwrights' suspensions of judgment also demonstrate an intense engagement with the realities they stage. These city comedies are indeed fictions of unsettlement.

Notes

INTRODUCTION: THEATER'S JANUS FACE

1. Thomas Browne, *Religio Medici*, in *The Major Works* (Harmondsworth, England: Penguin, 1977), 148.
2. A. A. Long, *Hellenistic Philosophy: Stoics, Epicureans, Sceptics* (London: Duckworth, 1974).
3. Sextus Empiricus, *Outlines of Pyrrhonism*, trans R. G. Bury (Cambridge: Harvard University Press, 1933), 7.
4. Richard Popkin, *The History of Skepticism from Erasmus to Spinoza* (Berkeley: University of California Press); see also Victoria Kahn, *Rhetoric, Prudence and Skepticism in the Renaissance* (Ithaca: Cornell University Press, 1985).
5. Michel Montaigne, *Apology for Raymond Sebond*, in *The Complete Essays*, trans. Donald Frame (Stanford, Calif.: Stanford University Press, 1958), 419.
6. René Descartes, *Meditations*, in *Discourse on Method and the Meditations*, trans. F. E. Sutcliffe (Harmondsworth, England: Penguin, 1968), 96.
7. Ibid.
8. Ludwig Wittgenstein, *Philosophical Investigations*, trans. G. E. M. Anscombe (Oxford: Blackwell, 1963), 61.
9. J. L. Austin, *How to Do Things with Words* (Cambridge: Harvard University Press, 1962), 22.
10. Francis Bacon, *The New Organon*, ed. Fulton Anderson (Englewood Cliffs, N.J.: Prentice-Hall, 1960), 49.
11. Steven Mullaney, *The Place of the Stage: License, Play and Power in Renaissance England* (Chicago: University of Chicago Press, 1988).
12. Jonas Barish, *The Antitheatrical Prejudice* (Berkeley: University of California Press, 1981).
13. Norbert Elias, *The Civilizing Process*, trans. E. Jephcott (Oxford: Blackwell, 1994).
14. Niccolo Machiavelli, *The Discourses*, in *The Prince and The Discourses*, trans. L. Ricci and C. Detmond (New York: Random House, 1940).
15. See Robert Brenner, "Agrarian Class Structure and Economic Development in Pre-Industrial Europe," *Past and Present* 97 (1982).
16. See Christopher Hill, *Reformation to Industrial Revolution: A Social and Economic History of Britain, 1530–1780* (London: Weidenfeld and Nicolson, 1967); A. L. Beier and R. Findlay eds, *The Making of the Metropolis: London, 1500–1700* (London: Longman, 1986).
17. Joyce Appleby, *Economic Thought and Ideology in Seventeenth-Century England* (Princeton: Princeton University Press, 1978).

18. L. C. Knights, *Drama and Society in the Age of Jonson* (New York: Stewart, 1936), 202.

19. Alexander Leggatt, *Citizen Comedy in the Age of Shakespeare* (Toronto: University of Toronto Press, 1973), 150.

20. Brian Gibbons, *Jacobean City Comedy*, 2d ed. (London: Methuen, 1980).

21. Douglas Bruster, *Drama and the Market in the Age of Shakespeare* (Cambridge: Cambridge University Press, 1992), 3.

22. Don Wayne, "*Drama and Society in the Age of Jonson:* An Alternative View," *Renaissance Drama*, n.s., 13 (1982): 106.

23. Jean-Christophe Agnew, *Worlds Apart: The Market and the Theater in Anglo-American Thought, 1550–1750* (Cambridge: Cambridge University Press, 1986), 11.

24. Gail Kern Paster, *The Idea of the City in the Age of Shakespeare* (Athens: University of Georgia Press, 1985), 3.

25. Lawrence Manley, *Literature and Culture in Early Modern England* (Cambridge: Cambridge University Press, 1995), 127.

Chapter 1: *Volpone* and the Dystopian Turn of Utopian Discourse

1. R. C. Elliot argues that utopian literature is inevitably critical: "even without overt attack on contemporary society, utopia necessarily wears a Janus-face. The portrayal of an ideal commonwealth has a double function: it establishes a standard, a goal; and by virtue of its existence alone it casts a critical light on society as presently constituted" (*The Shape of Utopia: Studies in a Literary Genre* [Chicago: University of Chicago Press, 1970], 22). Not surprisingly, the social theories of radical Christian sects and Marxists have significant utopian elements. For the connection between utopian ideas and radical Christianity in the Middle Ages, see Norman Cohn's *The Pursuit of the Millennium*. In *The World Turned Upside-Down*, Christopher Hill discusses this connection in relation to the radical social thought that flourished in England between 1640 and 1660. Herbert Marcuse in *The Aesthetic Dimension* places the utopian impulse at the center of his Marxist aesthetics. In *Marxism and Form* Frederic Jameson argues the importance of the utopian element in the thought of such key twentieth-century Marxists as Benjamin and Bloc, and in *The Political Unconscious* it plays a central role in Jameson's own dialectical hermeneutics, in which "a Marxist negative hermeneutic, a Marxist practice of ideological analysis proper, must in the practical work of reading and interpretation be exercised *simultaneously* with a Marxist positive hermeneutic, or a decipherment of the Utopian impulses of these same still ideological cultural texts" (*The Political Unconscious: Narrative as a Socially Symbolic Act* [Ithaca: Cornell University Press, 1981], 296). Indeed, the post-Marxist Left's greatest difficulty has been finding a unifying platform of critique to replace old and no longer tenable Marxist utopian visions. As Laclau and Mouffe put it, "What is now in crisis is a whole conception of socialism which rests upon the ontological centrality of the working class, upon the role of Revolution, with a capital 'r', as the founding moment in the transition from one type of society to another, and upon the illusory prospect of a perfectly unitary and homogeneous collective will that will render pointless the moment of politics" (*Hegemony and Socialist Strategy: Towards a Radical Democratic Politics* [London: Verso, 1985], 2).

2. Douglas Bruster in *Drama and the Market* argues that the inclusion of plays such as *Volpone*, which is set in Venice not London, in the category of city comedy renders it

meaningless. Bruster's Aristotelian genus-species model of definition, however, seems unduly restrictive. City comedy, and *Volpone*'s place within the genre, can more usefully be considered in the Wittgensteinian terms of family resemblances. Ralph Cohen argues that, although "the Venice of *Volpone* does not grow transparent and reveal, as the play progresses, a thinly disguised London beneath an Italian setting" ("The Setting of *Volpone*," *Renaissance Papers,* 1978, 66), Venice does embody the type of urban and commercial reality at the heart of Jonson's London city comedies. Other critics have noted that London may have been on Jonson's mind in more specific ways. Robert Evans argues that Volpone is modeled on and in ways recognizable to a Jacobean audience alludes to Thomas Sutton, Jacobean England's richest commoner. Richard Dutton sees both Nano and Sir Pol as satiric allusions to Robert Cecil.

3. Plato, *The Republic*, trans. Desmond Lee, 2d ed. (Harmondsworth, England: Penguin, 1974), 297–98; all subsequent citations are to this edition.

4. Ben Jonson, dedication to *Volpone*, in vol. 3 of *The Complete Plays of Ben Jonson*, ed. G. A. Wilkes (Oxford: Clarendon, 1982), line 112; all subsequent citations are to this edition.

5. William Shakespeare, *The Comedy of Errors*, ed. Stanley Wells (Harmondsworth, England: Penguin, 1972), 1.2.97–101.

6. Ibid., 5.1.398.

7. Michel Montaigne, "Of the power of the imagination," in *The Complete Essays*, trans. Donald Frame (Stanford, Calif.: Stanford University Press, 1958), 68.

8. Alexander Lyle, "Volpone's Two Worlds," *Yearbook of English Studies* 4 (1974): 72.

9. David McPherson in *Shakespeare, Jonson, and the Myth of Venice* (London: University of Delaware Press, 1990) makes the comparison between Volpone's shrine and Saint Mark's treasury.

10. Hesiod, *Works and Days*, in *Hesiod and Theognis*, trans. Dorothea Wender (Harmondsworth, England: Penguin, 1973), 109, 112.

11. Alexander Leggatt, *Ben Jonson: His Vision and His Art* (London: Methuen, 1981), 2.

12. In *Beyond the Pleasure Principle*, Freud divides instincts into Thanatos and Eros, those that seek to return the organism to its initial inanimate and dead state and those that are life-preserving, sexual. Freud comments that "For a long time, perhaps, living substance was thus being constantly created afresh and easily dying, till decisive external influences altered in such a way as to oblige the still living substance to diverge ever more widely from its original course of life and make ever more complicated *detours* before reaching its aim of death" (*Beyond the Pleasure Principle*, in *On Metapsychology: The Theory of Psychoanalysis*, trans. J. Strachey [London: Penguin, 1984], 311). Freud later claims that Eros cannot be reduced to Thanatos, but to make such a claim he must suppress the strange interrelationship between the two, in which Eros can be seen, as Derrida comments, as simply the frisson of death's detour, as "expenditure without reserve, as the irreparable loss of presence, the irreversible usage of energy, that is, as the death instinct, and as the entirely other relationship that apparently interrupts every economy" ("*Différance*," in *Margins of Philosophy*, trans. A. Bass [Chicago: University of Chicago Press, 1982], 19). Marx notes a similar disruption in the logic of economic exchange: "If circulation is looked at not as a constant alternation, but as a series of circular motions which it describes within itself, then this circular path appears as a double one: Commodity-Money-Money-Commodity; and in the other direction Money-Commodity-Commodity-Money. . . . The circle Money-Commodity-Commodity-Money, which we then drew from the analysis of circulation, would then appear to be merely an arbitrary and senseless abstraction, roughly as if

one wanted to describe the life cycle as Death-Life-Death" (*Grundrisse*, trans. M. Nicolaus [London: Penguin, 1973], 202). Jonson does not question the senselessness of the economic and sexual logic defined in terms of Money-Commodity-Money and Death-Life-Death; he does, with Derrida, question the essentialism—of Eros, of the commodity—by which Freud and Marx seek to contain these logics' disruptiveness.

13. Plato, *The Republic*, 218.

14. Thomas Greene, "Ben Jonson and the Centred Self," *Studies in English Literature* 10 (1970): 329.

15. Ibid., 337.

16. In his *Discourse on Method* Descartes's radical skepticism leads him to conclude that he is "a substance, of which the whole essence or nature consists in thinking, and which, in order to exist, needs no place and depends on no material thing: so that this 'I', that is to say, the mind, by which I am what I am, is entirely distinct from the body, and that it is easier to know than the body, and, moreover, that even if the body were not, it would not cease to be all that it is" (René Descartes, *Discourse on Method*, in *Discourse on Method and the Meditations*, trans F. E. Sutcliffe [Harmondsworth: Penguin, 1968], 54.)

17. Francis Barker, *The Tremulous Private Body: Essays on Subjection*, 2nd ed. (Ann Arbor: University of Michigan Press), 58–59.

18. In *The Tremulous Private Body*, Barker reads for historical difference and so finds attempts to locate the Cartesian subject and body in pre-Cartesian and prebourgeois Jacobean theater problematic. While the warning against anachronistic and unreflexive interpretations of the subjectivity staged in Jacobean drama is salutary, Barker both ignores the work of such critics as Catherine Belsey, the thesis of whose *Subject of Tragedy* is that Jacobean theater was the site of the fashioning of a unified, gendered interiority, and overstates Descartes significance and originality as the founding moment of a new "dispensation." Two useful correctives to Barker are Katharine Eisaman Maus's *Inwardness and Theater in the English Renaissance* (Chicago: University of Chicago Press, 1995) and Jonathan Sawday's *The Body Emblazoned: Dissection and the Human Body in Renaissance Culture* (London: Routledge, 1995.)

19. Harold Skulsky, "Cannibals vs. Demons in *Volpone*," *Studies in English Literature* 29, no. 2 (1989): 291–308.

20. Stephen Greenblatt, "The False Ending in *Volpone*," *Journal of English and Germanic Philology* 75 (1976): 101.

21. According to Plato, individual "justice consists in minding your own business and not interfering with other people" (*Republic* 204); justice in the state is analogous to individual justice: "when each of our three classes (businessmen, Auxilliaries, and Guardians) does its own job and minds its own business, that . . . is justice and makes our state just" (206). Plato banishes actors, poets, and Sophists from his republic because they undermine justice, undermine the unity of the self, by encouraging the imitation of other constructions of the self and the indulgence of passions, which should be under reason's control.

22. Jonas Barish, "Feasting and Judging in Jonsonian Comedy," *Renaissance Drama*, n.s., 5 (1972): 20.

23. Krishan Kumar, *Utopia and Anti-Utopia in Modern Times* (Oxford: Blackwell, 1987), 99, 102.

24. Jeffrey Knapp argues that *Utopia* is vexed at the level of literary representation by the paradoxicality embodied in Hythloday: "The unworldly (literary) product of an otherworld (England) that self-reflexively takes an otherworld (Utopia) as its subject, *Utopia*, to More's mind, sublimely mocks the worldly standards that would condemn it, but by the same token acknowledges its sequestration from the world's positive life" (*An Empire Nowhere: England, America, and Literature from Utopia to The Tempest* [Berkeley: University of Cali-

fornia Press, 1992], 53). As I will argue, *The Republic* and *Volpone* are also deeply perplexed by the paradoxes involved in representing utopia.

25. Michel Foucault, *Power/ Knowledge*, ed. Colin Gordon (New York: Pantheon, 1980), 133.

26. Robert N. Watson, *Ben Jonson's Parodic Strategies: Literary Imperialism in the Comedies* (Cambridge: Harvard University Press, 1987), 90.

27. Charles Hallett presents this thesis in "Jonson's Celia: A Reinterpretation of *Volpone*," *Studies in Philology* 68 (1971).

28. In his fine and complex article, Ronald Broude outlines the moral theme and basic plot structure of the Triumph of Truth tradition, established first in morality plays, taken over by revenge tragedy in the 1580s, and extending into comedy by the accession of James. The moral theme is homiletic: divine providence has ordained that even the most secret crime will be uncovered, either by the errors created by the criminal's overreaching cunning or by the direct intervention of providence. The plot structure elaborates the theme. As Broude notes, however, not all plays that reproduce this tradition's conventions unambiguously endorse its moral: "[I]n plays which, like *The Jew of Malta*, may reflect skepticism regarding the officially sanctioned view of Divine Providence, recognition of the possibility of reading events as providentially arranged is a necessary precondition for the appreciation of whatever irony may be present" ("Volpone and the Triumph of Truth: Some Antecedents and Analogues to the Main Plot in *Volpone*," *Studies in Philology* 77 [1980]: 238). Broude observes a similar ambiguity in *Volpone* but is inclined to see the play as a relatively straightforward instance of Triumph of Truth drama, largely because he considers Volpone's unmasking to be unproblematic: Volpone unmasks, and "with the true state of affairs at last revealed, the court must willy-nilly right the wrongs which have been done and pass sentences which affirm the justice on which society must be based" (244). While I agree with Broude that *Volpone* reproduces Triumph of Truth conventions, I argue that it does so far less straightforwardly than Broude allows, foregrounding through its lengthy court scenes and multiple versions of the same event both the need to find truth in order to act justly and the impossibility of finding truth in the avocatori's dystopian world. Even if the avocatori could with certainty recognize an undisguised Volpone, knowledge of the "true state of affairs" does not follow from this mere fact; but, as I have argued, the avocatori have no way of certainly knowing the identity of the disrobing commandadore.

29. This is, of course, to some extent a matter of degree. In Marlowe's *The Jew of Malta*, the truth of Barabas's villainy is unmistakable simply because it backfires: only because he has been preparing a trap for his enemies can he be caught in it himself. In Marlowe's play the irony turns on the moral hypocrisy of those who pronounce judgment on Barabas, not their epistemological limitations. In Kyd's *The Spanish Tragedy*, Hieronimo has room to doubt the letter from Bel-Imperia outlining the circumstances of Horatio's death, and initially he does. He determines to test the letter's truth and evidence such as Pedringano's letter—which comes into Hieronimo's possession accidentally but is nonetheless unmistakable in its import—confirms it. From the time Hieronimo reads Bel-Imperia's letter, he observes only details that work to confirm her account; no alternative account is presented to complicate the matter. Unlike *The Jew of Malta* or *The Spanish Tragedy*, *Volpone* foregrounds the question of truth, and the avocatori's epistemological limitations far more than their moral faults generate the irony of the play's ending. For *Volpone*, truth is not simply the byproduct of or an unproblematic bridge to justice but justice's essential, and unavailable, precondition (perhaps, in relation to *The Spanish Tragedy*, because Jonson is concerned with public justice, not revenge.)

30. Ben Jonson, *Discoveries*, in *The Complete Poems*, ed. George Parfitt (London: Penguin, 1988), line 1277.

CHAPTER 2: "[B]EGOT BETWEEN TIREWOMEN AND TAILORS":
COMMODIFIED SELF-FASHIONING IN *MICHAELMAS TERM*

1. Paul Yachnin, "Social Competition in Middleton's *Michaelmas Term*," *Explorations in Renaissance Culture* 13 (1987): 87.

2. Lawrence Stone's work on social mobility in early modern England is still valuable. See his *The Crisis of the Aristocracy, 1558–1641* (Oxford: Clarendon, 1965) and "Social Mobility in England, 1500–1700," *Past and Present* 33 (1966). Although recent historians have contested aspects of Stone's arguments, Stone's thesis that the early modern period in England was a time of great social mobility remains generally accepted. Barry Coward states that "Though there are serious disagreements among historians about the changes that were taking place in English society and in the varying fortunes of different social groups before 1650, no one challenges the view that inflationary and demographic pressures made the period one of great social mobility" (*The Stuart Age: England, 1603–1714*, 2d ed. [London: Longman, 1994], 62).

3. In this short historical summary I have attempted to do no more than sketch widely agreed-upon outlines of certain economic changes occurring in the period. C. G. A. Clay's two-volume *Economic Expansion and Social Change: England, 1500–1700* (Cambridge: Cambridge University Press, 1984) treats these economic changes and their social implications in detail. The articles in *The Making of the Metropolis: London, 1500–1700*, edited by A. L. Beier and R. Findlay (London: Longman, 1986), document the role of the nation's capital in these changes. Dietz's article, "Overseas trade and metropolitan growth," and Beier's article, "Engine of manufacture: the trades of London," were particularly helpful. Joan Thirsk discusses the development of a national domestic economy in *Economic Policy and Projects: The Development of a Consumer Society in Early Modern England* (Oxford: Clarendon, 1978). In the second chapter of his *The City of London in International Politics at the Accession of Elizabeth Tudor* (Manchester: Manchester University Press, 1975), G. D. Ramsay outlines the strain that wealthy members of the Merchant Adventurers placed on the guild structure. This is pursued further in I. W. Archer's *The Pursuit of Stability: Social Relations in Elizabethan London* (Cambridge: Cambridge University Press, 1991) and Robert Ashton's *The City and the Court, 1603–1642* (Cambridge: Cambridge University Press, 1979). Joyce Appleby's *Economic Thought and Ideology in Seventeenth-Century England* (Princeton: Princeton University Press, 1978) documents the difficulties that commonwealth ideology, which subordinated the economic to the moral and sought to preserve the divinely sanctioned status quo, had in dealing with these economic changes.

4. See Richard Grassby's "The Personal Wealth of the Business Community in Seventeenth-Century England," *Economic History Review* 23, no. 2 (1970).

5. Stone argues that "merchants were a mobile group of transients, very many of whom moved into and out of the group in a single lifetime, and nearly all in two generations: as a contemporary put it at the time, merchants 'do attain to great wealth and riches, which for the most part they employ in purchasing land and little by little they do creep and seek to be gentlemen.'" ("Social Mobility," 19). R. G. Lang argues that this is both an exaggeration and something of a misunderstanding of why merchants purchased land: "Few of the merchants best furnished with land and wealth to enter the gentry manifested a desire to do so, of by entering the gentry we mean, in part, a retirement to the country and a withdrawal from civic life. The great merchants did not retire to the country; neither did they dissociate themselves from city affairs" ("Social Origins and Social Aspirations of Jacobean London Merchants," *Economic History Review* 27, no. 1 [1974]: 46–47). But granted that urban merchants did not want to adopt the lifestyle of the traditional country

gentleman, the possession of land was still a marker of status. Furthermore, gentry lifestyles were changing: country gentleman were urbanizing their lifestyles, buying large houses in the city and remaining there for extended periods of time.

6. See Stone's *The Crisis of the Aristocracy, 1558–1641*, particularly chapter 3, "The Inflation of Honours." Stone states that "With the failure of the Great Contract in 1610 and the abrupt dissolution of the Addled Parliament in 1614, the Crown had lost hope of parliamentary supplies and was trying to manage without them. The pressure to use the sale of titles as rewards for the hungry Villiers family, as compensation for the outgoing politicians, and as a means to raise ready cash was therefore almost irresistible" (103–4).

7. See Robert Brenner's article "Agrarian Class Structure and Economic Development in Pre-Industrial Europe," *Past and Present* 97 (1982) for an in-depth analysis of the development of agrarian capitalism in early modern England.

8. See Paul Slack's *Poverty and Policy in Tudor and Stuart England* (London: Longman, 1988) for a thorough treatment of poverty and the social dislocations it created, and state attempts to contain the problem.

9. Thomas Harman, *A Caveat for Common Cursitors Vulgarly Called Vagabonds*, in *Rogues, Vagabonds and Sturdy Beggars*, ed. Arthur Kinney (Amherst: University of Massachusetts Press, 1990).

10. Slack, *Poverty and Policy*, 118.

11. This body of Elizabethan literature, which includes Deloney's novels and Dekker's plays, is the focus of L. C. Stevenson's *Praise and Paradox: Merchants and Craftsmen in Elizabethan Popular Literature* (Cambridge: Cambridge University Press, 1984). Stevenson's thesis is that, while the new visibility of London's merchant elite drew writers to attempt to find positive places for them in the commonwealth, these writers were not able to articulate a distinctly middle-class consciousness and value system. Rather, "Elizabethan praise of bourgeois men was expressed in the rhetoric—and by extension, in terms of the social paradigms—of the aristocracy" (6).

12. Ruth Kelso in *The Doctrine of the English Gentleman in the Sixteenth Century* (1929; reprint, Gloucester, Mass.: Peter Smith, 1964) charts these developments. She notes that "when war ceased to be the gentleman's chief profession, and he was challenged to help solve the complicated problems of an increasingly complicated world, something more [than military prowess] was needed, and thoughtful men were not slow to point the need, and to warn of the results of the current scorn for learning among the nobility. Higher public affairs would suffer, or their management would pass out of the hands of the old nobility into the hands of men of low origin" (116). Even so, "blurred as class lines became during the sixteenth century, and new as many of England's prominent families were, the idea that *gentility* meant fundamentally gentle birth was never lost" (20).

13. See F. J. Fisher's "The Development of London as a Centre of Conspicuous Consumption in the Sixteenth and Seventeenth Centuries," *Transactions of the Royal Historical Society,* 4th ser., 30 (1948).

14. In *Vagrant Writing: Social and Semiotic Disorder in the English Renaissance* (Toronto: University of Toronto Press, 1991) Barry Taylor discusses the social mobility of the vagrant in terms of a crisis in social perception: "The undoing of the fundamental category distinction between the true and the feigned produces a crisis of thinking, a disjunction between the world's appearance and the established categorical system through which the subject orders it into perceptual coherence, and into meaning. The disguising of the vagrant tips the world towards illegibility" (3).

15. Philip Stubbes, *Anatomie of Abuses* (1583; reprint, New York: Garland, 1973), B5v.

16. Ibid., C3r.

17. Lawrence Stone, *The Crisis of the Aristocracy, 1558–1641* (Oxford: Clarendon, 1965), 29.

18. Theodore Leinwand, *The City Staged: Jacobean City Comedy, 1603–1613* (Madison: University of Wisconsin Press, 1986), 19.

19. Thomas Smith, *De Republica Anglorum* (1583; reprint, New York: Da Capo Press, 1970), 27.

20. Stone, *Crisis*, 36.

21. Francis Bacon, "Of Nobility," reprinted in *Francis Bacon: A Selection of His Works*, ed. Sidney Warhaft (Toronto: Macmillan, 1965), 78.

22. Thomas Middleton, induction to *Michaelmas Term*, in *A Mad World, My Masters and Other Plays*, ed. Michael Taylor (Oxford: Oxford University Press, 1995), 32–35.

23. "Does my boy pick and I steal to enrich myself, to keep her, to maintain him? Why, this is right the sequence of the world. So in like manner the pocket keeps my boy, I keep her, she keeps him; it runs like quicksilver from one to another" (*Your Five Gallants* 3.2.100–107), the thief Pursenet exclaims after robbing another courtier of the purse he himself had given to his mistress. The band of thieves in *The Widow* sings roughly the same tune, "How round the world goes, and everything that's in it! / The tides of gold and ebb and flow in a minute" (3.1.110–11).

24. George Rowe, "Prodigal Sons, New Comedy, and Middleton's *Michaelmas Term*," *English Literary Renaissance* 7 (1977): 101.

25. Swapan Chakravorty, *Society and Politics in the Plays of Thomas Middleton* (Oxford: Clarendon, 1996), 46.

26. Thomas Middleton, *The Phoenix*, in vol. 1 of *The Works of Middleton*, ed. A. H. Bullen (1885; reprint, New York: AMS Press, 1964), 1.5.12, 13.

27. Thomas Middleton, *A Chaste Maid in Cheapside*, in *Thomas Middleton: Five Plays*, ed. Bryan Loughrey and Neil Taylor (London: Penguin, 1988), 2.1.59; all subsequent citations are to this edition.

28. C. L. Barber, *Shakespeare's Festive Comedy* (Princeton: Princeton University Press, 1959), 4.

29. Gail Kern Paster, "Quomodo, Sir Giles, and Triangular Desire: Social Aspiration in Middleton and Massinger," in *Comedy from Shakespeare to Sheridan*, ed. A. A. Braunmuller and J. C. Bulman (Toronto: Associated University Presses, 1986), 170.

30. Ibid., 168.

31. William Slights, "Unfashioning the Man of Mode: A Comic Countergenre in Marston, Jonson, and Middleton," *Renaissance Drama*, n.s., 15 (1984): 97.

32. Smith, *De Republica Anglorum*, 26.

33. Ibid., 28.

34. Ibid., 21–22.

35. Ibid., 22.

36. These details are taken from chapter 3, "The Inflation of Honours," of Stone's *The Crisis of the Aristocracy*.

37. Douglas Bruster, *Drama and the Market in the Age of Shakespeare* (Cambridge: Cambridge University Press, 1992), 69.

38. Jean-Christophe Agnew, *Worlds Apart: The Market and the Theater in Anglo-American Thought, 1550–1750* (Cambridge: Cambridge University Press, 1986), 85–86.

39. Leinwand, *The City Staged*, 91.

40. Thomas Middleton, *A Trick to Catch the Old One*, in *A Mad World, My Masters and Other Plays*, ed. Michael Taylor (Oxford: Oxford University Press, 1995), 4.2.88–89.

41. William Shakespeare, *Hamlet*, ed. Willard Farnham, in *William Shakespeare: The Complete Works*, ed. Alfred Harbage (London: Penguin, 1969), 1.2.85.

42. Smith, *De Republica Anglorum*, 27–28; Tudor and Stuart governments viewed

false pretensions to gentility to be a serious social problem. J. F. Day remarks that "In the sixteenth and seventeenth centuries a series of Visitations was conducted by the heralds in various counties of England to establish 'gentlemen of coat armour' and their genealogies, and to deface false armory. By the time of Elizabeth and James, the heralds were appointed by the court to safeguard that all-important distinction between those who were not and those were gentlemen, the latter group comprising not only the titled aristocracy but also the gentry" ("Trafficking in Honor," *Renaissance Papers* [1987]: 61-62).

43. Barbara Shapiro in *Probability and Certainty in Seventeenth-Century England* (Princeton: Princeton University Press, 1987) observes that seventeenth-century English historiography was influenced by a broader movement away from the pursuit of absolute certainty toward more probabilistic epistemological theories (138). It is interesting to note, then, that just at the moment at which historians began to ground historical knowledge in records, documents, and testimonies, the reliability of these documents, their status as fact and not fiction, is rendered dubious by their commodification.

CHAPTER 3: *EPICOENE* AND KNOWING BY TRADITION

1. L. C. Knights calls *Epicoene* "pure entertainment" (*Drama and Society in the Age of Jonson* [New York: Stewart, 1936], 196). Alan Dessen contrasts "the searching moral comedy of *Volpone* and the lighthearted exposes of *Epicoene*" (*Jonson's Moral Comedy* [Evanston, Ill.: Northwestern University Press, 1971], 108).

2. Emrys Jones, "The First West End Comedy," *Proceedings of the British Academy* 68 (1982): 233.

3. Paul Kristeller, "Humanism," in *The Cambridge History of Renaissance Philosophy*, ed. Charles Schmitt and Quentin Skinner (Cambridge: Cambridge University Press, 1988), 114.

4. Buckley notes that medieval thought divided the classics into those whose contents could be reconciled with Christian doctrine and were therefore held to be forerunners of Christianity, and those whose contents could not be so reconciled and were therefore "minions of Satan, to be accursed and damned and if possible run to earth and slain" (*Atheism in the English Renaissance* [Chicago: University of Chicago Press, 1932], 2). According to Buckley, Renaissance humanism is characterized by a movement away from this dichotomy to an attempt to read the classics in their own terms; thus the classics became a potent source of skeptical and atheist ideas. As Allen argues, most Renaissance Christians, especially after the Reformation, were deeply ambivalent about classical thought, regarding it at best as the product of natural reason but in need of revelation, and at worst as a major source of growing atheism (*Doubt's Boundless Sea: Skepticism and Faith in the Renaissance* [Baltimore: Johns Hopkins University Press, 1964], 4-6).

5. See Kahn's *Rhetoric, Prudence, and Skepticism in the Renaissance* (Ithaca: Cornell University Press, 1985). Kahn argues that humanism's Pyrrhonian crisis forced writers such as Erasmus, Montaigne, and Hobbes to doubt language's ability to persuade or instruct, and that these writers' rhetorical strategies manifest this doubt and their attempts to come to terms with it. See also Schiffmann's "Montaigne and the Rise of Skepticism in Early Modern Europe: A Reappraisal," *Renaissance Essays II* (1993). Schiffmann argues that the Renaissance Pyrrhonian crisis was largely the result of "the failure of the humanist program of education [which] . . . united a normative view of the world with a skeptical mode of thinking, balancing one against the other" (390). The increasing diversity of opinion, according to Schiffmann, destroyed the possibility of a normative view of the world on which to base arguments; consequently, skeptical habits of thought cultivated by humanist educators, such as arguing *in utramque partem*, inevitably led to a Pyrrhonist position.

NOTES TO CHAPTER THREE

6. Brian Copenhaver and Charles Schmitt, *Renaissance Philosophy* (Oxford: Oxford University Press, 1992), 196.

7. W. Scott Blanchard, *Scholars' Bedlam: Menippean Satire in the Renaissance* (Lewisburg, Pa.: Bucknell University Press, 1995).

8. Barbara Shapiro, *Probability and Certainty in Seventeenth-Century England* (Princeton: Princeton University Press, 1983).

9. Francis Bacon, *The Advancement of Learning*, ed. G. W. Kitchin (London: Dent, 1973), 31.

10. Francis Bacon, *The New Organon*, ed. Fulton Anderson (Englewood Cliffs, N.J.: Prentice-Hall, 1960), 47.

11. Ibid., 20.

12. Ibid., 113.

13. Bacon, *The Advancement of Learning*, 28.

14. Bacon, *The New Organon*, 49.

15. Ben Jonson, *Discoveries*, in *The Complete Poems*, ed. George Parfitt (London: Penguin, 1988), ll. 2596–2603.

16. Ibid., ll. 2611–14.

17. John Enck, *Jonson and the Comic Truth* (Madison: University of Wisconsin Press, 1957), 113.

18. Ben Jonson, *Epicoene*, ed. L. A. Beaurline (Lincoln: University of Nebraska Press, 1966), 1.2.64; all subsequent citations are to this edition.

19. Baldassare Castiglione, *The Book of the Courtier*, trans. Sir Thomas Hoby (1561; reprint, New York: Dutton, 1928).

20. Jonson, *Discoveries*, 1349–51.

21. Ben Jonson, *Every Man Out of His Humour*, in vol. 1 of *The Complete Plays of Ben Jonson*, ed. G. A. Wilkes (Oxford: Clarendon, 1981), 5.11.52–53.

22. Tom Wolfe, *The Pumphouse Gang* (New York: Noonday Press, 1968), 6.

23. P. K. Ayers, "Dreams of the City: The Urban and the Urbane in Jonson's *Epicoene*," *Philological Quarterly* 66, no. 1 (1987): 74–75.

24. Jonathan Haynes, *The Social Relations of Jonson's Theater* (Cambridge: Cambridge University Press, 1992), 93.

25. Thomas Wright, *The Passions of the Mind in General*, ed. W. W. Newbold (New York: Garland, 1986), 97.

26. Ibid., 126.

27. M. M. Bakhtin, *The Dialogic Imagination*, trans. Caryl Emerson and Michael Holquist (Austin: University of Texas Press, 1981), 12.

28. Katherine Eiseman Maus, *Inwardness and Theater in the English Renaissance* (Chicago: University of Chicago Press, 1995), 146.

29. Ayers, "Dreams of the City," 77.

30. Ian Donaldson, *The World Upside-Down: Comedy from Jonson to Fielding* (Oxford: Clarendon, 1970), 30.

31. Steven Fuller, *Social Epistemology* (Bloomington: Indiana University Press, 1988), 28.

32. Charles Lyons, "Silent Women and Shrews: Eroticism and Conventions in *Epicoene* and *Measure for Measure*," *Comparative Drama* 23, no. 2 (1989): 131.

33. Phyllis Rackin, "Androgyny, Mimesis, and the Marriage of the Boy Heroine on the English Renaissance Stage," *PMLA* 102, no. 1 (1987): 36.

34. Jonas Barish, "Ovid, Juvenal, and *The Silent Woman*," *PMLA* 71 (1956): 224.

35. Ibid., 222.

36. Lorraine Helms, "Roaring Girls and Silent Women: The Politics of Androgyny on the Jacobean Stage," in *Women in Theatre*, ed. J. Redmond (Cambridge: Cambridge University Press, 1989): 68.

37. Linda Woodbridge, *Women in the English Renaissance: Literature and the Nature of Womankind, 1540–1620* (Urbana: University of Illinois Press, 1984), 181.

38. Jean Howard, *The Stage and Social Struggle in Early Modern England* (London: Routledge, 1994), 106.

39. Ibid., 109.

40. In *Jonson and the Psychology of the Public Theater* (Princeton: Princeton University Press, 1985), Sweeney argues that the play's antifeminism is in part a symptom of an "essential male anxiety [that] mother-wives are self-sufficient—they do not need men, or, to twist this proposition to reflect the fear implicit in the idea of female promiscuity, any man will do" (119). Jonson, according to Sweeney, had more than his fair share of this essential male anxiety: "Jonson's aggression toward women in this play serves two psychological ends: first, it is a confession, an acknowledgment of the fear suppressed in the earlier plays, that women are really nasty creatures; second, to portray them as nasty is revenge against them, not just for their malignancy but also for their rejection of males" (120).

41. Alvin Kernan, *The Cankered Muse: Satire of the English Renaissance* (New Haven: Yale University Press, 1959), 114, 142–43.

42. Lyons, "Silent Women and Shrews," 135.

43. J. L. Austin, *How To Do Things With Words* (Cambridge: Harvard University Press, 1962), 103.

44. Jonas Barish, *Ben Jonson and the Language of Prose Comedy* (Cambridge: Harvard University Press, 1967), 157.

45. William Slights, "*Epicoene* and the Prose Paradox," *Philological Quarterly* 49 (1970): 179.

46. Slights argues that mock encomia satirize while seeming to praise, but as the paradigmatic example of the Renaissance mock encomium, Erasmus's *Praise of Folly*, illustrates, the mock encomium is more ambivalent than this, skeptically balancing satire and praise. Kahn in *Rhetoric, Prudence, and Skepticism in the Renaissance* argues that Erasmus's rhetorical strategies force the reader into a suspension of judgment: the reader has no way of deciding if Folly is wisdom or folly.

47. John Marston, *What You Will*, in vol. 2. of *The Works of John Marston*, ed. A. H. Bullen (New York: Georg Olms, 1970), 2.2.151; all subsequent citations are to this edition.

48. Diana Benet, "'The Master-Wit is the master-fool': Jonson, *Epicoene*, and the Moralists," *Renaissance Drama*, n.s., 16 (1985): 137.

49. Bruce Thomas Boehrer, "*Epicoene*, Charivari, Skimmington," *English Studies* 75, no. 1 (1994): 32.

50. Ayers, "Dreams of the City," 78.

51. W. David Kay, "Jonson's Urbane Gallants: Humanistic Contexts for *Epicoene*," *Huntington Library Quarterly* 39 (1976): 266.

CHAPTER 4: THE RISE OF *HOMO ECONOMICUS* IN *A TRICK TO CATCH THE OLD ONE*

1. Ervin Beck, "Terence Improved: The Paradigm of the Prodigal Son in English Renaissance Comedy," *Renaissance Drama*, n.s., 6 (1973): 119.

2. Ibid.

3. Richard Henry Tawney, *Religion and the Rise of Capitalism* (1926; reprint, London: Penguin, 1938), 43–44.

4. Richard Hooker, *Of the Laws of Ecclesiastical Polity*, in *The Works of That Learned and Judicious Divine Mr. Richard Hooker*, ed. J. Kebble (1888; reprint, New York: Burt Franklin, 1970), book 8, chap. i., 4.

5. Francis Bacon, "Of Riches," in *Francis Bacon: A Selection of His Works*, ed. Warhaft, 136–37.

6. Tawney, *Religion*, 158, 163–65.

7. Stephen Greenblatt, "Murdering Peasants: Status, Genre, and the Representation of Rebellion," in *Learning to Curse* (New York: Routledge, 1990).

8. Thomas Middleton, *A Trick to Catch the Old One*, in *A Mad World, My Masters and Other Plays*, ed. Michael Taylor (Oxford: Oxford University Press, 1995), 1.1.13, 16; all subsequent citations are to this edition.

9. *The First and Second Prayer Books of Edward VI* (1549–52; reprint, London: Dent, 1910), 252.

10. Michel Foucault, *The History of Sexuality: An Introduction*, trans. R. Hurley, vol. 1 (New York: Pantheon, 1978), 93.

11. Leonard Tennenhouse, *Power on Display: The Politics of Shakespeare's Genres* (New York: Methuen, 1986), 153, 154.

12. George Rowe, *Thomas Middleton and the New Comedy Tradition* (Lincoln: University of Nebraska Press, 1979), 83.

13. David Mount, "The '[Un]reclaymed forme' of Middleton's *A Trick to Catch the Old One*," *Studies in English Literature, 1500–1900* 31, no. 2 (1991): 261.

14. Derek Sayer, *Capitalism and Modernity: An excursus on Marx and Weber* (London: Routledge, 1991), 18.

15. Max Weber, *The Protestant Ethic and the Spirit of Capitalism* (1930; reprint, London: Routledge, 1992), 181.

16. Karl Marx, *Grundrisse*, trans. M. Nicolaus (London: Penguin, 1973), 243, 163.

17. Pierre Bourdieu, *The Field of Cultural Production* (New York: Columbia University Press, 1993), 7.

18. Ibid.

19. Stephen Greenblatt, *Renaissance Self-Fashioning: From More to Shakespeare* (Chicago: University of Chicago Press, 1980), 9.

20. Weber, *The Protestant Ethic*, 53.

21. P. K. Ayers, "Plot, Subplot, and the Uses of Dramatic Discord in *A Mad World, My Masters* and *A Trick to Catch the Old One*," *Modern Language Quarterly* 47, no. 1 (1986): 12.

22. Joseph Messina, "The Moral Design of *A Trick to Catch the Old One*," in *Accompaninge the Players: Essays Celebrating Thomas Middleton, 1580–1980* (New York: AMS, 1983).

23. Terry Eagleton, *Ideology: An Introduction* (London: Verso, 1991), 1.

24. Richard Levin, "The Dampit Scenes in *A Trick to Catch the Old One*," *Modern Language Quarterly* 25, no. 2 (1964): 144, 147.

25. Scott Cutler Shershow, "The Pit of Wit: Subplot and Unity in Middleton's *A Trick to Catch the Old One*," *Studies in Philology* 88, no. 3 (1991): 365.

26. Ibid., 366.

27. Ibid., 376.

28. Richard Bowers, "Middleton's *A Trick to Catch the Old One*," *Explicator* 51, no. 4 (1993): 211.

CHAPTER 5: PLAY AND PLAGUE IN *THE ALCHEMIST*

1. Ben Jonson, Letter to The Reader, *The Alchemist*, in vol. 3 of *The Complete Plays of Ben Jonson*, ed. G. A. Wilkes (Oxford: Clarendon, 1982), line 6; all subsequent citations are to this edition.

2. Paul Slack's *The Impact of Plague in Tudor and Stuart England* (London: Routledge and Kegan Paul, 1985) is my main source of information about the plague, but I have also consulted F. P. Wilson's *The Plague in Shakespeare's London* (Oxford: Clarendon, 1927). See Slack, pp. 28–29, for a discussion of the intersections of medical and theological discourses about the plague.

3. Jacques Derrida, *Dissemination*, trans. Barbara Johnson (Chicago: University of Chicago Press, 1981), 99.

4. See Slack, *Impact of Plague,* chapter 8, "Public Authority and Policy for Control" and chapter 10, "Towns Under Stress" for the details concerning plague policy, the problems faced by authorities in implementing plague policy, the stress such policy placed on the urban fabric, and particularly pp. 256–66 for the various responses, including flight, of urban magistrates to the plague. See Slack, chapter 11, "Police and People" for a comparison of England's plague policies with those on the continent and for a discussion of popular resistance to the plague orders.

5. Thomas Dekker, *The Wonderfull Yeare,* in *The Plague Pamphlets of Thomas Dekker,* ed. F. P. Wilson (Oxford: Clarendon, 1925), 27.

6. See Slack, *Impact of Plague,* chapter 9, "Controversy and compromise" for a discussion of the government's position and its elaboration in opposition to other stances on the plague.

7. Michel Foucault, *Discipline and Punish,* trans. A. Sheridan (New York: Random House, 1977), 198.

8. Ibid., 197.

9. See Slack, *Impact of Plague,* p. 230 and Wilson, *Plague in Shakespeare's London,* pp. 93–99 for the details of contemporary descriptions of carnivalesque behavior during the plague.

10. Robert Lerner, "The Black Death and Western Escatological Mentalities," *American Historical Review* 86, no. 3 (1981): 551.

11. Katherine Firth, *The Apocalyptic Tradition in Reformation Britain, 1530–1645* (Oxford: Oxford University Press, 1979).

12. Alexander Nowell, "An Homily concerning the Justice of God in punyshyng of impenitent sinners, and of his mercies towardes all such as theyr afflictions unfaynedly turne unto hym," in *The Remains of Archbishop Grindal,* ed. W. Nelson (Cambridge: Cambridge University Press, 1843), 97.

13. Ibid., 108.

14. John Donne, "After Our Dispersion, by the Sickness," in *London in the Age of Shakespeare,* ed. Lawrence Manley (London: Pennsylvania State University Press, 1986), 115.

15. See Slack, *Impact of Plague,* chapter 9, "Controversy and compromise," particularly pp. 227–35, for the details of the extreme spiritualist view.

16. Ludwig Wittgenstein, *Philosophical Investigations,* trans. G. E. M. Anscombe (Oxford: Blackwell, 1963), 11.

17. Dekker, *The Wonderfull Yeare,* 36.

18. Ibid., 37.

19. Keith Thomas, *Religion and the Decline of Magic* (1971; reprint, London: Penguin, 1973).

20. Dekker, *The Wonderfull Yeare,* 37.

21. Alan Dessen, "*The Alchemist*: Jonson's 'Estates' Play," *Renaissance Drama* 7 (1964): 49.

22. Jonathan Haynes, "Representing the Underworld: *The Alchemist,*" *Studies in Philology* 86, no. 1 (1989): 35–36.

23. R. L. Smallwood, "'Here in the Friars': Immediacy and Theatricality in *The Alchemist,*" *Review of English Studies,* n.s., 32 (1980): 147.

24. Robert N. Watson, *Ben Jonson's Parodic Strategies: Literary Imperialism in the Comedies* (Cambridge: Harvard University Press, 1987), 114.

25. Ian Donaldson, *Jonson's Magic Houses: Essays in Interpretation* (Oxford: Clarendon, 1997), 77.

26. William Slights, *Ben Jonson and the Art of Secrecy* (Toronto: University of Toronto Press, 1994), 107.

27. Frank Kermode, *The Sense of an Ending: Studies in the Theory of Fiction* (New York: Oxford University Press, 1967), 8.

28. Geraldo de Sousa, "Boundaries of Genre in Ben Jonson's *Volpone* and *the Alchemist*," *Essays in Theater* 4, no. 2 (1986): 135.

29. See Robert Schuler's "Jonson's Alchemists, Epicures, and Puritans," *Medieval and Renaissance Drama in England* 2 (1985) for a full discussion of the significance of the links between the Brethren and the Anabaptists. Schuler states that "the anti-social, anti-government, and communistic attitudes of the Anabaptists made them a threat not only to the theological but also to the political order as well. That this fear was well founded, history seemed to demonstrate all to clearly, and the social disruption generally associated with Puritanism looked pale when compared to the millenarian anarchy of radical Anabaptism" (176).

30. See John Mebane's *Renaissance Magic and the Return of the Golden Age* (Lincoln: University of Nebraska Press, 1989), esp. pp. 153–54, for a detailed discussion of Mammon's visions in the context of myths of the golden age.

31. Cheryl Lynn Ross, "The Plague of *The Alchemist*, " *Renaissance Quarterly* 41, no. 3 (1988): 443.

32. Haynes, "Representing the Underworld," 31–32.

33. Judd Arnold, "Lovewit's Triumph and Jonsonian Morality: A Reading of *The Alchemist*," *Criticism* 11 (1969): 166.

34. Wayne Rebhorn, "Jonson's 'Jovy Boy': Lovewit and the Dupes in *The Alchemist*," *Journal of English and Germanic Philology* 79 (1980): 356.

35. Ian Donaldson, "Language, Noise, and Nonsense: *The Alchemist*," in *Seventeenth-Century Imagery: Essays on the Use of Figurative Language from Donne to Farquhar* (Berkeley: University of California Press, 1971), 78.

36. Ross, "The Plague of *The Alchemist*," 454.

37. See Lindberg, *The Beginnings of Western Science* (Chicago: University of Chicago Press, 1992), 287–90 for a discussion of the development of alchemy within the framework of Aristotelian natural philosophy.

38. Subtle's speech here can create difficulties for critics intent on dismissing all the play's alchemical language as sheer jargon. Linden, in his admirable study of the ways in which the play incorporates its numerous alchemical sources, argues that "Subtle's speech serves as a marvelous instance of alchemical foolishness, one of the myriad examples of the hocus-pocus characteristic of the *ignotum per ignocius* tradition," yet concedes that "the passage is also a very accurate reflection of alchemical theory" (*Darke Hierogliphicks: Alchemy in English Literature from Chaucer to the Restoration* [Lexington: University of Kentucky Press, 1996], 122). I argue both that the passage is less obscure than Linden makes it out to be and that Jonson allowed Subtle's alchemical discourse here to be more coherent than elsewhere for dramatic reasons, not just to display his own learning.

39. Walter Ralegh, "What is our life? a play of passion," in *The Metaphysical Poets*, ed. Helen Gardner, 3d ed. (London: Penguin, 1972), l. 5.

Chapter 6: Paradox, Wonder, and the Reproduction of Patriarchy in *A Chaste Maid in Cheapside*.

1. Covatta argues that Middleton applies "surface characteristics—names, occupations, settings—to the constant patterns of comic human conduct. He worked in universals" (*Thomas Middleton's City Comedies* [Lewisburg, Pa.: Bucknell University Press, 1973], 36). Similarly, Rowe argues that city comedy "seldom did more than impose apparently realistic and contemporary veneers on what are basically New Comedy plots" (*Thomas Middleton and the New Comedy Tradition* [Lincoln: University of Nebraska Press, 1979], 4). In their discussion of *A Chaste Maid*, both critics treat the play's ironies and paradoxes as complications of the universal comic paradigm that declare its meaninglessness. Yet, as Altieri observes, such arguments ignore "the intense specific sociality of his [Middleton's] plays, carried especially in the materialism of his dramaturgy" ("Against Moralizing Jacobean Comedy: Middleton's *Chaste Maid*," *Criticism* 30, no. 2 [1988]: 173). By paying attention to the specifically social in *A Chaste Maid*, I argue that the play's paradoxes do not render the forms they complicate meaningless but performative, not devoid of truth but not possessing absolute truth either.

2. Frederic Jameson, *The Political Unconscious: Narrative as a Socially Symbolic Act* (Ithaca: Cornell University Press, 1981), 77.

3. Thomas Middleton, *A Chaste Maid in Cheapside*, in *Thomas Middleton: Five Plays*, ed. Bryan Loughrey and Neil Taylor (London: Penguin, 1988), 2.1.8–9; all subsequent citations are to this edition.

4. Arthur Marotti, "Fertility and Comic Form in *A Chaste Maid in Cheapside*," *Comparative Drama* 3 (1969): 72.

5. Stephen Wigler, "Thomas Middleton's *A Chaste Maid in Cheapside*: The Delicious and the Disgusting," *American Imago* 33 (1976): 199.

6. Gail Kern Paster, *The Body Embarrassed: Drama and the Disciplines of Shame in Early Modern England* (Ithaca: Cornell University Press, 1993), 57.

7. Ibid., 63.

8. Mark Breitenberg, *Anxious Masculinity in Early Modern England* (Cambridge: Cambridge University Press, 1996), 22.

9. Ingrid Hotz-Davies, "*A Chaste Maid in Cheapside* and *Women Beware Women*: Feminism, Anti-Feminism and the Limitations of Satire," *Cahiers Elisabethains* 39 (1991): 31.

10. Colie notes that classical rhetoric defined the rhetorical paradox as a "defense, organised along the lines of traditional *encomia*, of the unexpected, unworthy, or indefensible subject" (*Paradoxia Epidemica: The Renaissance Tradition of Paradox* [Princeton: Princeton University Press, 1966], 3). Allwit's encomium is particularly paradoxical because it manipulates the logical incoherence of an aspect of patriarchal thought.

11. Ronald Huebert, "Middleton's Nameless Art," *Sewanee Review* 95, no. 4 (1987): 598.

12. Paster, *The Body Embarrassed*, 63.

13. Heidi Hartmann, "The Unhappy Marriage of Marxism and Feminism: Towards a More Progressive Union," in *Women and Revolution: A Discussion of the Unhappy Marriage of Marxism and Feminism*, ed. Lydia Sargent (Boston: South End Press, 1981), quoted in Eve Kosofsky Sedgwick, *Between Men: English Literature and Male Homosocial Desire* (New York: Columbia University Press, 1985), 3.

NOTES TO CHAPTER SEVEN

14. Richard Levin, "The Four Plots of *A Chaste Maid in Cheapside*," *Review of English Studies*, n.s., 16 (1965).
15. Eve Kosofsky Sedgwick, *Between Men: English Literature and Male Homosocial Desire* (New York: Columbia University Press, 1985).
16. Paster, *The Body Embarrassed*, 57.
17. Sedgwick, *Between Men*, 50.
18. Hotz-Davies, "Limitations of Satire," 30.
19. M. M. Bakhtin, *Rabelais and His World*, trans. H. Iswolsky (1668; reprint, Bloomington: Indiana University Press, 1984), 19–20.
20. In the Church of England christening ceremony, the priest invokes Christ to "recyue you [the infant] into his holy householde, and to kepe and gouerne you alwaye in the same, that you may have euerlasting lyfe" (*The First and Second Prayer Books of Edward VI*, 239). See Amussen's *An Ordered Society: Gender and Class in Early Modern England* (Oxford: Blackwell, 1988), 34–66, for a full discussion of the analogies between church, state, and household in sixteenth- and seventeenth-century English thought.
21. J. L. Austin, *How to Do Things with Words* (Cambridge: Harvard University Press, 1962), 14.
22. Swapan Chakravorty, *Society and Politics in the Plays of Thomas Middleton* (Oxford: Clarendon, 1996), 104.
23. Anthony Covatta, *Thomas Middleton's City Comedies* (Lewisburg, Pa.: Bucknell University Press, 1973), 142–43.
24. George Wilkins, *The Miseries of Inforst Marriage* (1607; reprint, Oxford: Oxford University Press, 1964), 430.
25. See Houlbrooke's *The English Family, 1450–1700* (London: Longman, 1984), 63–95, for discussion of the changes in common law's stance to precontracts and of the attitudes toward parental authority in the matter of marriage.
26. William Shakespeare, *Othello*, ed. G. Bentley (Harmondsworth, England: Penguin, 1970), 1.3.292–93.
27. Susan Wells, "Jacobean City Comedy and the Ideology of the City," *English Literary History* 48 (1981): 58.
28. George Puttenham, *The Arte of English Poesie*, ed. G. D. Willcock and A. Walker (Cambridge: Cambridge University Press, 1936), 226.

CHAPTER 7: SKEPTICAL LAUGHTER IN THE BRAVE NEW WORLD OF *BARTHOLOMEW FAIR*

1. See Marvin Herrick's *Comic Theory in the Sixteenth Century* (Urbana: University of Illinois Press, 1964), esp. the third chapter, "The Function of Comedy."
2. Philip Sidney, *The Defence of Poesy*, in *Sir Philip Sidney*, ed. K. Duncan-Jones (Oxford: Oxford University Press, 1989), ll. 1340–41, 1357–60.
3. M. M. Bakhtin, *Rabelais and His World*, trans. H. Iswolsky (1968; reprint, Bloomington: Indiana University Press, 1984), 15.
4. Ben Jonson, *Bartholomew Fair*, in vol. 3 of *The Complete Plays of Ben Jonson*, ed. G. A. Wilkes (Oxford: Clarendon Press, 1982), 5.4.87; all subsequent citations are to this edition.
5. Jonas Barish, "*Bartholomew Fair* and Its Puppets," *Modern Language Quarterly* 20 (1959): 4.
6. Ibid.
7. Neil Rhodes, *Elizabethan Grotesque* (London: Routledge and Kegan Paul, 1980), 152.

8. Jonson, *Discoveries*, ll. 2328–30.
9. Ibid., ll. 3311–13.
10. David McPherson in "The Origins of Overdo: A Study in Jonsonian Invention," *Modern Language Quarterly* 37 (1976): convincingly argues that Sir Thomas Middleton, London's mayor 1613–14, Whetstone's pamphlet and the anonymous *Look on me London* (1613) provide examples on which Overdo fashions his behavior. McPherson also discusses the disguised-duke tradition of which Overdo is a parody.
11. Thomas Cartelli, "*Bartholomew Fair* as Urban Arcadia: Jonson Responds to Shakespeare," *Renaissance Drama,* n.s., 14 (1983): 156.
12. Jonas Barish, "Feasting and Judging in Jonsonian Comedy," *Renaissance Drama,* n.s., 5 (1972): 30.
13. Michael McCanes, "Festival in Jonsonian Comedy," *Renaissance Drama,* n.s., 8 (1977): 209.
14. Ibid., 204.
15. Rhodes, *Elizabethan Grotesque*, 154.
16. Bakhtin, *Rabelais*, 11.
17. Ibid., 24.
18. Michael Bristol, "Acting Out Utopia: The Politics of Carnival," *Performance* 6 (1973): 25.
19. Michael Bristol, *Carnival and Theater: Plebeian Culture and the Structure of Authority in Renaissance England* (London: Methuen, 1985), 52.
20. Peter Stallybrass and Allon White, *The Poetics and Politics of Transgression* (Ithaca: Cornell University Press, 1986), 27–28.
21. Ibid., 37.
22. Jonathan Haynes, "Festivity and the Dramatic Economy of Jonson's *Bartholomew Fair,*" *English Literary History* 51, no. 4 (1984): 647.
23. Ibid., 649.
24. Ibid., 640.
25. Jonathan Haynes, "Representing the Underworld: *The Alchemist,*" *Studies in Philology* 86, no. 1 (1989): 20.
26. Rebecca Ann Bach, "Jonson's 'Civil Savages,'" *Studies in English Literature, 1500–1900* 37, no. 2 (1997): 289.
27. Jonathan Dollimore, *Sexual Dissidence: Augustine to Wilde, Freud to Foucault* (Oxford: Clarendon, 1991), 33.
28. Thomas Harman, *A Caveat for Common Cursitors Vulgarly Called Vagabonds*, in *Rogues, Vagabonds and Sturdy Beggars*, ed. Arthur Kinney (Amherst: University of Massachusetts Press, 1990), 110.
29. Ibid., 109, 111.
30. Haynes, "Representing the Underworld," 29.
31. Michel Montaigne, "Of Cannibals," in *The Complete Essays*, trans. Donald Frame (Stanford, Calif.: Stanford University Press, 1958).
32. Harman, *Caveat*, 113.
33. Edward Said, *Orientalism* (New York: Vintage, 1979).
34. Keith Sturgess, *Jacobean Private Theatre* (New York: Routledge and Kegan Paul, 1987).
35. Thomas Browne, *Religio Medici*, in *The Major Works* (Harmondsworth, England: Penguin, 1977), 148.
36. Francis Bacon, *The Advancement of Learning*, ed. G. W. Kitchin (London: Dent, 1973), 132.
37. Ibid., 3, 113.

38. Henry Van Leeuwen, *The Problem of Certainty in English Thought, 1630–1690* (The Hague: Martinus Nijhoff, 1970), 12.

39. Francis Bacon, *The New Organon*, ed. Fulton Anderson (Englewood Cliffs, N.J.: Prentice-Hall, 1960), 29.

40. Bacon, *Advancement of Learning*, 205, 206; in *James I and the Politics of Literature: Jonson, Shakespeare, Donne, and Their Contemporaries* (Baltimore: Johns Hopkins University Press, 1983), Jonathan Goldberg argues that James likewise fashioned himself as both inscrutable and omniscient, surrounded by secrets but able to see into all others' secrets.

41. Julian Martin argues that, in fact, Bacon's natural philosophy is based on the legal methods in which Bacon's daily life as lawyer and spymaster was immersed: "[C]ertain procedures in legal investigation and court trials, when linked with Bacon's own proposals for legal reform, not only exactly parallel his procedure for a reformed natural philosophy, but they were the model for it" (*Francis Bacon, the State, and the Reform of Natural Philosophy* [Cambridge: Cambridge University Press, 1992], 73).

42. Jackson Cope, "*Bartholomew Fair* as Blasphemy," *Renaissance Drama* 8 (1965).

43. R. B. Parker in "The Themes and Staging of *Bartholomew Fair*," *University of Toronto Quarterly* 39 (1970), describes the echoes of medieval theater that the play's staging may have evoked. Assuming that Ursula's booth is stage-left and Littlewit's house/ the puppet play booth is stage-right, and that these two booths remain on stage for the duration of the play's action, it is possible to see them as "the 'hell' and the 'heaven' of the fair" (295). The stocks, if placed center-stage, become an "emblem of life-as-tribulation" (295). Kathleen Lynch argues that "Overdo is probably separating the saved on stage right from the damned on stage left when he is persuaded by evidence of his own fallibility to abandon the plan" ("The Dramatic Festivity of *Bartholomew Fair*," *Medieval and Renaissance Drama in England* 8 [1996], 130). While disagreeing with Parker about the booth's continual presence on stage, Keith Sturgess concludes that "The farcical business is overlaid on a morality play armature" (*Jacobean Private Theatre* 186).

44. Jeffrey Knapp, *An Empire Nowhere: England, America, and Literature from Utopia to The Tempest* (Berkeley: University of California Press, 1992).

45. Barish, "*Bartholomew Fair* and Its Puppets," 17.

46. Bristol, *Carnival and Theater*, 201.

47. In *Forms of Nationhood: The Elizabethan Writing of England* (Chicago: University of Chicago Press, 1992), Richard Helgerson dates the professional theater's shift away from an artisan-based, collaborative theater to an author-based theater of the script as beginning in the 1590s, with the influx of university-educated playwrights whose sole function was to write plays and who gradually displaced the player-writer (195–204).

48. Sturgess, *Jacobean Private Theatre*, 179.

49. Ibid., 189.

50. Ben Jonson, "To King James," epigram IV, in *The Complete Poems*, ed. George Parfitt (London: Penguin, 1988).

51. Sturgess, *Jacobean Private Theatre*, 176.

52. Ben Jonson, *The Masque of Blackness*, in *Court Masques: Jacobean and Caroline Entertainments, 1605–1640*, ed. David Lindley (Oxford: Oxford University Press, 1995), ll. 8, 7.

53. Susan Wells, "Jacobean City Comedy and the Ideology of the City," *English Literary History* 48 (1981): 53.

54. Jonathan Goldberg, *James I and the Politics of Literature: Jonson, Shakespeare, Donne, and Their Contemporaries* (Baltimore: Johns Hopkins University Press, 1983), 83.

Conclusion

1. Thomas Dekker, *The Gulls Horn-Book*, in vol. 2. of *The Non-Dramatic Works of Thomas Dekker*, ed. A. Grossart (New York: Russell and Russell, 1963), 246.

Bibliography

Agnew, Jean-Christophe. *Worlds Apart: The Market and the Theater in Anglo-American Thought, 1550–1750*. Cambridge: Cambridge University Press, 1986.

Allen, Donald Cameron. *Doubt's Boundless Sea: Skepticism and Faith in the Renaissance*. Baltimore: Johns Hopkins University Press, 1964.

Altieri, Joan. "Against Moralizing Jacobean Comedy: Middleton's *Chaste Maid*." *Criticism* 30, no. 2 (1988): 171–87.

Amussen, Susan Dwyer. *The Ordered Society: Gender and Class in Early Modern England*. Oxford: Blackwell, 1988.

Appleby, Joyce. *Economic Thought and Ideology in Seventeenth-Century England*. Princeton: Princeton University Press, 1978.

Archer, I. W. *The Pursuit of Stability: Social Relations in Elizabethan London*. Cambridge: Cambridge University Press, 1991.

Aristophanes. *The Complete Plays of Aristophanes*. Edited by M. Hadas. New York: Bantam, 1962.

Arnold, Judd. "Lovewit's Triumph and Jonsonian Morality: A Reading of *The Alchemist*." *Criticism* 11 (1969): 151–66.

Artaud, Antonin. "The Theater and the Plague." In *The Theater and Its Double*, translated by M. C. Richards, 15–32. New York: Grove Press, 1958.

Ashton, Robert. *The City and the Court, 1603–1643*. Cambridge: Cambridge University Press, 1979.

Austin, J. L. *How To Do Things With Words*. Cambridge: Harvard University Press, 1962.

Ayers, P. K. "Plot, Subplot, and the Uses of Dramatic Discord in *A Mad World, My Masters* and *A Trick to Catch the Old One*." *Modern Language Quarterly* 47, no. 1 (1986): 3–18.

———. "Dreams of the City: The Urban and the Urbane in Jonson's *Epicoene*." *Philological Quarterly* 66, no. 1 (1987): 73–86.

Bach, Rebecca. A. "Ben Jonson's 'Civil Savages'." *Studies in English Literature 1500–1900* 37, no. 2 (spring 1997): 277–93.

Bacon, Francis. *The New Organon* (1620). Edited by F. H. Anderson. Englewood Cliffs, N.J.: Prentice-Hall, 1960.

———. "Of Nobility." Reprinted in *Francis Bacon: A Selection of His Works*, edited by S. Warhaft. Toronto: Macmillan, 1965.

———. "Of Riches." Reprinted in *Francis Bacon: A Selection of His Works*, edited by S. Warhaft. Toronto: Macmillan, 1965.

---. *The New Atlantis*. In *Francis Bacon: A Selection of His Works*. Toronto: Macmillan, 1965.

---. *The Advancement of Learning*. Edited by G. W. Kitchin. London: Dent, 1973.

Bakhtin, M. M. *Rabelais and His World*. Translated by H. Iswolsky. 1968. Reprint, Bloomington: Indiana University Press, 1984.

---. *The Dialogic Imagination*. Translated by C. Emerson and M. Holquist. Austin: University of Texas Press, 1981.

Barber, C. L. *Shakespeare's Festive Comedy*. Princeton: Princeton University Press, 1959.

Barish, Jonas. "Ovid, Juvenal, and *The Silent Woman*." *PMLA* 71 (1956): 213–24.

---. "*Bartholomew Fair* and Its Puppets." *Modern Language Quarterly* 20 (1959): 3–17.

---. *Ben Jonson and the Language of Prose Comedy*. Cambridge: Harvard University Press, 1967.

---. "Feasting and Judging in Jonsonian Comedy." *Renaissance Drama*, n.s., 5 (1972): 3–35.

---. "Jonson and the Loathed Stage." In *A Celebration of Ben Jonson*, edited by W. Blissett, J. Patrick, and R. W. Van Fossen, 27–54. Toronto: University of Toronto Press, 1973.

---. *The Antitheatrical Prejudice*. Berkeley: University of California Press, 1981.

Barker, Francis. *The Tremulous Private Body: Essays on Subjection*. 1984. Reprint, Ann Arbor: University of Michigan Press, 1995.

Beck, Ervin. "Terence Improved: The Paradigm of the Prodigal Son in English Renaissance Comedy." *Renaissance Drama*, n.s., 6 (1973): 107–22.

Beier, A. L., and R. Finlay, eds. *The Making of the Metropolis: London, 1500–1700*. London: Longman, 1986.

Belsey, Catherine. *The Subject of Tragedy*. London: Methuen, 1985.

Benet, Diana. "'The Master-Wit is the master-fool': Jonson, *Epicoene*, and the Moralists." *Renaissance Drama*, n.s., 16 (1985): 121–39.

Blanchard, W. Scott. *Scholars' Bedlam: Menippean Satire in the Renaissance*. Lewisburg, Pa.: Bucknell University Press, 1995.

Boehrer, Bruce Thomas. "*Epicoene*, Charivari, Skimmington." *English Studies* 75, no. 1 (1994): 17–33.

Bourdieu, Pierre. *The Field of Cultural Production*. New York: Columbia University Press, 1993.

Bowers, Richard. "Middleton's *A Trick to Catch the Old One*." *Explicator* 51, no. 4 (1993): 211–14.

Breitenberg, Mark. *Anxious Masculinity in Early Modern England*. Cambridge: Cambridge University Press, 1996.

Brenner, Robert. "Agrarian Class Structure and Economic Development in Pre-Industrial Europe." *Past and Present* 97 (1982): 16–113.

Bristol, Michael. "Acting Out Utopia: The Politics of Carnival." *Performance* 6 (1973): 13–28.

---. *Carnival and Theater: Plebeian Culture and the Structure of Authority in Renaissance England*. London: Methuen, 1985.

Broude, Ronald. "Volpone and the Triumph of Truth: Some Antecedents and Analogues of the Main Plot in Volpone." *Studies in Philology* 77 (1980): 227–46.

Browne, Thomas. *Religio Medici*. 1642. Reprinted in *The Major Works*. Harmondsworth, England: Penguin, 1977.

Bruster, Douglas. *Drama and the Market in the Age of Shakespeare*. Cambridge: Cambridge University Press, 1992.

Buckley, G. *Atheism in the English Renaissance*. Chicago: University of Chicago Press, 1932.

Cartelli, Thomas. "*Bartholomew Fair* as Urban Arcadia: Jonson Responds to Shakespeare." *Renaissance Drama,* n.s., 14 (1983): 151–72.

Castiglione, Baldassare. *The Courtier*. Translated by T. Hoby. 1561. Reprint, New York: Dutton, 1928.

Cavell, Stanley. *Disowning Knowledge in Six Plays of Shakespeare*. Cambridge: Cambridge University Press, 1987.

Chakravorty, Swapan. *Society and Politics in the Plays of Thomas Middleton*. Oxford: Clarendon, 1996.

Clay, C. G. A. *Economic Expansion and Social Change: England, 1500–1700*. 2 vols. Cambridge: Cambridge University Press, 1984.

Cohen, Roger. "The Setting of Volpone." *Renaissance Papers,* 1978, 64–75.

Cohn, Norman. *The Pursuit of the Millennium: Revolutionary Millenarians and Mystical Anarchists of the Middle Ages*. New York: Oxford University Press, 1970.

Colie, Rosalie. *Paradoxia Epidemica: The Renaissance Tradition of Paradox*. Princeton: Princeton University Press, 1966.

Cope, Jackson. "*Bartholomew Fair* as Blasphemy." *Renaissance Drama* 8 (1965): 127–52.

Copenhaver, Brian, and Charles Schmitt. *Renaissance Philosophy*. Oxford: Oxford University Press, 1992.

Covatta, Anthony. *Thomas Middleton's City Comedies*. Lewisburg, Pa.: Bucknell University Press, 1973.

Coward, Barry. *The Stuart Age: England, 1603–1714*. 2d ed. London: Longman, 1994.

Cummins, John. *Francis Drake*. 1995. Reprint, London: Phoenix, 1997.

Davis, J. C. *Utopia and the Ideal Society: A Study of English Utopian Writings, 1516–1700*. Cambridge: Cambridge University Press, 1981.

Day, J. F. "Trafficking in Honor: Social Climbing and the Purchase of Gentility in the English Renaissance." *Renaissance Papers,* 1987, 61–70.

Dekker, Thomas. *The Wonderfull Yeare*. 1603. Reprinted in *The Plague Pamphlets of Thomas Dekker*, edited by F. P. Wilson, 1–62. Oxford: Clarendon, 1925.

———. *The Gulls Horn-Book*. Vol. 2 of *The Non-Dramatic Works of Thomas Dekker*. Edited by A. Grossart. 5 vols. New York: Russell and Russell, 1963.

Derrida, Jacques. *Dissemination*. Translated by B. Jonson. Chicago: University of Chicago Press, 1981.

———. "*Différance*." In *Margins of Philosophy*, translated by Alan Bass. Chicago: University of Chicago Press, 1982.

Descartes, René. *Discourse on Method and the Meditations*. Translated by F. E. Sutcliffe. Harmondsworth, England: Penguin, 1968.

de Sousa, Geraldo. "Boundaries of Genre in Ben Jonson's *Volpone* and *The Alchemist*." *Essays in Theater* 4, no. 2 (May 1986): 134–46.

Dessen, Alan. "*The Alchemist*: Jonson's 'Estates' Play." *Renaissance Drama* 7 (1964): 35–54.

———. *Jonson's Moral Comedy*. Evanston, Ill.: Northwestern University Press, 1971.

Diogenes Laertius. *Lives and Opinions of Eminent Philosophers in Ten Books*. Translated by R. Hicks. 2 vols. Cambridge: Harvard University Press, 1925.

Dollimore, Jonathan. *Sexual Dissidence: Augustine to Wilde, Freud to Foucault*. Oxford: Clarendon, 1991.

———. *Radical Tragedy: Ideology and Power in the Drama of Shakespeare and His Contemporaries*. 2d ed. Durham, N.C.: Duke University Press, 1993.

Donaldson, Ian. *The World Upside-Down: Comedy from Jonson to Fielding*. Oxford: Clarendon, 1970.

———. "Language, Noise, and Nonsense: *The Alchemist*." In *Seventeenth-Century Imagery: Essays on Uses of Figurative Language from Donne to Farquhar*, 69–82. Berkeley: University of California Press, 1971.

———. *Jonson's Magic Houses: Essays in Interpretation*. Oxford: Clarendon, 1997.

Donne, John. "After Our Dispersion, by the Sickness" (1625). Reprinted in *London in the Age of Shakespeare*, edited by L. Manley, 115–17. London: Pennsylvania State University Press, 1986.

Duncan, Douglas. *Ben Jonson and the Lucianic Tradition*. Cambridge: Cambridge University Press, 1979.

Dutton, Richard. *Ben Jonson: To the First Folio*. Cambridge: Cambridge University Press, 1983.

Eagleton, Terry. *Ideology: An Introduction*. London: Verso, 1991.

Elias, Norbert. *The Civilizing Process*. Translated by E. Jephcott. 1939. Reprint, Oxford: Blackwell, 1994.

Elliott, R. C. *The Shape of Utopia: Studies in a Literary Genre*. Chicago: University of Chicago Press, 1970.

Enck, John. *Jonson and the Comic Truth*. Madison: University of Wisconsin Press, 1957.

Evans, R. C. "Thomas Sutton: Ben Jonson's Volpone?" *Philological Quarterly* 68, no. 3 (1989): 295–314.

The First and Second Prayer Books of Edward VI. 1549–52. Reprint, London: Dent, 1910.

Firth, Katharine. *The Apocalyptic Tradition in Reformation Britain, 1530–1645*. Oxford: Oxford University Press, 1979.

Fisher, F. J. "The Development of London as a Centre of Conspicuous Consumption in the Sixteenth and Seventeenth Centuries." *Transactions of the Royal Historical Society*, 4th ser., 30 (1948): 37–50.

Foucault, Michel. *The Order of Things: An Archaeology of the Human Sciences*. 1966. Reprint, New York: Random House, 1970.

———. *Discipline and Punish*. 1975. Translated by A. Sheridan. Reprint, New York: Random House, 1977.

———. *The History of Sexuality*, vol. 1: *An Introduction*. Translated by R. Hurley. New York: Pantheon, 1978.

———. *Power/Knowledge*. Edited by C. Gordon. New York: Pantheon, 1980.

Freud, Sigmund. *Beyond the Pleasure Principle*. In *On Metapsychology: The Theory of Psychoanalysis*, translated by James Strachey, 269–338. London: Penguin, 1984.

Fuller, Stephen. *Social Epistemology*. Bloomington: Indiana University Press, 1988.

Gibbons, Brian. *Jacobean City Comedy*. 1968. Reprint, London: Methuen, 1980.

Goldberg, Jonathan. *James I and the Politics of Literature: Jonson, Shakespeare, Donne, and Their Contemporaries*. Baltimore: Johns Hopkins University Press, 1983.

Grassby, Richard. "The Personal Wealth of the Business Community in Seventeenth-Century England." *Economic History Review* 23, no. 2 (August 1970): 220–34.

Greenblatt, Stephen. "The False Ending in Volpone." *Journal of English and Germanic Philology* 75 (1976): 90–104.

———. *Renaissance Self-Fashioning: From More to Shakespeare*. Chicago: University of Chicago Press, 1980.

———. "Murdering Peasants: Status, Genre, and the Representation of Rebellion." In *Learning to Curse*. New York: Routledge, 1990.

Greene, Thomas. "Ben Jonson and the Centred Self." *Studies in English Literature* 10 (1970): 325–48.

Hallett, Charles. "Jonson's Celia: A Reinterpretation of *Volpone*." *Studies in Philology* 68 (1971): 50–69.

Harman, Thomas. *A Caveat for Common Cursitors Vulgarly Called Vagabonds* (1566). In *Rogues, Vagabonds and Sturdy Beggars*, edited by A. F. Kinney. Amherst: University of Massachusetts Press, 1990.

Hartmann, Heidi. "The Unhappy Marriage of Marxism and Feminism: Towards a More Progressive Union." Cited in Sedgwick, *Between Men: English Literature and Male Homosocial Desire*. New York: Columbia University Press, 1985.

Haynes, Jonathan. "Festivity and the Dramatic Economy of Jonson's *Bartholomew Fair*." *English Literary History* 51, no. 4 (winter 1984): 645–68.

———. "Representing the Underworld: *The Alchemist*." *Studies in Philology* 86, no. 1 (winter 1989): 18–41.

———. *The Social Relations of Jonson's Theater*. Cambridge: Cambridge University Press, 1992.

Helgerson, Richard. *Forms of Nationhood: The Elizabethan Writing of England*. Chicago: University of Chicago Press, 1992.

Helms, Lorraine. "Roaring Girls and Silent Women: The Politics of Androgyny on the Jacobean Stage." In *Women in Theatre*, edited by J. Redmond. Cambridge: Cambridge University Press, 1989.

Herrick, Marvin. *Comic Theory in the Sixteenth Century*. Urbana: University of Illinois Press, 1964.

Hesiod. *Works and Days. Hesiod and Theognis*. Translated by D. Wender. Harmondsworth, England: Penguin, 1973.

Hill, Christopher. *Reformation to Industrial Revolution: A Social and Economic History of Britain, 1530–1780*. London: Weidenfeld and Nicolson, 1967.

———. *The World Turned University Pressside Down: Radical Ideas during the English Revolution*. London: Temple Smith, 1972.

Hooker, Richard. *Of the Laws of Ecclesiastical Polity. The Works of That Learned and Judicious Divine Mr. Richard Hooker*. Edited by J. Keble. 1888. Reprint, New York: Burt Franklin, 1970.

Hotz-Davies, Ingrid. "*A Chaste Maid in Cheapside* and *Women Beware Women*: Feminism, Anti-Feminism and the Limitations of Satire" *Cahiers Elisabethains* 39 (1991): 29–39.

Houlbrooke, Ralph. *The English Family, 1450–1700*. London: Longman, 1984.

Howard, Jean. *The Stage and Social Struggle in Early Modern England*. London: Routledge, 1994.

Huebert, Ronald. "Middleton's Nameless Art." *Sewanee Review* 95, no. 4 (1987): 591–609.

Jameson, Frederic. *Marxism and Form: Twentieth-Century Dialectical Theories of Literature*. Princeton: Princeton University Press, 1971.

———. *The Political Unconscious: Narrative as a Socially Symbolic Act*. Ithaca: Cornell University Press, 1981.

Jones, Emrys. "The First West End Comedy." *Proceedings of the British Academy* 68 (1982): 125–258.

Jonson, Ben. *Epicoene* (1616). Edited by L. A. Beaurline. Lincoln: University of Nebraska Press, 1966.

———. *Every Man Out of His Humour*. In vol. 1. of *The Complete Plays of Ben Jonson*, edited by G. A. Wilkes. Oxford: Clarendon Press, 1981.

———. *The Alchemist*. In vol. 3 of *The Complete Plays of Ben Jonson*, edited by G. A. Wilkes. Oxford: Clarendon Press, 1982.

———. *Bartholomew Fair*. In vol. 3. of *The Complete Plays of Ben Jonson*, edited by G. A. Wilkes. Oxford: Clarendon Press, 1982.

———. *Volpone*. In vol. 3 of *The Complete Plays of Ben Jonson*, edited by G. A. Wilkes. Oxford: Clarendon Press, 1982.

———. *Discoveries*. In *The Complete Poems*, edited by G. Parfitt. London: Penguin, 1988.

———. Epigram IV: "To King James." In *The Complete Poems*, edited by G. Parfitt. London: Penguin, 1988.

———. *The Masque of Blackness*. In *Court Masques: Jacobean and Caroline Entertainments, 1605–1640*, edited by D. Lindley. Oxford: Oxford University Press, 1995.

Kahn, Victoria. *Rhetoric, Prudence, and Skepticism in the Renaissance*. Ithaca: Cornell University Press, 1985.

Kay, W. David. "Jonson's Urbane Gallants: Humanistic Contexts for *Epicoene*." *Huntington Library Quarterly* 39 (1976): 251–66.

Kelso, Ruth. *The Doctrine of the English Gentleman in the Sixteenth Century*. 1929. Reprint, Gloucester, Mass.: Peter Smith, 1964.

Kermode, Frank. *The Sense of an Ending: Studies in the Theory of Fiction*. New York: Oxford University Press, 1967.

Kernan, Alvin. *The Cankered Muse: Satire of the English Renaissance*. New Haven: Yale University Press, 1959.

Knapp, Jeffrey. *An Empire Nowhere: England, America, and Literature from* Utopia *to* The Tempest. Berkeley: University of California Press, 1992.

Knights, L. C. *Drama and Society in the Age of Jonson*. New York: Stewart, 1936.

Kristeller, Paul. "Humanism." In *The Cambridge History of Renaissance Philosophy*, edited by C. Schmitt and Q. Skinner. Cambridge: Cambridge University Press, 1988.

Kumar, Krishan. *Utopia and Anti-Utopia in Modern Times*. Oxford: Blackwell, 1987.

Kyd, Thomas. *The Spanish Tragedy*. Edited by J. R. Mulryne. 2nd ed. New York: Norton, 1989.

Laclau, Ernst, and Chantelle Mouffe. *Hegemony and Socialist Strategy: Towards a Radical Democratic Politics*. London: Verso, 1985.

Lang, R. G. "Social Origins and Social Aspirations of Jacobean London Merchants." *Economic History Review* 27, no. 1 (February 1974): 28–47.

Leggatt, Alexander. *Citizen Comedy in the Age of Shakespeare*. Toronto: University of Toronto Press, 1973.

———. *Ben Jonson: His Vision and His Art*. London: Methuen, 1981.

Leinwand, Theodore. *The City Staged: Jacobean Comedy, 1603–1613*. Madison: University of Wisconsin Press, 1986.

Lerner, Robert. "The Black Death and Western Eschatological Mentalities." *American Historical Review* 86, no. 3 (1981): 533–52.

Levin, Richard. "The Dampit Scenes in *A Trick to Catch the Old One*." *Modern Language Quarterly* 25, no. 2 (1964): 140–52.

———. "The Four Plots of *A Chaste Maid in Cheapside*." *Review of English Studies*, n.s., 16 (1965): 14–24.

Lindberg, David. *The Beginnings of Western Science*. Chicago: University of Chicago Press, 1992.

Linden, S. *Darke Hierogliphicks: Alchemy in English Literature from Chaucer to the Restoration*. Lexington: University Press of Kentucky, 1996.

Long, A. A. *Hellenistic Philosophy: Stoics, Epicureans, Sceptics*. London: Duckworth, 1974.

Lucian. *Selected Satires of Lucian*. Edited and translated by L. Casson. New York: Norton, 1962.

Lyle, Alexander. "Volpone's Two Worlds." *Yearbook of English Studies* 4 (1974): 70–76.

Lynch, Kathleen. "The Dramatic Festivity of *Bartholomew Fair*." *Medieval and Renaissance Drama in England* 8 (1996): 128–45.

Lyons, Charles. "Silent Women and Shrews: Eroticism and Conventions in *Epicoene* and *Measure for Measure*." *Comparative Drama* 23, no. 2 (1989): 123–40.

Machiavelli, Niccolò. *The Prince and the Discourses*. Translated by L. Ricci and C. Detmond. New York: Random House, 1940.

Manley, Lawrence. *Literature and Culture in Early Modern England*. Cambridge: Cambridge University Press, 1995.

Marlowe, Christopher. *The Jew of Malta*. Edited by T. W. Craik. London: Ernest Benn, 1966.

Marotti, Arthur. "Fertility and Comic Form in *A Chaste Maid in Cheapside*." *Comparative Drama* 3 (1969): 65–74.

Marston, John. *The Fawn*. In vol. 2. of *The Works of John Marston*, edited by A. H. Bullen. New York: Georg Olms, 1970.

———. *What You Will*. In vol. 2 of *The Works of John Marston*, edited by A. H. Bullen. New York: Georg Olms, 1970.

Martin, Julian. *Francis Bacon, the State, and the Reform of Natural Philosophy*. Cambridge: Cambridge University Press, 1992.

Marx, Karl. *The Grundrisse*. Translated by M. Nicolaus. London: Penguin, 1973.

Maus, Katharine Eisaman. *Inwardness and Theater in the English Renaissance*. Chicago: University of Chicago Press, 1995.

McCanles, Michael. "Festival in Jonsonian Comedy." *Renaissance Drama*, n.s., 8 (1977): 203–19.

McPherson, David. "The Origins of Overdo: A Study in Jonsonian Invention." *Modern Language Quarterly* 37 (1976): 221–33.

———. *Shakespeare, Jonson, and the Myth of Venice*. London: University of Delaware Press, 1990.

Mebane, John. *Renaissance Magic and the Return of the Golden Age: The Occult Tradition and Marlowe, Jonson, and Shakespeare*. Lincoln: University of Nebraska Press, 1989.

Messina, Joseph. "The Moral Design of *A Trick to Catch the Old One*." In *Accompaninge the Players: Essays Celebrating Thomas Middleton, 1580–1980*, 109–32. New York: AMS, 1983.

Middleton, Thomas. *The Phoenix*. In vol. 1 of *The Works of Middleton*, edited by A. H. Bullen. 1885. Reprint, New York: AMS Press, 1964.

———. *Your Five Gallants*. In vol. 3 of *The Works of Middleton*,. edited by A. H. Bullen. 1885. Reprint, New York: AMS Press, 1964.

———. *The Widow*. In vol. 5 of *The Works of Middleton*, edited by A. H. Bullen. 1885. Reprint, New York: AMS Press, 1964.

———. *A Chaste Maid in Cheapside*. In *Thomas Middleton: Five Plays*, edited by B. Loughrey and N. Taylor. London: Penguin, 1988.

———. *A Trick to Catch the Old One*. In *A Mad World, My Masters and Other Plays*, edited by M. Taylor. Oxford: Oxford University Press, 1995.

———. *Michaelmas Term*. In *A Mad World, My Masters and Other Plays*, edited by M. Taylor. Oxford: Oxford University Press, 1995.

Montaigne, M. *The Complete Essays*. Translated by D. Frame. Stanford, Calif.: Stanford University Press, 1958.

More, Thomas. *Utopia*. Translated by P. Turner. London: Penguin, 1965.

Mount, David. "The '[Un]reclaymed forme' of Middleton's *A Trick to Catch the Old One*." *Studies in English Literature 1500 –1900* 31, no. 2 (1991): 259–72.

Mullaney, Steven. *The Place of the Stage: License, Play, and Power in Renaissance England*. Chicago: University of Chicago Press, 1988.

Nowell, Alexander. "An Homily concerning the Justice of God in punyshyng of impenitent sinners, and of his mercies towardes all such as theyr afflictions unfaynedly turne unto hym." In *The Remains of Archbishop Grindal*, edited by W. Nicholson, 95–110. Cambridge: Cambridge University Press, 1843.

Parker, R. B. "The Themes and Staging of *Bartholomew Fair*." *University of Toronto Quarterly* 39 (1970): 293–309.

Paster, Gail Kern. *The Idea of the City in the Age of Shakespeare*. Athens: University of Georgia Press, 1985.

———. "Quomodo, Sir Giles, and Triangular Desire: Social Aspiration in Middleton and Massinger." In *Comedy from Shakespeare to Sheridan*, edited by A. A. Braunmuller and J. C. Bulman, 165–78. Toronto: Associated University Presses, 1986.

———. *The Body Embarrassed: Drama and the Disciplines of Shame in Early Modern England*. Ithaca: Cornell University Press, 1993.

Plato. *The Republic*. Translated by D. Lee. 2d ed. Harmondsworth, England: Penguin, 1974.

Popkin, Richard. *The History of Skepticism from Erasmus to Spinoza*. Berkeley: University of California Press, 1979.

Puttenham, George. *The Arte of English Poesie*. Edited by G. D. Willcock and A. Walker. Cambridge: Cambridge University Press, 1936.

Rackin, Phyllis. "Androgyny, Mimesis, and the Marriage of the Boy Heroine on the English Renaissance Stage." *PMLA* 102, no. 1 (1987): 29–41.

Ralegh, Walter. "What is our life? a play of passion." In *The Metaphysical Poets*, edited by H. Gardner, 35. 3d ed. London: Penguin, 1972.

Ramsey, G. D. *The City of London in International Politics at the Accession of Elizabeth Tudor*. Manchester. Manchester University Press, 1975.

Rebhorn, Wayne. "Jonson's 'Jovy Boy': Lovewit and the Dupes in *The Alchemist*." *Journal of English and Germanic Philology* 79 (1980): 355–75.

Rhodes, Neil. *Elizabethan Grotesque*. London: Routledge and Kegan Paul, 1980.

Ross, Cheryl Lynn. "The Plague of *The Alchemist*." *Renaissance Quarterly* 41, no. 3 (autumn 1988): 439–58.

Rowe, George. "Prodigal Sons, New Comedy, and Middleton's *Michaelmas Term*." *English Literary Renaissance* 7 (1977): 90–107.

———. *Thomas Middleton and the New Comedy Tradition*. Lincoln: University of Nebraska Press, 1979.

Said, Edward. *Orientalism*. New York: Vintage, 1979.

Sawday, Jonathan. *The Body Emblazoned: Dissection and the Human Body in Renaissance Culture*. London: Routledge, 1995.

Sayer, Derek. *Capitalism and Modernity: An Excursus on Marx and Weber*. London: Routledge, 1991.

Schiffmann, Z. "Montaigne and the Rise of Skepticism in Early Modern Europe: A Reappraisal." *Renaissance Essays II,* 1993, 330–47.

Schuler, Robert. "Jonson's Alchemists, Epicures, and Puritans." *Medieval and Renaissance Drama in England* 2 (1985): 171–208.

Sedgwick, Eve Kosofsky. *Between Men: English Literature and Male Homosocial Desire*. New York: Columbia University Press, 1985.

Sextus Empiricus. *Outlines of Pyrrhonism*. Translated by R. G. Bury. Cambridge: Harvard University Press, 1933.

Shakespeare, William. *Hamlet*. Edited by W. Farnham. In *William Shakespeare: The Complete Works*, edited by A. Harbage. London: Penguin, 1969.

———. *Othello*. Edited by G. Bentley. Harmondsworth, England: Penguin, 1970.

———. *The Comedy of Errors*. Edited by S. Wells. Harmondsworth, England: Penguin, 1972.

Shapiro, Barbara. *Probability and Certainty in Seventeenth-Century England*. Princeton: Princeton University Press, 1983.

Shershow, Scott Cutler. "The Pit of Wit: Subplot and Unity in Middleton's *A Trick to Catch the Old One*." *Studies in Philology* 88, no. 3 (1991): 363–81.

Sidney, Philip. *The Defence of Poesy*. In *Sir Philip Sidney,* edited by K. Duncan-Jones. Oxford: Oxford University Press, 1989.

Skulsky, Harold. "Cannibals vs. Demons in Volpone." *SEL* 29, no. 2 (1989): 291–308.

Slack, Paul. *The Impact of Plague in Tudor and Stuart England*. London: Routledge and Kegan Paul, 1985.

———. *Poverty and Policy in Tudor and Stuart England*. London: Longman, 1988.

Slights, William. "*Epicoene* and the Prose Paradox." *Philological Quarterly* 49 (1970): 178–87.

———. "Unfashioning the Man of Mode: A Comic Countergenre in Marston, Jonson, and Middleton." *Renaissance Drama*, n.s., 15 (1984): 69–91.

———. *Ben Jonson and the Art of Secrecy*. Toronto: University of Toronto Press, 1994.

Smallwood, R. L. "'Here in the Friars': Immediacy and Theatricality in *The Alchemist*." *Review of English Studies,* n.s., 32 (1980): 142–60.

Smith, Thomas. *De Republica Anglorum*. 1583. Reprint, New York: Da Capo Press, 1970.

Stallybrass, Peter, and Allon White. *The Politics and Poetics of Transgression.* Ithaca: Cornell University Press, 1986.

Stevenson, Laura. C. *Praise and Paradox: Merchants and Craftsmen in Elizabethan Popular Literature.* Cambridge: Cambridge University Press, 1984.

Stone, Lawrence. *The Crisis of the Aristocracy, 1558–1641.* Oxford: Clarendon, 1965.

———. "Social Mobility in England, 1500–1700." *Past and Present* 33 (April 1966): 16–55.

Stubbes, Philip. *The Anatomie of Abuses.* New York: Garland, 1973.

Sturgess, Keith. *Jacobean Private Theatre.* New York: Routledge and Kegan Paul, 1987.

Sweeney, John. *Jonson and the Psychology of the Public Theater.* Princeton: Princeton University Press, 1985.

Tawney, R. H. *Religion and the Rise of Capitalism.* 1926. Reprint, London: Penguin, 1938.

Taylor, Barry. *Vagrant Writing: Social and Semiotic Disorders in the English Renaissance.* Toronto: University of Toronto Press, 1991.

Tennenhouse, Leonard. *Power on Display: The Politics of Shakespeare's Genres.* New York: Methuen, 1986.

Thirsk, Joan. *Economic Policy and Projects: The Development of a Consumer Society in Early Modern England.* Oxford: Clarendon, 1978.

Thomas, Keith. *Religion and the Decline of Magic.* London: Penguin, 1973.

Van Leeuwen, Henry. *The Problem of Certainty in English Thought, 1630–1690.* The Hague: Martinus Nijhoff, 1970.

Watson, Robert. N. *Ben Jonson's Parodic Strategy: Literary Imperialism in the Comedies.* Cambridge: Harvard University Press, 1987.

Wayne, Don. "*Drama and Society in the Age of Jonson:* An Alternative View." *Renaissance Drama*, n.s., 13 (1982): 103–29.

Weber, Max. *The Protestant Ethic and the Spirit of Capitalism.* 1930. Reprint, London: Routledge, 1992.

Wells, Susan. "Jacobean City Comedy and the Ideology of the City." *English Literary History* 48 (1981): 37–60.

Wigler, Stephen. "Thomas Middleton's *A Chaste Maid in Cheapside:* The Delicious and the Disgusting." *American Imago* 33 (1976): 197–215.

Wilkins, George. *The Miseries of Inforst Marriage.* Oxford: Oxford University Press, 1964.

Wilson, F. P. *The Plague in Shakespeare's London.* Oxford: Clarendon, 1927.

Wittgenstein, Ludwig. *Philosophical Investigations.* Translated by G. E. M. Anscombe. Oxford: Blackwell, 1963.

Wolfe, Tom. *The Pumphouse Gang.* New York: The Noonday Press, 1968.

Woodbridge, Linda. *Women and the English Renaissance: Literature and the Nature of Womankind, 1540–1620.* Urbana: University of Illinois Press, 1984.

Wright, Thomas. *The Passions of the Mind in General.* Edited by W. W. Newbold. New York: Garland, 1986.

Yachnin, Paul. "Social Competition in Middleton's *Michaelmas Term.*" *Explorations in Renaissance Culture* 13 (1987): 87–99.

Index

Academica (Cicero), 14
Advancement of Learning, The (Bacon), 60, 61, 144, 145
Agnew, Jean-Christophe, 51; *Worlds Apart,* 20
agriculture: capitalization of, 18
Agrippa: *De incertitudine,* 60
Alchemist, The (Jonson), 21, 22, 95–114, 133, 136, 150, 155
alchemy, 107–8, 109, 112–13
Anatomie of Abuses (Stubbes), 42–43
Anatomy of Melancholy (Burton), 60
anti-Platonism, 27, 29
Antitheatrical Prejudice, The (Barish), 17
Anxious Masculinity in Early Modern England (Breitenberg), 121
Apocalyptic Tradition, The (Firth), 97
Apology for Raymond Sebond (Montaigne), 15
appearance vs. being, 27
Appleby, Joyce: *Economic Thought and Ideology,* 19
Aristophanes, 24; *The Clouds,* 16
Aristotelian natural philosophy, 112–13
Arnold, Judd, 110
Arte of English Poesie, The (Puttenham), 132
Austin, J. L., 16, 72
Ayers, P. K., 64, 66, 76; "Plot, Subplot," 90

Bach, Rebecca Ann: "Ben Jonson's 'Civil Savages'," 139–40
Bacon, Francis, 45, 51, 60, 61, 67, 72, 79, 143, 144, 145; *The Advancement of Learning,* 60, 61, 144, 145; and knowing by tradition, 61; *New Atlantis,* 145; *The New Organon,* 60, 144; "Of Nobility," 44; on philosophy and theater, 16–17; and the theater, 61
Bakhtin, M. M., 66, 134, 137, 138
Barish, Jonas, 32, 70, 71, 73, 74, 134, 137, 150; *The Antitheatrical Prejudice,* 17
Barker, Francis, 29
Bartholomew Fair (Jonson), 21, 22, 75, 100, 115, 133–53
Beck, Ervin, 78
Beginnings of Western Science, The (Lindberg), 112–13
Bergson, Henri, 134
Benet, Diana, 75
"Ben Jonson's 'Civil Savages'" (Bach), 139–40
Between Men (Kosofsky), 123
Blanchard, W. Scott: *Scholar's Bedlam,* 59
body, the, 29, 30, 31
Body Embarrassed, The (Paster), 119
Book of Common Prayer, The, 82
Book of the Courtier, The (Castiglione), 18
Bourdieu, Pierre, 88
Brave New World (Huxley), 33
Breitenberg, Mark: *Anxious Masculinity in Early Modern England,* 121
Bristol, Michael, 138
Broude, Ronald, 37
Browne, Thomas, 144; *Religio Medici,* 13
Bruster, Douglas, 20, 51
Burton, Robert, *The Anatomy of Melancholy,* 60

Calvin, John, 59
Cankered Muse, The (Kernan), 71

INDEX

"Cannibals vs. Demons in *Volpone*" (Skulsky), 30
capitalism, 18–19, 20, 105
Capitalism and Modernity (Sayer), 86
carnival, 133, 135, 137–39
Cartelli, Thomas, 136
Castiglione, 62, 76; *The Book of the Courtier*, 18
Catholic Church, 15
Caveat for Common Cursitors, A (Harman), 41, 140
Cavell, Stanley: *Disowning Knowledge*, 17–18
Chakravorty, Swapan, 46, 127
Chapman, Henoch, 74, 98
Chaste Maid in Cheapside, A (Middleton), 21, 22, 36, 47, 81, 115–32, 154–55
Christie, Agatha: *The Mousetrap*, 36
Cicero, 59; *Academica*, 14
citizen comedy, 20
Citizen Comedy in the Age of Shakespeare (Leggatt), 20
citizen-gentry conflict, 44, 49
city comedy, 18, 19–20, 40, 44, 53, 74, 83, 93, 100, 101, 115, 155; as moral critique, 20
City Staged, The (Leinwand), 20
Civilizing Process, The (Elias), 18, 83
classical (pagan) literature, 59
Clouds, The (Aristophanes), 16
comedy, 133
Comedy of Errors, The (Shakespeare), 24
commonwealth, English, 79, 80
Copenhaver, Brian, 59
Cope, Jackson, 146
Covatta, Anthony, 115, 129
Cranfield, Lionel, 50

"Dampit Scenes, . . . The" (Levin), 92, 93
Defence of Poesy (Sidney), 133
Dekker, Thomas, 99; *The Wonderfull Yeare*, 96
Deloney, Thomas, 102
De incertitudine (Agrippa), 60
De Republica Anglorum (Smith), 44, 49–50, 54, 55, 143
Derrida, Jacques, 96
Descartes, René, 13; *Discourses on Method*, 29; *Meditations*, 16; on theater, 95
Dessen, Alan, 100–101

Devil Is An Ass, The (Jonson), 155
Diogenes Laërtius: *Lives of Eminent Philosophers*, 14
Discourses, The (Machiavelli), 18
Discourses on Method (Descartes), 29
Disowning Knowledge (Cavell), 17–18
divine order, 40
divine-right monarchy, 130
Dollimore, Jonathan, 140
Donaldson, Ian, 102, 111; *The World Upside Down*, 135
Donne, John, 98
Drama and Society in the Age of Jonson (Knights), 20
dress, 42–43
Dr. Faustus (Marlowe), 108
Dürer, Albrecht: "Monument," 80
dystopia, 23, 27, 31, 33, 34, 37

Economic Thought and Ideology (Appleby), 19
economics, 79
economy, capitalist, 40; dystopian, 27; exchange, 23, 31, 55
Elias, Norbert: *The Civilizing Process*, 18, 83
Elizabeth I, 19, 43
Empire Nowhere, An (Knapp), 148
Enck, John, 61
Epicoene (Jonson), 21, 22, 26, 36, 58–78, 95, 100; and collegiate ladies of, 63, 64, 68, 69, 70, 72, 73; and learning, 73, 74; wits in, 76
Epicureanism, 14
epistemology, 14–16, 26–27, 61–62, 65, 67–68, 74, 76–77, 98, 99, 100, 102, 109, 114, 144, 145, 146, 148
Erasmus, 76
Essays (Montaigne), 60
Essays of a Prentise, The (James I), 151
Estienne, Henri, 14
Every Man In His Humor (Jonson), 72
Every Man Out of His Humor (Jonson), 63, 67

fairs, 138
Fawn, The (Marston), 75
feminism, 125
feudalism, 18, 83
Firth, Katharine: *The Apocalyptic Tradition*, 97

Fletcher, John, 155
food imagery, 30, 117
Ford, John, 155
Foucault, Michel, 36, 83, 96–97
Fourme to be used in Common prayer, 96, 98
"Four Plots of *A Chaste Maid in Cheapside,* The" (Levin), 123, 125
Freud, Sigmund: on death, 28

Gargantua and Pantagruel (Rabelais), 60
gentlemen: defined, 49–50
Gibbons, Brian: *Jacobean City Comedy,* 20
Goldberg, Jonathan, 152
Good, 37
Greenblatt, Stephen, 31; "Murdering Peasants," 80; *Renaissance Self-Fashioning,"* 89
Greene, Thomas, 29
Gresham's Royal Exchange, 19
"grotesque realism," 134
Grundisse (Marx), 87

Harman, Thomas: *A Caveat for Common Cursitors,* 41, 140
Hartmann, Heidi, 122
Haynes, Jonathan, 64, 101, 139, 140
Hellenistic Philosophy (Long), 14
Helms, Lorraine, 71
History of Scepticism (Popkin), 14, 59
Homily Concerning the Justice of God, A (Nowell), 98
Homo economicus, 78, 89
Hooker, Richard, 80, 91; *The Laws of Ecclesiastical Polity,* 79, 136
Hotz-Davies, Ingrid, 121, 125
Howard, Jean, 71
Huebert, Ronald: "Middleton's Nameless Art," 121
humanism, 15, 60
humanist, the, 137
humanist project, 58, 59
humors play, 61, 63, 67, 103
humors psychology, 65
Huxley, Aldous: *Brave New World,* 33

incontinence, 119
intriguer: tragic, 74

Jacobean City Comedy (Gibbons), 20

"Jacobean City Comedy and the Ideology of the City" (Wells), 132, 152
James I, 14, 44, 50, 130, 143, 145, 151, 152; *The Essays of a Prentise,* 151
Jameson, Frederic: *The Political Unconscious,* 115
Jones, Emrys, 58
Jonson, Ben, 13, 14, 18, 20, 105, 154, 155; *The Alchemist,* 21, 22, 95–114, 133, 136, 150, 155; *Bartholomew Fair,* 21, 22, 75, 100, 115, 133–53; *The Devil Is An Ass,* 155; *Epicoene,* 21, 22, 26, 36, 58–78, 95, 100; *Every Man In His Humor,* 72, *Every Man Out of His Humor,* 63, 67; and knowing by tradition, 61; and misogyny, 71; *The New Inn,* 155; *The Sad Shepherd,* 155; *Volpone,* 21, 22, 23–38, 48, 56, 58, 78, 95, 100, 115, 118, 132, 133, 150, 152, 154, 155
"Jonson's Urbane Gallants" (Kay), 76
Juvenal, 70–71

Kay, W. David: "Jonson's Urbane Gallants," 76
Kermode, Frank, 103
Kernan, Alvin: *The Cankered Muse,* 71
Knapp, Jeffrey: *An Empire Nowhere,* 148
Knight of the Burning Pestle, The, 42
knights, 50, 51, 55
Knights, L. C.: *Drama and Society in the Age of Jonson,* 20
Knowledge, 14, 58, 61
Kristeller, Paul, 59
Kumar, Krishan, 32

language, 99, 111, 135
laughter, 133, 137
Laws of Ecclesiastical Polity, The (Hooker), 79, 136
Legitimation, 40, 49; strategies of, 65
Leinwand, Theodore, 44, 50; *The City Staged,* 20
Levin, Richard, 116; "The Dampit Scenes," 92, 93; "The Four Plots of *A Chaste Maid in Cheapside,"* 123, 125
Lindberg, David: *The Beginnings of Western Science,* 112–13
Lives of Eminent Philosophers (Diogenes), 14
London, 42, 49, 52, 66, 69, 76, 80, 91, 93,

94; economic importance of, 18–19; during the plague, 95–99
Long, A. A.: *Hellenistic Philosophy*, 14
Lucian, 24; *Philosophers For Sale*, 16
Lyons, 72
Lyotard, Jean-François, 83
Luther, Martin, 59

Machiavelli, Niccolò, 33; *The Discourses*, 18; *The Prince*, 18
Manley, Laurence, 21
Marlowe, Christopher, 102; *Dr. Faustus*, 108
Marston, John, 21; *The Fawn*, 75; *What You Will*, 74
Marx, Karl, 86; *Grundisse*, 87
masques, 155
Maus, Katharine, 66
McCanles, Michael, 137
medicine, Galenic, 97, 99
Meditations (Descartes), 16
Menippus, 59–60
Messina, Joseph: "The Moral Design of *A Trick to Catch the Old One*," 90
Michaelmas Term (Middleton), 21, 22, 39–57, 78, 81, 83, 86, 110, 115, 132, 154; and gentle birth, 46; and money, 46, 47, 48; and sex, 46, 47, 48
Middleton, Thomas, 13, 14, 18, 20, 154, 155; *A Chaste Maid in Cheapside*, 21, 22, 36, 47, 81, 115–32, 154–55; *Michaelmas Term* (Middleton), 21, 22, 39–57, 78, 81, 83, 86, 110, 115, 132, 115, 132; *The Roaring Girl*, 125; *A Trick to Catch the Old One*, 21, 22, 54, 78–94
"Middleton's Nameless Art" (Huebert), 121
Mirour for Magestrates of Cyties, A (Whetstone), 136
Miseries of Inforst Marriage, The (Wilkin), 129
Montaigne, Michel, 25, 95, 140; *Apology for Raymond Sebond*, 15; *Essays*, 60; on skepticism, 15
"Monument to Commemorate a Victory" (Dürer), 80
"Moral Design of *A Trick...* , The" (Messina), 90
morality play, 94, 100, 148
More, Thomas, 76; *Utopia*, 32, 33

Mount, David: "The '[Un]reclaymed forme'," 85
Mousetrap, The (Christie), 36
Mullaney, Steven: *The Place of the Stage*, 17, 150
"Murdering Peasants" (Greenblatt), 80
Münster Anabaptists, 105

New Atlantis (Bacon), 145
New Comedy, 18, 84
New Exchange, 19
New Inn, The (Jonson), 155
"new men," 41, 42
New Organon, The (Bacon), 60, 144
Nineteen Eight-Four (Orwell), 33
Nowell, Alexander: *An Homily Concerning the Justice of God*, 98

"Of Nobility" (Bacon), 44
Orientalism (Said), 143
origins: in *Michaelmas Term*, 50–54
Orwell, George: *Nineteen Eighty-Four*, 33
Othello (Shakespeare), 130
Other, the, 31, 66, 89, 140
Outlines of Pyrrhonism (Empiricus), 14
Ovid, 68, 69, 70, 71

paradox, 115–32
Passions of the Mind in General, The (Wright), 65
Paster, Gail Kern, 21, 49; *The Body Embarrassed*, 119, 122
patriarchy, 115–32
pharmakon, 95, 96
Philosophical Investigations (Wittgenstein), 99
Philosophers For Sale (Lucian), 16
philosophy: Hellenistic, 13, 14; post-Hellenistic, 14
"Pit of Wit, The" (Shershow), 92–93, 94
Place of the Stage, The (Mullaney), 17, 150
plague, the, 95–99; response to, 96, 97
Plato, 29, 31, 32, 37, 38; *Republic*, 16, 22, 23, 24, 31–34
Platonic Academy, 14
playhouses, 19, 20
"Plot, Subplot..." (Ayers), 90
Political Unconscious, The (Jameson), 115
Popkin, Richard: *The History of Skepticism*, 14, 59

potency, sexual, 119
power, 83
Prince, The (Machiavelli), 18
Probability and Certainty (Shapiro), 60
Puritans, 98
Puttenham, George: *The Arte of English Poesie*, 132
Pyrrho of Elis, 14
Pyrrhonism, 14, 15, 59, 155

Rabelais, François: *Gargantua and Pantagruel*, 60
Rackin, Phyllis, 70
reason, 60
Rebhorn, Wayne, 110
Reformation, the, 15, 59
Religio Medici (Browne), 13
Religion and the Decline of Magic (Thomas), 99
Religion and the Rise of Capitalism (Tawney), 79
Renaissance, the, 73, 74
Renaissance Self-Fashioning (Greenblatt), 89
Republic (Plato), 16, 22, 23, 24, 31–34
Rhodes, Neil, 135, 137
Roaring Girl, The (Middleton), 125
rogue pamphlets, 140
Romeo and Juliet (Shakespeare), 132
Ross, Cheryl Lynn, 108, 111
Rowe, George, 46, 115; *Thomas Middleton and the New Comedy Tradition*, 85

Sad Shepherd, The (Jonson), 155
Said, Edward: *Orientalism*, 143
satire, 71–72, 137–38
Sayer, Derek: *Capitalism and Modernity*, 86
Scarborrow, William, 129
Schmitt, 59
Scholar's Bedlam *(Blanchard)*, 59
Scott, William, 51
Sedgwick, Eve Kosofsky: *Between Men*, 123
self, the, 86, 87, 107; economic, 89, 90, 91; anti-Platonic, 29–31; commodified, 51–57
sense perceptions, 24, 25
sex, 116
sex-money calculus, 46, 81
Sextus Empiricus, 15, 59; *Outlines of Pyrrhonism*, 14

sexuality, female, 119, 120
Shakespeare, William, 17, 47; *The Comedy of Errors*, 24; *Othello*, 130; *Romeo and Juliet*, 132; *The Winter's Tale*, 132
Shapiro, Barbara: *Probability and Certainty*, 60
Shershow, Scott: "The Pit of Wit," 92–93, 94
Sidney, Philip, 102; *Defence of Poesy*, 133
skepticism, 13, 14, 15, 16, 59–60, 95, 114, 133, 134, 144, 150, 154, 155
Skulsky, Harold: "Cannibals vs. Demons in *Volpone*," 30
Slack, Paul, 41
Slights, William, 49, 102
Smallwood, R. L., 101, 102
Smith, Thomas, 50; *De Republica Anglorum*, 44, 49, 54, 55, 143
social mobility, 40–43
social order, 39, 40, 41–43, 115
Spenser, Edmund, 102
stage: Elizabethan, 17; Jacobean, 17
Stallybrass, Peter, 138
state and church: unity of, 79
status, 88
Stoicism, 14
Stubbs, Philip, 51, 54; *Anatomie of Abuses*, 42–43
Sturgess, Keith, 143, 151, 152

Tawney, R. H., 80; *Religion and the Rise of Capitalism*, 79
Tennenhouse, Leonard, 83
theater, 17, 95, 100–102
Thomas, Keith: *Religion and the Decline of Magic*, 99
Thomas Middleton and the New Comedy Tradition (Rowe), 85
Tourneur, Cyril, 74
Trick to Catch the Old One, A (Middleton), 21, 22, 54, 78–94, 154
truth vs. falsehood, 25

"'[Un]reclaymed forme' . . . The" (Mount), 85
usury, 80, 92, 93
Utopia, 23, 24, 32, 33, 34, 39
Utopia (More), 32, 33

vagrants, 41
Van Leeuwen, Henry, 144

Volpone (Jonson), 21, 22, 23–28, 48, 56, 58, 78, 95, 100, 115, 118, 132, 133, 150, 152, 154, 155

Watson, R. N., 37, 102, 136
Wayne, Don, 20
Weber, Max, 87, 89
Wells, Susan: "Jacobean City Comedy," 132, 152
What You Will (Marston), 74
Whetstone, George: *A Mirour for Magestrates of Cyties,* 136
White, Allon, 138
Wilkins, George: *The Miseries of Inforst Marriage,* 129

Winter's Tale, The (Shakespeare), 132
wits: and gulls, 75, 78
Wittgenstein, Ludwig, 13, 16; *Philosophical Investigations,* 99
Wolfe, Thomas, 63
Wonderfull Yeare, The (Dekker), 96
Woodbridge, Linda, 71
World Upside Down, The (Donaldson), 135
Worlds Apart (Agnew), 20
Wright, Thomas, 51; *The Passions of the Mind in General,* 65

Yachnin, Paul, 40